SWEET FREEDOM'S SONG

SWEET FREEDOM'S SONG

"My Country 'Tis of Thee"
and Democracy in America

Robert James Branham &
Stephen J. Hartnett

OXFORD
UNIVERSITY PRESS

2002

OXFORD

UNIVERSITY PRESS

Oxford   New York

Athens   Auckland   Bangkok   Bogotá   Buenos Aires   Cape Town
Chennai   Dar es Salaam   Delhi   Florence   Hong Kong   Istanbul   Karachi
Kolkata   Kuala Lumpur   Madrid   Melbourne   Mexico City   Mumbai   Nairobi
Paris   São Paulo   Shanghai   Singapore   Taipei   Tokyo   Toronto   Warsaw

and associated companies in
Berlin   Ibadan

Copyright © 2002 by Oxford University Press

Published by Oxford University Press, Inc.
198 Madison Avenue, New York, New York 10016

Oxford is a registered trademark of Oxford University Press

Library of Congress Cataloging-in-Publication Data
Branham, Robert J.
Sweet freedom's song : "My country 'tis of thee" and democracy in America
Robert James Branham and Stephen J. Hartnett.
p.   cm.
ISBN 0-19-513741-8
1. God save the King.   2. Democracy—United States.   I. Hartnett, Stephen J.   II. Title.
ML3561.A51 B73   2002
782.42'1599'0973—dc21   2001036275

1 3 5 7 9 8 6 4 2

Printed in the United States of America
on acid-free paper

TO NOAH AND CELESTE

Preface

ROBERT James Branham began this study in 1994. Like many historiographical adventures it began as a potluck of random footnotes, lightning flashes of "what if?"s, and a playful sense of having stumbled into a marvelous story waiting to be constructed from enticing fragments. Pursuing his hunch regarding the remarkable role of the song "My Country 'Tis of Thee" throughout our national history enabled Bob in turn to explore the promises, possibilities, and compromises of democracy in America. Indeed, while undertaken as a cultural history of the varied uses of "My Country 'Tis of Thee," this work also aspires to stand as a rhetorical history of democracy in America, of how we have come through the years to express our varied senses of nationalism, our competing notions of pride and place, and our ever-changing frustrations with corruption and greed and racism and sexism—in short, our kaleidoscopic sense of what it means to be Americans. While immersed in rich historical details, this book strives for the big picture, the broad view, as the song "My Country 'Tis of Thee" provides a wonderful opportunity to offer a humble rendering of our national history that is thrilled by the glories of our triumphs and saddened by the tragedies of our failures, but mostly just convinced that we make our own history, that democracy is as grand or as crass as our individual and collective actions.

In the spring of 1998, while happily grappling with the complexities of our national history as expressed through the hundreds of variations employed through the years of "God Save the King/Queen," "America," and "My Country 'Tis of Thee"—songs that share the same melody and line structure—Bob was diagnosed with cancer. He died that October, with this book unfinished.

Before succumbing to the cancer, Bob asked me to try to complete his project; hence the attribution of shared authorship on the title page. In keeping with Bob's original intentions, I have resisted the all-too-common practice of cluttering the text with rarified academic jargon and instead have sought to produce a narrative that is clear and accessible while still honoring the awesome complexity of the materials addressed here.

Stephen Hartnett

Champaign, November the First,
of the year Two-Thousand and One A.D., and
of our National Independence the Two-Hundred and Twenty-fifth.

Acknowledgments

A N early overview of the project appeared as "'Of Thee I Sing': Contesting 'America'" in *American Quarterly* 48:4 (December 1996): 623–652; that material appears here courtesy of the American Studies Association. A draft of chapter 1 appeared as "'God Save the _____!': American National Songs and National Identities, 1760–1798" in the *Quarterly Journal of Speech* 85 (1999): 17–37; that material appears here courtesy of the National Communication Association. For their comments on those early drafts, Bob thanks Rob Farnsworth, Mary Hunter, Jim Parakilas, Cully Clark, and Jim Leamon. For assistance with processing early drafts, Bob thanks Ann Fadiman and Eric Wollman. For assistance finding songbooks and broadsides, Bob thanks Elaine Ardia and the interlibrary loan staff at Bates College and Wayne Hammond of Rare Books at Williams College. Bob and Stephen both thank Larry Frey for his support and famously precise editing skills. For his tenacity in the dreaded microfilm basement at the University of Illinois, Stephen thanks Donovan Conley. For assistance locating rare books and song sheets, Stephen thanks the staff of the University of Illinois Rare Book and Special Collections Library, and Richard Griscom and the staff of the University of Illinois Music Library's Special Collections. For processing image requests, locating images, and making photocopies of archival materials not available on microfilm or microfiche, Stephen thanks Clark Evans of the Library of Congress, Nicole Finzer of the Art Institute of Chicago, Kathy Shoemaker of Special Collections at Emory University, Jean Rainwater of Special Collections at Brown University, Jean Gaudette of the American Antiquarian Society, Robert Zonghi and R. Eugene Zepp of Rare Books and Manuscripts at the Boston Public Library, the Photographic

Services of the British Museum, and Nicole Wells of the New York Historical Society. Considering the subject matter of this book, it is important for Stephen to thank WEFT, 90.1 FM, Champaign-Urbana, the best little community radio station in the land, not only for filling his days with joy, but for proving that fine music, progressive politics, and local democracy are better things when freed from the imposed banality of the corporate bottom line. Here as always, Stephen thanks Brett Kaplan for everything. Finally, Bob and Stephen thank everyone at Oxford University Press for shepherding this project toward completion, and the Press's three remarkable reviewers, whose work on our behalf epitomizes constructive criticism.

Contents

SWEET FREEDOM'S SONG

Introduction

"You Can Sing What Would Be Death to Speak"

Fɪʀsᴛ published in 1854, Joshua McCarter Simpson's *The Emancipation Car, Being an Original Composition of Anti-Slavery Ballads* is a remarkable collection of three prayers, two essays, and fifty-two abolitionist songs set to popular "airs," including "America" ("My Country 'Tis of Thee"), "Marseilles' Hymn," and "Hail Columbia." In Simpson's opening "Note to the Public, by the Author," he tells the story of his slow maturation into an abolitionist, his slow realization that those whom he once saw as "fools, devils, mischief-makers, &c," were in fact fighting for justice. Simpson was a "free black" in Morgan County, Ohio, where as a child he "served under a hard master until twenty-one years old," after which he attended Oberlin Collegiate Institute. In writing his abolitionist song-book, then, Simpson was culminating a climb from "believing that it was all right for us to be slaves" to fighting for abolition, from the drudgery of manual labor to the thrill of cultural production, from the privacy of his own doubts and fears to the self-revealing and self-creating sphere of public participation. Simpson's use of songs to facilitate this wonderful series of transformations is based on his belief that *"you can sing what would be death to speak."*[1]

This book is, in large part, a celebration of what Simpson understood to be the enabling power of music. More specifically, this book explores how words and melody and harmony and rhythm merge to form shimmering patterns of sound that float across the air, carrying political words that "would be death to speak" in the form of musical messages that somehow weave their way into consciousness, infiltrating prejudice, melting anger, nudging the listener toward the willingness to consider new ideas, new images, new possibilities. And while music may be studied from a technical perspective that explains the intricacies of how sound and consciousness interweave, we are interested in the question of how music functions as political persuasion. We pursue this question by tracking the hundreds of lyrical variations, political situations, and cultural contexts of one song: "America." Popularly known as "My Country 'Tis of Thee"—and as "God Save the King/Queen" before that—this song may arguably be situated as the most important, or at least the most commonly used, political song in our national history. Indeed, as we demonstrate hereafter, for over 250 years "America" has been one of the most popular songs of choice—from early revolutionary America through President Grover Cleveland's National Thanksgiving Festival in 1894 up to Richard Nixon's nationally televised funeral a century later—whenever Americans have felt the impulse to sing their politics, to voice their frustrations, to share their hopes, *to render democracy musical.*[2]

Exploring the remarkably complicated and compelling history of "America" has led us to consider five historical moments in which music played an integral role in both shaping and expressing political consciousness:

- In chapter 1 we examine the earliest moments of cultural appropriation and autonomy in the colonies (as witnessed through the colonists' multiple uses of "God Save the King!"), the struggle for independence in the American Revolution, and the ensuing use of song to construct early American nationalism, circa 1750–98.
- In chapter 2 we explore both the formative events behind the writing and premiere of "America" in Boston in 1831 and the subsequent popularization of the song through hundreds of versions employed in the 1830s and 1840s by the music education, temperance, labor, and suffrage movements.
- In chapter 3 we address the variations of "America" used by abolitionists, circa 1831–61, and focus in particular on the abolitionists' use of song to contest what William Lloyd Garrison lambasted as "The mockery of mockeries": July Fourth celebrations in the shadow of slavery.
- In chapter 4 we consider the various revisions of "America" employed to construct both regional and national identities during the Civil War and early Reconstruction periods, from the first battle songs of 1861 up through the spectacular 1869 National Peace Jubilee in Boston.
- In chapter 5 we analyze the roles of "America" in the late-Reconstruction, Gilded Age, and early-twentieth-century struggles of Americans against capitalism, decadence, and sexism via the labor, temperance, and women's suffrage movements, circa 1870–1932.

We thus offer five extended case studies, organized chronologically, that examine the roles of "America" in radical grassroots activism. Our primary concerns are political, historical, and cultural; hence we do not engage in elaborate discussions of music theory, instead approaching the performance of "America" as a political act, a historical artifact, and a cultural text. Our interest is in demonstrating how each of these three conditions (act, artifact, and text) are both implicated in and indicative of the practices and promises of grassroots activism in America. Ultimately, then, reconstructing the fascinating history of "America"—referred to in Samuel Smith's 1831 version as "sweet freedom's song"—enables us to venture some provisional observations on the history of democracy in America.

THE great philosopher of music Ernst Bloch observed that "The vibrating note travels. It does not remain in its place, as color does. True, color is likewise emitted to catch the attention, but then it stays put. For a white to detach itself from a garment, or a wall, is unthinkable. In contrast, the whole of the surrounding air can be full of a sound." Anyone who has ever grooved to a swinging jazz band, or sat stunned before a glorious symphony, or moshed along with a hammering rock-and-roll band, or reeled and cavorted amid a shower of bluegrass riffs, or trembled at the harmonics of a tight barbershop quartet—anyone who has ever felt his or her world expanded and made more beautiful by music—anyone who has ever been alive with sound will immediately recall his or her own experiences with the truth of Bloch's claim. For regardless of genre, one of the most powerful and magical aspects of music is its sheer physicality: we are overcome by it, we are propelled by it; as the air fills with sound, so music washes through us. Thus Bloch observes that "the ear perceives more than can be explained conceptually." How else can one "explain" the dramatic appeal of "My Country 'Tis of Thee," a song that, speaking musically, is childish, banal, and embarrassing? Most listeners know, cognitively, that the song is silly, goofy, bound up in the worst forms of nationalism, yet the ear perceives something more, perhaps demonstrating what Bloch called "feeling extensively." For Bloch this meant both *listening through* the music to grasp the component parts of the composition and *listening beyond* the music to catch a glimmer of its hopes, the "unsayable" that nonetheless embodies "our utopia calling."[3] What if the power of "My Country 'Tis of Thee" flows, then, from the fact that every time Americans hear it sung, every time we find ourselves awash in a sea of "vibrating notes" filling the air with sound, we *listen beyond* the song, thus hearing not so much the song itself, trite and simple, but the promise of democracy, grand and complex?

This political, historical, and cultural consideration of "My Country 'Tis of Thee" strives to demonstrate how such musical and political promises accrue over time, slowly adding up to something like tradition or custom. Unfortunately, tradition and custom tend to crystallize national memory in ways that marginalize oppositional politics. As Nathan Huggins has argued recently, "The need to define the nation as a coherent whole obliges one to obliterate or subordinate those particular groups who would lay claim to an independent or alternative generalization."[4] Our work struggles to recover those independent and alternative voices filtered out by obliterating nationalist memories, thus offering a study that celebrates American democracy while simultaneously pausing to observe where we were misled by fear and laziness, where we stopped listening to those musical voices that struggled to teach us how to be better, how to be more true to the promises of democracy.

Americans have always seen music in this way, as an emotional lightning rod for slicing through the stultifying obduracy of politics to the heart of the matter. For example, in the preface to his 1844 anthology of abolitionist songs, *The Liberty Minstrel*, compiler George Clark described the antislavery singing groups he hoped would use his collection. "Let associations of singers, having the love of liberty in their hearts, be immediately formed in every community," Clark declared. "Let them study thoroughly, and make themselves perfectly familiar with both the poetry and the music, and enter into the *sentiment* of the piece they perform, that they may *impress it* upon their hearers."[5] And so the singers, gathered in kitchens and parlors and barbershops and church basements, teach themselves about poetry and music, contemplate how to address their neighbors' support for slavery, rehearse their songs, and then venture out into the public to strike at their listeners' political beliefs through their sentiments.

In fact, a few generations earlier, during the American Revolution, some of the leading revolutionaries, including Tom Paine, Ben Franklin, John Dickinson, Arthur Lee, and Joseph Warren, penned their own lyrics for the cause. Noted schemer, rabble-rouser, and arch propagandist Samuel Adams, he of the Boston Tea Party, formed among Boston mechanics political singing groups so successful (or at least notorious) that his Tory detractor Peter Oliver later credited them with "inculcating Sedition, 'till it had ripened into Rebellion."[6] That rebellion eventually took many forms, but even the military actions of Adams's "Sons of Liberty" were accompanied by music; we know that the tea partiers, while dumping the East India Company's tea into Boston Harbor on 16 December 1773, sang their way through the night, chanting "Rally, Mohawks! Bring our your axes, / and tell King George we'll pay no taxes / on his foreign tea."[7] Two years and one month later, in January 1776, Tom Paine published *Common Sense*, a pamphlet widely considered to be one of the, if not *the*, most important pieces of revolutionary persuasion. The previous year Paine had voiced some of the concerns that would later become famous in *Common Sense* in the form of "The Liberty Tree," a popular ballad set to the tune of "The Gods of Greece." The song is no masterpiece; one can nonetheless imagine Paine and his comrades parading audaciously through the streets of Philadelphia singing

> From the East to the West blow the trumpet to arms,
> Thro' the land let the sounds of it flee:
> Let the far and the near all unite with a cheer,
> In defense of our Liberty Tree.[8]

The interlacing of music and politics has also served causes decidedly less radical than those pursued by Adams, Franklin, Paine, and their revolutionary colleagues. Indeed, as the revolutionary energies of the founders turned toward the boggling question of how to put democratic ideals into practice, so America's music was put to different purposes as well. James Morton Smith notes, for example, that during the infamous xyz Affair of 1798, when President John Adams and the Federalists led a blistering assault on Jefferson and the Democratic-Republicans, whom they accused of collaborating with France, "'Hail Columbia' was sung to the tune of the 'President's March' and served unofficially as the national anthem."[9] Written by Joseph Hopkins, "Hail Columbia," "swept the country, arousing fervent patriotic emotions."[10] Along with "Yankee Doodle," which quickly became a folk standard, "Hail Columbia" contributed mightily to the xenophobic and authoritarian backlash institutionalized in the 1798 Alien and Sedition Acts, bills that stand now, in retrospect, as gross violations of the Constitution, not the least because they identify respect for the Constitution as consent to the political ploys of a specific party (the Federalists). This collapsing of the Constitution's protected rights into the Federalists' dubious political imperatives was made possible, in part, by the sense that the Federalists spoke, organically, directly, intuitively, for all democracy-loving Americans. Xenophobic sentiments ran so high in both politics and music that even one's instruments were subject to questions of national loyalty. Thus on 23 June 1798 Benjamin Franklin Bache's oppositional *Philadelphia Aurora* reported, in its typically biting, anti-Federalist tone, that "Cremona fiddles are to be ordered out of the kingdom under the Alien Bill," as their fine Italian tones were considered likely to "bring the *constitutional* music of organs and kettle-drums into contempt."[11] In the face of such bitter sarcasm, Federalists sang that "Frenchmen's songs, so full of wrongs / Are scorn'd by Yankee heroes," to which Democratic-Republicans responded that "Hail Columbia" was "an aristocratic tune" full of "ridiculous bombast."[12] Regardless of one's position on the xyz Affair and the ensuing Alien and Sedition Acts of 1798, then, it is clear that hotly contested folk songs played significant roles both in shaping public opinion regarding current affairs and in voicing competing ideals regarding the promises and practices of democracy in America.

A generation later, in the Jacksonian period, Americans found their cities flooded with immigrants fleeing Europe's famines and wars. Contrary to "melting pot" mythology, these immigrants were not welcomed with open arms.

Rather, they were hounded into ghettoes, treated like "vermin," and subjected to a historically unprecedented disciplinary onslaught (carried out by police and fire departments, schools, churches, and other "reform" groups) that sought to change their languages, their dress, their food, their politics, and their music. William Woodbridge was one of the leading figures in this disciplinary movement; his contribution to the cause was a lifetime of activism supporting music education as a means of socialization. For example, in his front-page editorial in the inaugural issue of the *American Annals of Education and Instruction*, in August 1830, Woodbridge expressed grave anxieties about the fate of the nation and its rapidly expanding population. Demonstrating the ease with which reformers of the era moved from liberalizing impulses to disciplinary practices, he warned of the threat to democracy posed by ignorance, corruption, and the "irreligion" of Irish Catholic immigrants: "If we slumber over our danger or shrink back from the contest, our country is lost, our institutions must be trampled under foot, and the name of America is inscribed on the broken column which records the weakness and the ruin of republics."[13] Woodbridge spent the better part of his life defending the nation from this epic threat through music, which he believed could inculcate proper emotions, discipline, and nationalism. The story of Mr. Woodbridge and his fellow "reformers" (to which we turn in chapter 2) demonstrates that the use of music as a persuasive tool can serve multiple and often contradictory political impulses. Indeed, whereas Simpson's *Emancipation Car* would soon be offering antislavery ballads to abolitionists in 1854, proslavery songsters would be publishing similar collections for their neighbors. As we demonstrate in chapters 3 and 4, one could sing just as persuasively of white supremacy as of emancipation.

One of the most obvious reasons why "America" has been so consistently employed in these multiple and contradictory political movements is its lyrical and musical simplicity, which enables even marginally talented poets to rewrite its lyrics without much effort, while even the tone-deaf can learn quickly to sing along with its simple tune. Rather than shrinking from such lyrical and musical simplicity, Lowell Mason was convinced that it was a key component of any attempt to use music as a persuasive weapon, particularly in the realm of moral reform, where psalms and hymns were popular. One of the most important liberal reformers and proponents of music education in America from roughly 1825–60 and one of the driving forces behind the popularization of "America" as the "national hymn" and "national psalm" in the 1830s, Mason wrote that "One of the most important characteristics of a good psalm tune is simplicity, or such arrangement with respect both to melody and harmony as shall render the design intelligible, and the execution easy."[14] If we take Mason's argument seriously—his fellow reformers certainly did at the time—then it leads to the thesis that nationalism in general and nationalizing songs such as "America" in particular necessarily entail the simplification of culture, the rendering of complex factors in forms trivial and banal.

While European nations and cultures are no less open to this change than America, European observers have nonetheless taken great pleasure in deriding both American nationalism and musical culture as particularly vulgar. For example, writing in 1835, Gustave de Beaumont (Tocqueville's traveling companion) confessed: "I deplore that blind national pride in Americans." "When they abandon themselves to their national pride," Beaumont warned, "they lose all reason entirely."[15] Almost seventy years later, Max Weber, a thinker not known as a musical critic, could not resist commenting condescendingly on what he saw in 1904 as "that absolute musical vacuum" of America, where "one hears as community singing in general only a noise which is intolerable to German ears."[16] At the time of Weber's launching this chauvinist barrage, "community singing" in our "absolute musical vacuum" would have certainly included "America," particularly among the radical farmers and factory workers who (as we demonstrate in chapter 5) were fighting precisely the grassroots political battles necessary to forestall the construction in America of what Weber saw in Europe as an inescapably bureaucratized world of disempowered automatons. While the folk music of the period may not have been as complicated or sophisticated as that listened to by Weber and his fellow highbrow critics, and while it is granted here that many forms of American nationalism in fact amount to little more than Beaumont's dreaded sense of "blindness," we should not forget that many national songs are deeply intertwined with a thriving political culture that produces its own musical sites and situations and that takes the possibility of employing songs as political weapons seriously.

Weber argued from Europe in 1904 that "the tremendous cosmos of the modern economic order . . . is now bound to the technical and economic conditions of machine production which today determine the lives of all the individuals who are born into the mechanism." This "iron cage" exerts "an inexorable power over the lives of men as at no previous period in history," hence producing a hellish world of "mechanized petrification, embellished with a sort of convulsive self-importance."[17] Americans at the time were far from petrified, however, as the nation was awash in an era of radical political activism that targeted precisely the inexorable power of big money and bureaucracies that Weber feared. Indeed, Philip Foner's glorious collection, *American Labor Songs of the Nineteenth Century*, offers us a remarkable opportunity to hear what our forebears had to say and sing about the "iron cage" of modernity. *The Alliance and Labor Songster* of 1891, for example, included "A New National Anthem" (see appendix A), set to the tune of "America," that argued in the second verse: "[I] hate thy usury mills, / That fill the bankers' tills / Till they overflow." The first verse begins with "My country, 'tis of thee / *Once* land of liberty," indicating the nation's slide toward injustice, and concludes with a desperate description of a "Land of the Millionaire; / Farmers with pockets bare; / Caused by the cursed snare — / The money ring."[18] These are hardly the sentiments of someone in the throes either of "convulsive self-importance" or disempowered defeatism.

In fact, contrary to the charge that America was an "absolute musical vacuum," it is clear that the nation was on fire with protest songs. Set both to familiar tunes such as "When Johnny Comes Marching Home," "Susannah, Don't You Cry," and "America" and to original "airs" composed for the moment, the period featured hundreds of political songs, including "Ring the Bells of Freedom," "To the Polls," "Storm the Fort," "Our Battle Song," an anticapitalist and anticorruption version of the "Star-Spangled Banner," "Shouting the Battle-Cry of Labor," "The March of Labor," and so on.[19] These were not musical masterpieces of high art, nor were they intended to be; rather, these simple songs served the more pressing function of voicing oppositional politics. While some versions of "America" lamented lost liberties (such as in "A New National Anthem"), others looked forward to a day of achievement and fulfillment. For example, Harvey Moyer's 1913 "My Country, A New National Hymn" begins with the claim: "My country thou shalt be / Sweet land of liberty / When justice reigns." Included in Moyer's popular *Songs of Socialism* (see figure I.1), this utopian version of the song imagines an America where "Poverty shall cease / Wealth, comforts, joys increase / on ev'ry hand."[20]

Despite the obviously important roles such songs have played in radical grassroots movements in America, one of the aspects of American folk culture that has most annoyed highbrow critics such as Weber and Theodor Adorno is its apparent lack of self-reflexive consciousness and irony.[21] The history of "America" demonstrates, however, that the song has been rewritten according to a wide range of rhetorical strategies, with parody and irony chief among them. For example, in the early stages of the Civil War, when Northerners feared that Britain would side with the South, the *New York Evening Post* offered a "New Version of an Old Song." Considering that the *London Times* had recently editorialized in sympathy with the rebellion, one can imagine the venom with which these brilliantly sarcastic lines, set to the tune of "America," must have been sung.

> God save Cotton, our King!
> God save our noble King!
>   God save the King!
> Send him the sway he craves,
> Britons his willing slaves,
> "Rule," Cotton! "Rule the waves!"
>   God save the King!

Later verses (see appendix A) decry the hypocrisy of a world in which "Freedom" is but "an empty name . . . Careless of good or ill . . . While we our pockets fill"

SONGS OF SOCIALISM

FOR

Local Branch and Campaign Work, Public Meetings, Labor, Fraternal, and Religious Organizations, Social Gatherings, and the Home

EDITED BY

Harvey P. Moyer,

Author of Vital Problems, The A B C of Socialism, Socialism Simplified, A Socialist Catechism, The Christianity of Socialism, &c.

Love is the greatest thing in the world.—*Drummond*

 33

PRICES.

In Strong Paper Cover.
Single Copy, postpaid, 20 cents; Six Copies, $1.00;
Per Dozen, $1.75; Special rates for 100 Copies.
In Beautiful Crimson Cloth.
Single Copy, postpaid, 30 cents; Four Copies, $1.00;
Per Dozen, $2.50; Special rates for 100 Copies.

Seventh Edition.
Thirtieth Thousand.

The Co-Operative Printing Company

5443 Drexel Ave,   1913   Chicago, Ill., U. S. A.

Figure I.1. The title page of Harvey Moyer's 1913 *Songs of Socialism*. Courtesy of The University of Illinois Rare Book and Special Collections Library.

through lucrative dealings based on slavery.[22] This mocking, ironic 1861 celebration of the rampant greed driving Britain's feared alliance with slavemasters might just as effectively be sung today as a damning lullaby for those who justify labor relations in much of the world that amount to little more than slavery. Indeed, given the fact that America's military and economic interests now straddle the globe, patriotism is a numbingly complicated matter, for it is not clear where or when supporting the national interest makes one complicit with programs and policies that may be politically questionable, if not ethically untenable.

As a host of observers have noted, it is difficult to speak of patriotism in such a situation: does loving America mean endorsing the unfair labor practices of those U.S. corporations that fill our stores with commodities? Does loving America mean supporting the environment-destroying practices of those U.S. corporations that fill our cars with gasoline and our stoves with natural gas? Does loving America mean accepting its failed "war on drugs" and its cruel prisons, now bursting with over two million of our neighbors? Clearly, loving one's country has become immensely complicated. In fact, more than a year before the terrorist attacks of 11 September 2001 the noted American historian David Kennedy wrote in an editorial printed on the Fourth of July that "perhaps in no age have patriots been deemed more foolish than in our own. To confess love of country today is to invite sneers from sophisticates, to court banishment to the supposedly lunatic fringe, to risk indictment as smug, stupid, or reactionary—or, vilest of all epithets, corny." Kennedy's claim reminds us just how tenuous patriotism had become before the terrorist strikes of the Autumn of 2001 launched Americans into a new phase of national concern. Indeed, following those brutal attacks Americans dug for flags long stowed away in basements and garages and called passionately for renewing the bonds of patriotism and duty. Most aptly for the subject of this book, in the days following the attacks Americans sang more renditions of national songs than at any time since the end of World War II.

As we demonstrate below, "My Country 'Tis of Thee" is historically the song more Americans embraced in more political crises to voice their concerns than any other. But as the *New York Times* reported eight days after the destruction of the World Trade Towers, it was not "My Country 'Tis of Thee" but Irving Berlin's "God Bless America" that was sung "from the steps of the Capitol to the stages of Broadway, from the National Cathedral and even the balcony of the New York Stock Exchange."[23] That Americans turned to song in our time of crisis indicates how deeply notions of nationalism and patriotism are entwined with the familiar narratives and melodies that constitute such an important part of our national culture. That "God Bless America" was the song of the moment —for reasons that critics more distanced from the tragedy will no doubt address —demonstrates how the ability of a given song to voice widespread political ambitions and anxieties is always contingent upon larger issues of cultural transformation and political expedience.

What makes my "My Country 'Tis of Thee" so historically interesting, politically powerful, and artistically fascinating is the fact that it has been sung since
1744 and has thus accrued a deep and resonant series of voicings, all offering nu-
anced versions not only of what it means to love your nation, but of how patriotism has always been the subject of heated contestation. Indeed, the fact that
the song has been appropriated in hundreds of competing versions means that
it embodies the very dialogue and debate that distinguishes American democracy. Patriotism, the song teaches us, is not only about supporting your nation's
policies, but also about questioning them when you think they need questioning
—after all, we are not a compliant and quietist nation; democracy does not
thrive without debate and debate cannot thrive without skepticism. Like patriotism, skepticism too has deep historical roots in our national history. One obvious reason for this skepticism is that the American public has clearly become
sensitive to state-orchestrated events that use patriotism as the veneer for obviously partisan or personal objectives. For example, on 3 June 1921, during National Music Week, fifty thousand schoolchildren formed a great "human wheel"
on the Ellipse in Washington, D.C. The embattled President Warren Harding
lumbered to the hub of the wheel and stood beside an eight-foot floral lyre honoring the Goddess of Music, as five bands and the assembled multitude performed "America."[24] Like so many of the stories that follow, this example highlights the tensions between sincere emotion and staged show, between citizens'
love of nation and politicians' need of spectacle. One wonders how many spectacles like this you can see before growing skeptical.

We would do well, then, to remember that our forebears sang "My Country
'Tis of Thee" not only to focus their political ideals and to persuade their neighbors, but also to express both their love of and dismay with their country. But
most of all, whereas we for the most part listen and buy and download, they
sang, they performed, they participated in the public production of their musical culture.[25] We close this introduction, then, by returning to Samuel Smith,
the author of "America," who argued during the early days of the Civil War, as
ever, that one should sing one's politics. Indeed, much as Joshua McCarter
Simpson understood that "you can sing what would be death to speak," and
much as Ernst Bloch understood that "the vibrating note travels," so Smith understood that music has a special power to transcend the factional, to leap
across space, to reach beyond prejudice; for

> Sound sweeps wildly o'er the land,
>   Sweeps o'er the bounding sea;
> It echoes, from each mountain-top,
>   The anthem of the free;
> It snaps the chain that sin has forged
>   It sings for liberty.[26]

ONE

"God Save the _____!"

Institutionalizing, Appropriating, and Contesting Nationalism through Song, 1744–1798

Iɴ his 1895 essay "Music in America," Antonin Dvorak wondered: "What songs, then, belong to the American and appeal more strongly to him than any others? What melody could stop him on the street if he were in a strange land and make the home feeling well up within him, no matter how hardened he might be or how wretchedly the tune were played?"[1] Much to the dismay of Dvorak and others, the national song that Americans were most likely to hear abroad, although not necessarily in honor of their own nation, was "America" ("My Country 'Tis of Thee"). Set to the highly recognizable melody of the unofficial British national anthem, no song more roused the wrath of those calling for a "true American" song. For example, Professor Thomas Lounsbury of Yale insisted that "there is nothing more impudent in the history of plagiarism than our appropriation of 'God Save the King' and calling it 'America.'" In the same spirit, the *New York Times* editorialized in 1889 that "'America' should be ignored by all persons who do not wish to be classed as receivers of stolen goods."[2] A nation of distinction, they reasoned, should have a distinctive anthem. Indeed, "America"'s borrowed melody—from the land of monarchy, no less—seemed to both Lounsbury and the *New York Times* to stand at odds with the emergence of the United States as a creative, self-generating, and democratic world power.

Compounding the sin of its foreign origin, "America" was set to the monarchical anthem of the nation's former colonizer, an adversary in two wars and a foil throughout much of the nineteenth century for American assertions of republican virtue. In fact, in the congressional hearings held in 1930 to select an official American anthem, Representative Louis McFadden argued that the meaning of the melody was forever fixed in its association with the British monarchy and that its use as our national anthem would amount to a betrayal of the American Revolution. "I have been educated to believe that our American freedom consisted of emancipation from monarchical forms of government, officialdom, divine right, the feudal system and its modern ramification," McFadden argued, "For us Americans now to claim it [the air of "God Save the King"], is as sensible as for us to claim all the other monarchical prerogatives and heritages."[3] Based in part on such appeals to an American nationalism drained of all historical precedents—a move consistent with the longstanding notion of our "exceptionalism," our somehow transcending the entangling snares of historical obligations—Congress selected the supposedly more authentic and original "Star-Spangled Banner" as the national anthem in 1931. While historians pointed out that its melody was equally British in origin, it at least had the virtue of being less well known and thus of less obviously harking back to our monarchical beginnings. From the earliest proponents of "God Save the King!" in 1744 up through Dvorak in 1895 and Representative McFadden in 1931, then, songs have been recognized as important rhetorical and political texts.[4]

It is thus no surprise that the emotional and symbolic power of national songs has made them a favored resource not only for those seeking to express their own patriotism or to instill a love of country in others, but also for those who wish to contest nationalist claims or to reconstitute national identities. Indeed, as citizens of a nation almost indescribably heterogeneous in race, class, religious beliefs, and ancestral homelands, we have never had a sense of ourselves as Americans that has been uniform or stable. Thus, as our national identities are multiple and mutable, socially and rhetorically constructed, so our national songs are among the most intriguing and ever-changing expressions of our national identities.

Much like other forms of public expression, national songs are subject to several distinct but interrelated forms of rhetorical action, including: *institutionalization*, by which governments promote and associate themselves with national songs; *contestation*, by which issues of national policy or identity are disputed through the use of national songs; and *appropriation*, by which American identities are constructed through the borrowing of national songs from other nations. This chapter explores these three processes in early American uses of "God Save the King." As we demonstrate, in the period from 1744 to 1798, many Americans experienced profound transformations of national identity, from loyal colonial subjects of the British king, to antimonarchical revolutionaries or embattled loyalists, to citizens of an emerging and distinctive nation. The melody of "God Save the King" was one constant throughout this period, as it was used in hundreds of lyrical variations to express in widely, almost comically different ways what it meant to be an American. Reconstructing this story in turn enables us to visit some of the figures, controversies, songs, events, and movements that contributed to the production of American political culture circa 1744–98.

Institutionalization: The "Perpetual Reminder" of Nationalism

To identify oneself as a member of a nation is to place oneself within a "people" mythically connected by blood, belief, custom, or heritage. As argued by a number of recent theorists and historians of nation formation, the modern nation is a complex and frequently convoluted social construction rather than simply a geographic or demographic entity; it is an "imagined political community" that is real yet fictional, physical yet rhetorical.[5] Nationhood is thus an inherently elusive concept, as indicated in Margaret Canovan's observation that it entails

> a polity that feels like a community, or conversely a cultural or ethnic community politically mobilized; it cannot exist without subjective identification, and therefore is to some extent dependent on free individual choice, but that choice is nevertheless experienced as a destiny transcending individuality; it turns political institutions into a kind of extended family inheritance, although the kinship ties in question are highly metaphorical; it is a contingent historical product that feels like part of the order of nature; it links individual and community, past and present; it gives to cold institutional structures an aura of warm, intimate togetherness.[6]

This complicated sense of feeling that one is part of something that is simultaneously bigger than oneself yet intimately linked to one's individual choice is crucial for both the promotion of national affiliation and the mobilization of mass force, as the sense that one chooses or participates in the production of nationalism both depends on and generates collective power through inspirational myths and symbols. Nationalism thus *appears* natural, even organic, yet as Canovan and others have noted, the "warm, intimate togetherness" of nationhood is constructed through relatively spontaneous cultural and rhetorical acts and the most carefully choreographed institutional efforts. The "nation," then, is fundamentally a set of ideas, an overlapping series of cultural and historical artifacts sustained through ongoing rhetorical performances and negotiated institutionalization. Given these premises, national songs are among the clearest and most common enactments of our laying claim to the "extended family inheritance" of nationhood, as they are an important element of civic ceremonies, national holidays, state functions, and, prior to the rise of electronic mass media, the daily cultural life of families and neighborhoods. Indeed, for many citizens, their performance is, as Reverend Elias Nason described it in 1869, an "enchanted key to memory's deepest cells" that "kindles sacred flames in chambers of the soul unvisited by other agencies."[7]

What does it mean, then, to sing a national song? What does one *say* or *do* by singing such material? In large part, singing a national song is a statement of citizenship, an enactment of identity and belonging that is either explicit within the lyrics themselves (such as when one sings of "*our* King," or "*My* country 'tis of thee") or implicit in the complicated ways that all public performance claims relevancy and legitimacy for the performers. As Whitman boasts in the stunning opening lines of *Leaves of Grass*, "One's self I sing, a simple separate person, / Yet utter the word Democratic, the word En-Masse."[8] Thus, like Whitman (although perhaps with less bravado), we too, in singing national songs, blend our own individual voices and lives in an imagined yet inescapably real community built on the words and melodies crafted, sanctioned, and performed by others. In public settings, we merge our voices with others, and on the occasions in which our voices are called forth we sing of our rights and responsibilities, both of what we are entitled to expect as citizens of the country and what our country in turn is entitled to expect of us.

National songs therefore advance, implicitly or explicitly, at least two types of claims regarding national identity: claims about the nation and claims about the relationship between singer(s) and nation. These claims may be advanced textually (through lyrics), musically (through familiar melodies), or socially (through political or performative context) and usually entail rich combinations of all three. For example, national songs make explicit claims about the nation when their lyrics stipulate essential national characteristics, elements of shared history, geography, and blood, or principles used both to define the nation and set it apart from others. The United States is thus imagined in song as a "land of the free and home of the brave" or as a "sweet land of liberty" where one's "fathers died" and in which the Pilgrims took "pride." Depending on one's political beliefs, this idealized nation may be temporally fixed in a glorious past to be celebrated or in a hypocritical past to be redeemed; it may be held up for praise or ridicule; it may be recognized as a fully embodied present or as a hopeful future to be achieved through activism; yet its singing invests the moment of performance with national memory and promise. In this sense, then, "all songs," writes the novelist E. L. Doctorow, "are songs of justification." Indeed, national songs justify allegiance not only by proclaiming the nation's virtues but also by creating performative contexts in which citizen-singers publicly honor their love for the nation. On the other hand, such performative situations frequently veer into an embarrassingly banal reverence for national songs and symbols, as citizens are expected to stand, to be silent, or (when hearing one's national anthem upon receiving an Olympic medal, for example) to revel in nationalist emotions that feel more imposed than organic, more obligatory than chosen. In some instances, such as when hearing "God Save the King/Queen' and "America" — or in the closing lines of the "Star-Spangled Banner" at ball games — the audience is expected to join in, yet again it is difficult to judge the political impulses behind such choreographed moments. Nonetheless, despite the complexities of such performative contexts, it is clear that the rhetorical power of national songs lies in their brevity and "single-mindedness," Doctorow explains, which "make them universally and instantly accessible as no other form is."[9]

National songs are "national" not only in their subject matter but in their associations with governments, policies, and the efforts of the state to promote or suppress the use of song for political goals. By symbolically invoking the nation, governments lay claim to traditions, heroes, principles, and popular affections, purporting that their actions are undertaken on behalf of the people. National songs performed in civic ceremonies thus generally affirm the legitimacy of the state and equate the idealized nation of song with the state in fact. Despite the obvious contradictions buried within the slippage between idealized song and political reality, citizens continue to sing national songs. Governments and citizens therefore work hand-in-hand to institutionalize the performance of national songs and to negotiate their meanings. Simultaneously, however, because national songs are such powerful expressions of individual and group identity, they function as highly volatile spaces for staging social conflict. Thus, while Paul Nettl argues in *National Anthems* that "nationalism and patriotism are a sort of collective self-confidence," it is also important to observe that national songs are often created in periods beset by social unrest and insecurity. Most European anthems, for example, were produced in the early nineteenth century, when revolutions and the Napoleonic conquests swept the continent (thus radically redrawing national boundaries) and the romantic movement spurred interest in ethnicity, folklore, symbolism, and the mythic past (thus introducing elements difficult for modern nation-states to manage).[10] The resulting national songs were produced in response to social exigencies and/or perceived threats from without or within, including the threat of invasion ("La Marseillaise"), insurrection ("God Save the King"), or loss of independence ("The Star-Spangled Banner"). These French, British, and American songs capture moments when the fate of the nation seems to hang in the balance and when mobilization of public opinion and action becomes imperative. "The Star-Spangled Banner," for example, ends not with a declaration of certain survival and prosperity but with an open question: "Oh, say does that star-spangled banner yet wave / O'er the land of the free / And the home of the brave?" Anthems born in crisis therefore impart the lesson that history is tenuous and that political fortunes change quickly; in so doing they recall legacies of sacrifice, of yearning, and of becoming.

"God Save the King," like many other national songs, was popularized under circumstances in which the nation seemed threatened and tenuous and hence most real to those subjects who feared its destruction. The earliest published version of "God Save the King" appeared in the 1744 version of the annual collection *Thesaurus Musicus*.[11] In mid-July of the following year "Bonnie Prince Charlie," the grandson of the exiled James II, landed on the western shore of Scotland with the intention of placing his father on the throne of England. With British forces already engaged on the continent in the Austrian War of Succession, he won a series of early victories in Scotland, entering Edinburgh on 18 September and crushing General Cope's forces at Prestonpans on 20 September. After receiving the news of Cope's defeat, the supporters of George II were terrified, as Percy Scholes observes, at the prospect of "London invaded by a horde of wild Highlanders, a Catholic king on the throne, the Protestant religion, and their hard-won and now traditional political liberties taken from them in the name of James III, as they had been taken from them by his father, James II." Just eight days after the battle at Prestonpans, on 28 September 1745, "God Save the King" was first performed in public by players at the Theatre-Royal in Drury Lane, London. A notice in the London *General Advertiser* that morning announced the intention of the master of the Drury Lane company to raise a force of two hundred soldiers "in Defence of His Majesty's Person and Government; in which the whole Company of Players are willing to engage." Audience members "were agreeably surpriz'd" when at the end of the evening's performance twenty singers joined in "performing the anthem of *God save our noble King*." "The universal Applause it met with," according to a report in the *Daily Advertiser* of 30 September, "being encored with repeated Huzzas, sufficiently denoted in how just an Abhorrence they hold the arbitrary Schemes of our invidious Enemies, and detest the despotick Attempts of Papal Power."[12]

The version sung that night (see appendix A) included the famous opening lines: "God save great George our King, / Long live our noble King, / God save the King." The song's declaration of loyalty and obedience ("Long to reign over us") was qualified, however, in a new third stanza, which first appeared in the *Gentleman's Magazine* in 1745 and is still sung today: "May he defend our laws, / And ever give us cause, / With Heart and Voice to sing, / God Save the King."[13] The act of singing the song implies that, so far at least, such "cause" has been given, while holding open the possibility that someday royal behavior might forfeit the allegiance of subjects now loyal. Despite this qualification, in the first two verses the implied singers claim George II as their ruler and his enemies as their own, thus blending their individual voices within the

Figure 1.1. William Hogarth, *The March to Finchley: A Representation of the March of the Guards Towards Scotland in the Year 1745.* Courtesy of The British Museum.

implied plural chorus of nationhood (as seen in "*our* King," "reign over *us*," "*our* God," "*our* hopes"). Hence, in the face of war on the Continent, invasion from the North, and the usual political intrigue brought on by such calamities, the singing of "God Save the King" stipulates a qualified yet nonetheless national polity.

"God Save the King" attained immediate popularity and, in addition to being widely performed in church services and secular gatherings, was published in numerous magazines, newspapers, and broadsides. The ubiquity of the song is captured in William Hogarth's 1745 engraving *The March to Finchley* (see figure 1.1). The image depicts the dissipated British army as it marches to Scotland in 1745 to fight Bonnie Prince Charlie. Its central soldier figure is torn between the entreaties of a pregnant ballad-singer holding a basket full of broadside copies of "God Save the King" on one side (see figure 1.2), and on the other an old woman, dressed in a black priest's robe with an enormous crucifix swinging from her neck, holding aloft a rolled opposition newspaper. Scholes reads the image as symbolizing the nation "wavering between the Hanoverian Protestant Succession and the Stuart Romanist Succession," with "God Save the King" "thoroughly associated with the former." Hogarth thus highlights the

Figure 1.2. Hogarth, *March to Finchley*, detail.

rapid popularization of "God Save the King" as a symbol of public support for the crown.[14]

Official symbols, such as anthems, flags, and emblems, and the ceremonies in which they are used, blur the distinctions between nation and state. "From the point of view of the state authorities," Zdzislaw Mach has observed, "it is essential that the symbols have proper respect and are *sacred for citizens*, since they represent the ideological and political unity of the nation and its political organization."[15] Although never officially designated as the British national anthem, "God Save the King" soon acquired a status close to sacred through its incorporation in civic and military ceremonies, its use by the royal family, and the eager hyperbole of publishers who referred to the song on the cover of broadsides and songbooks as "the National Anthem." Thus, within three years of the Drury Lane performance the chimes of St. Margaret's, Westminster (the official church of the House of Commons), were set to play the tune. By the reign of Queen Victoria, "God Save the Queen" was heard on virtually every occasion of state and every public appearance of the queen. On her first jubilee in 1887 an inventive subject presented her with a mechanical bustle that would play the tune whenever she sat down.[16] "God Save the Queen/King" was frequently adapted to suit specific royal occasions and exigencies, such as the long mental illness of George III, his attempted assassination in 1800, or the transfer of power to a new monarch. On such occasions, the performance of "God Save the King" equated the well-being of nation and monarch and expressed the singer-subject's continuing loyalty to both, despite the crises of the moment.

Given such widespread domestic support, it is no surprise that "God Save the King/Queen" soon gained international recognition as a symbol of the British nation. For example, in Beethoven's symphony *Wellington's Victory* and Weber's *Kampf und Sieg*, written to commemorate momentous battles, the musical quotation of "God Save the King" signals the arrival, engagement, and triumph or defeat of the British forces. These battle pieces proved immensely popular with middle-class audiences, who packed concert halls to hear them performed.[17] "God Save the King/Queen" was in turn performed throughout the empire. In the colonies in particular, the song had special significance both for agents of the crown and loyal subjects, as it exemplified both British domination (the state) and the culture of the homeland (the nation). In this sense the song serves what rhetorical scholars refer to as the function of metonymy, for in condensing the state and nation into the figure of the king or queen, who are in turn represented as the uniting force of the people, the song takes the slippery, intangible complexities of nationhood and reduces them into an easily recognizable symbol; hence the complex is made simple, the intangible is made real, and *the nation is embodied*. "The existence of a song of prayer for that central human figure, a song known to millions of citizens of those monarchical-republics," Scholes observes, "is of enormous value as a perpetual reminder of the central point at which they unite."[18]

In the American colonies, "God Save the King" was an emblem of the ancestral or native homeland of most colonists. The vast majority of white immigrants to the colonies were British Protestants who retained strong cultural and political attachments unsevered by their passage. British influence was predominant in colonial language, politics, arts, social organization, and folkways. Affluent American families sent their sons to British universities, and each colony maintained closer trade and commercial ties with England than with neighboring colonies. Most white colonists, notes David Hackett Fischer in *Albion's Seed*, retained a strong sense of British national identity; they "lived under British law and took pride in possessing British liberties" as subjects of a distant but revered king. Indeed, the king cast a towering figure in colonial society as commander-in-chief of the armed forces, leader of the church, head of state, and "wealthiest of the wealthy" all in one. Social rank in Virginia, the most populous and influential of the colonies, was organized in a rigid hierarchy of deferential relationships extending from Britain itself, with the top tiers occupied by the monarch and royal family. "Distant as the sovereign may have been," writes Fischer, "the gentry of Virginia thought much about him." Even in Massachusetts, the most independent of the colonies, words of respect and praise for the king opened and closed all public ceremonies and peppered government documents and proclamations. In short, the expression "God save the King" was a ubiquitous feature of public and private discourse.[19]

Respect for the British monarch was also, however, enforced by both law and rigid social custom. In 1725 Elizabeth Hansford was found guilty by a jury in York County, Virginia, of singing in public "a scandalous and opprobrious song" that "did curse and revile our said Lord the King." She and her husband were each fined twenty shillings, payable "for the use of our said Lord the King." The Hansford case was exceptional, however, for up until the radical transformations of the 1770s most white colonists praised and celebrated the king within the routines of daily life. Royal events, such as birthdays, coronations, military victories, child births and marriages, were also widely commemorated in song. For example, a huge crowd gathered in Boston on 30 December 1760 in observance of the death of George II and the coronation of George III. A proclamation read from the balcony of the courthouse pledged on behalf of the citizens in attendance "all Faith and constant Obedience, with all hearty and humble Affection: Beseeching GOD . . . To bless the Royal King GEORGE the Third, with long and happy Years to Reign over us." Huzzahs, cannon fire, and the singing of "God Save the King" concluded the ceremony.[20]

New songs, such as "God Save the King," were published in newspapers and sold as broadsides, single sheets of paper generally printed on one side from woodcuts. Broadsides were posted in public spaces or purchased from booksellers, street vendors, or ballad-mongers who sold them for a penny apiece at markets, fairs, horse races, and door to door. Virtually every colonial home had a collection of broadside songs that were used for family entertainment and as texts for the education of children. In fact, the American colonists, writes music historian John Anthony Scott, "sang under every conceivable kind of circumstance and on every occasion." And while they sang traditional British songs and ballads from memory and taught them to their children, the colonists also introduced hundreds of minor variations—in melody, emphasis, language, and tempo—reflecting the particularities of colonial life. These songs, wedding old and new, merging appropriation and invention, expressed both the colonists' sense of the distinctiveness of their experiences and their connectedness to the British empire and thus gave, Scott observes, "a scattered and struggling people a sense of unity and common destiny among new and difficult problems."[21]

The complicated diffusion of song culture is illustrated in the first published version of "God Save the King" in America. This occurred in 1761, in James Lyon's *Urania, or a Choice Collection of Psalm-tunes, Anthems, and Hymns* (see figure 1.3), where, under the subtitle "Hymns," Lyon included "Whitefields," a popular hymn based on the melody and line structure of "God Save the King." Lyon

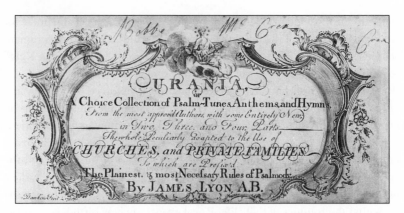

Figure 1.3. The title plate of James Lyon, *Urania, or A Choice Collection of Psalm-tunes, Anthems, and Hymns* (1761). Courtesy of The Library of Congress.

(1735–94) was born in Newark, New Jersey, and graduated from the College of New Jersey (later Princeton) in 1759. While in college, he began assembling a large collection of music both by British writers, who were transforming the practice of psalmody in the Church of England, and, as no previous collection had done, by Americans (including his classmate Francis Hopkinson). When no Philadelphia book dealer would finance its publication, Lyon sold subscriptions, with the promise that the collection would promote "the Art of Psalmody in its Perfection" among "the clergy of every denomination in America." *Urania* sold well in several editions and, for the first time, made the printed music of "God Save the King" available throughout the American colonies in a standardized form rather than in independently varying broadsides.[22]

"God Save the King" expressed for most white colonists the contractual basis of their allegiance to the state: loyalty was offered in return for protection of their lives, property, and liberties. In fact, it is no coincidence that Lyon published the song's melody during the Seven Years' War, when the British (at least according to loyalists; revolutionaries would later dispute this claim) sacrificed troops and treasure to protect the colonial frontier from French and Indian armies. During this period Britain cautiously promoted the idea of inter-colonial unity (while recognizing its potential danger for organized rebellion) in order to defend against the incursions of rival nations. When American colonists, such as Thomas Foxcroft in 1760, expressed their gratitude to the king "for his Paternal Goodness in sending such effectual Aids to his American subjects . . . when we so needed the Royal Protection," they both invoked this grow-ing sense of intercolonial unity and grounded that union in contractual alle-giance to the king, defining "we" as "his American subjects." Even the colonists' rising protests over British taxation and other issues of governance were long advanced as pleas for the king's protection of their rights as loyal British subjects. Thus, throughout the prerevolutionary period, "God Save the King" was widely, almost universally, accepted as a statement both of white colonists' national identity and their confidence in the king's regard for their interests and liberties.[23]

For the first decade of his reign, George III was popularly credited for British policies benefiting the colonists; he was held blameless for many unpopular actions, such as the Stamp Act of 1765 (which colonists blamed on scheming ministers and a corrupt Parliament). "No British king," writes William Liddle, "ever enjoyed the prestige, popularity, and influence in America that George III possessed in 1766."[24] In fact, between 1774 and 1776, as many colonists came to hold George III personally responsible for the repressive actions of the British government, even those sympathetic to the revolution were generally slow to renounce their loyalty to the king. Thus, during the American revolution approximately five hundred thousand out of two and a half million American colonists were loyalists; some nineteen thousand actually fought with the British; at the end of the war, between sixty thousand and one hundred thousand were eventually forced into exile and stripped of their property. Loyalty to the king among the colonists, however, extended beyond the life-threatening decision of openly opposing the revolution. Hence, at the outbreak of the revolution, Esmond Wright and others have argued, "most Americans" "were loyal if not Loyalist."[25]

Indeed, loyalists continued to sing "God Save the King" at ceremonial observances of the king's birthday and other occasions that marked the continuity of civil authority. Even after military hostilities were well commenced in America, loyalists celebrated the monarchy in part by honoring the loyalty of their fellow British subjects. For example, the Williamsburg *Virginia Gazette* of 17 February 1775 favorably reported the festivities of a tradesmen's meeting in London's King's Arms tavern to celebrate the birthday of the duke of Gloucester. A whip-maker and steward entertained the gathering by singing "God Save the King," with an additional stanza of hope that "the whole family / Live from all discord free, / In love and harmony, / 'Till time's no more." "Many loyal toasts," the report continues, were offered to the royal family and others, including one to the prospect of "A happy reconciliation between Great Britain and her Colonies." After his arrest in Philadelphia in 1775, the loyalist major Philip Skene was confined in the city tavern, where he gathered applause from passersby for his after-dinner renditions of "God Save the King."[26] When "a very respectable number of freeholders and inhabitants" of Westchester County gathered in White Plains, New York, on 11 April 1775 to select delegates for the upcoming Continental Congress, a rump meeting of loyalist "friends to order and government" assembled at a private home. The two groups later confronted each other at the courthouse. The loyalists professed their "determined resolution to continue steadfast in their allegiance to their gracious and merciful sovereign, King George the Third" and refused to participate in any vote to select delegates for an "unlawful congress." Then, after shouting "three huzzas," they marched away, "singing, as they went, with a loyal enthusiasm, the grand and animating song of 'God save great George our King, / Long live our noble King,' &c."[27] The rising tide of revolutionary sentiment was thus matched by public professions of loyalty to the king.

During the war, British forces used "God Save the King" to celebrate their victories and to mark control over occupied territories. After the six-week siege of Charleston in 1780, British troops led by Major General Alexander Leslie accepted the formal surrender of the city; as the British grenadiers reached the gate of the city their oboists played "God Save the King." In this context, the song marked the reassertion of British control and the forced obedience of rebels to the king. In an even more ominous display of the interweaving of song and discipline, of culture and state, oaths of allegiance and willingness to sing "God Save the King" provided public affirmation of loyalty in the occupied territories, particularly among those known to have supported the revolution.[28] Whereas the early publications and performances of the song appear to have been spontaneous eruptions of allegiance to state and love of country, these singing oaths mark a turn toward the use of song as a means of coercion, as a propagandizing tactic meant to strong-arm citizens or subjects into obedience.

As British control of the colonies slipped away, the performance of "God Save the King" for loyalists came to symbolize what had been lost. In 1777, Jonathan Odell of New Jersey lamented the revolt in a birthday poem for the king, beginning: "Time was when America hallow'd the morn / On which the lov'd monarch of Britain was born. / Hallow'd the day, and joyfully chanted / God save the King!" Odell yearned nostalgically for the vanished past and employed the song's decline in popularity as a figure for political decay:

> But see! How rebellion has lifted her head!
> How honor and truth are with loyalty fled;
> Few are there now who join us in chanting
> God save the King![29]

Odell's loyalist verses made him a target for those sympathetic to the revolution. In 1778 he escaped to the British stronghold of New York City, where he assisted in the defection of Benedict Arnold before fleeing to England.

Despite Odell's lament that "God Save the King" no longer played a role in American life, the song continued in frequent if quite different use. Where once the song had served to define colonial identity as loyal subjects of a distant protector-king, it now voiced the revolutionaries' alienation, republicanism, and desire for independence. Indeed, the symbolic and functional associations of song and state produced by its institutionalization during the colonial period in turn enabled the song to function as a site for contesting and reinventing the nation.

Contestation: "By FREEDOM Fir'd"

The institutionalization of national songs is intended to forge connections between citizens and government, culture and politics, self and society, present and past. When sung en masse in official ceremonies of civic affiliation, at political meetings and rallies, or at neighborhood gatherings, picnics, and parties, national songs offer clear and concise statements of national identity and belonging. These qualities make national songs valuable not only to the state but to its opponents, who may employ national songs for pointed parody or protest. Indeed, just as national songs can be used by governments to signify their own legitimacy and association with national heritages and principles, so opponents may employ national songs to highlight the disparity between national ideals and contemporary policies or circumstances. In short, while national songs may advance claims about the nation and the relationship between their citizen-singers and the nation, they may also dispute these claims and promote alternative understandings of how a particular government or administration should fulfill the promises of the nation. National songs thus inevitably occupy contested political territory and serve as objects of contention between groups competing to define the nation.

Given the fact that a song is a temporary conjunction of music, words, and one or more voices raised in a dizzying number of historical and performative contexts, it naturally follows that songs are subject to any number of changes that transform their meanings and political implications. Each element (melody, words, singers, and context) lends meaning to a song; alterations in any one of them, or in the composition of the audience, can dramatically alter meaning. Even if the words are identical in various renditions, the meanings of the song may be altered by changes in the instrumentation, the identity of the singer(s), or the circumstances under which it is sung. For example, "La Marseillaise" was written by a royalist yet became the battle song of the revolutionaries; it was sung by the Communards in 1848 as well as by the troops that opposed them.[30] Under the Vichy government it became the anthem of resistance to the collaborationist government; when Rick and other expatriate characters in *Casablanca* (1942) joined the free French in singing it, it became a call for American action. These brief examples demonstrate that the "same" song may support radically different visions of the nation and that meanings of national songs are mutable and contextually dependent.

The origins and authorship of "God Save the King" are uncertain, but it is clear that long before the song was used in support of George II against the Jacobites it was in fact a Jacobite anthem. A Jacobite drinking glass from 1725 is inscribed with a version of "God Save the King" written in honor of the birth of Prince Henry, Stuart heir to the throne. Other Jacobite relics date the song even earlier, probably during the reign of James II, when it may have been sung in Latin in the king's Catholic chapel. Even after its publication in 1744, the loyalties proclaimed in "God Save the King" remained ambiguous. For *which* king is God's blessing invoked? The first line in the 1744 printings of the song reads simply: "God save our Lord the King," leaving open the question of whether the singer acknowledges the Stuart "Old Pretender" James III or the Hanoverian Protestant George II as rightful occupant of the throne. Presumably to resolve this ambiguity after Bonnie Prince Charlie landed in Scotland, the first line was changed in the 1745 printings of the song to read "God save great GEORGE our King." Scholes concludes that "the nation, at that period (under the threat of conquest by an army with support from France, fighting on behalf of a king then resident in Rome), was fast shedding what Jacobitism it possessed, and from thence onwards *God Save the King* took on a truly national complexion and from some undecided period began to be called 'The National Anthem.'"[31]

However, as Scholes and others document, the national complexion of the anthem was never complete, as individuals and groups continued through the years to use the song for a multitude of competing political and cultural agendas. For example, long after "God Save the King" was published and popularized as a Whig national anthem, Jacobite versions were printed and performed in secret societies. During the Corn Laws conflict of the 1830s, those unable to buy bread sang "God Save the People," not the monarch. In Montreal in 1894 and at Dublin University in 1905, orchestras refused to play the anthem, finding it in conflict with their own sense of nationalism. More recently, the Sex Pistols' deliriously snide version of "God Save the Queen" (1977) demolished any illusion that the song, monarch, or national government were objects of universal affection among Britons or that the nation of worshipful singers imagined in earlier versions of the song was in any way related to a bruised citizenry struggling through a recession under the bumbling and famously unpopular Wilson administration. Thus, as Graeme Turner has observed, "although nationalism normally serves a hegemonic function, its articulation through popular representational forms provides it with the potential for recovering class divisions and for challenging the dominant points of view of the culture."[32] Indeed, precisely because national songs conjure "the nation" and "the people" in widely recognizable fashion, they open nationalist claims to interrogation, parody, and appropriation.

It comes as no surprise, then, to observe that alternative and oppositional lyrics to "God Save the King" appeared in England almost immediately after its first publication. For example, a cheeky "Extempore Catch for the Westminster Fish Market, to the tune of 'God Save the King,'" appeared in a newspaper advertisement in 1748. The song expresses the proprietor's hope: "O may this market thrive / Whilst there's a fish alive; / Nature's best treat." The most popular early variation was "Come, Thou Almighty King," printed initially as a leaflet in 1757 and included in George Whitefield's collection of hymns from 1761. Although its authorship is unknown, Whitefield helped popularize it during his itinerant preaching tours of both Britain and the American colonies, where it was widely published in songbooks and hymnals.[33] Until 1769, when it acquired a tune of its own, "Come, Thou Almighty King" was sung to the tune of "God Save the King." Like many of the alternative versions from this era, "Come, Thou Almighty King" incorporates language from the British anthem while revising the object of the singer's affection. For while the original version sang of "great George our King," this new version asked: "Come, thou Almighty King, / Help us Thy name to sing, / Help us to praise." The second half of the first verse makes this shift in allegiance even more explicit, as it requests: "Father! All-glorious, / O'er all victorious, / Come, and reign over us, / Ancient of days." In his report of his nineteenth-century travels in North America, the novelist Anthony Trollope deplores that in singing "God Save the King," "we used to declare how certain we were that we should achieve all that was desirable, not exactly by trusting to our prayer to heaven, but by relying almost exclusively on George the Third or George the Fourth." "That," he declares, "was a rather poor patriotism." "Come, Thou Almighty King" responds to such concerns. Whereas in "God Save the King" divine blessings are invoked on behalf of the earthly monarch, in "Come, Thou Almighty King" Christ is identified as the only true lord, asked, as in "God Save the King," to "reign over us" in the opening verse and praised as a "sovereign majesty" in the final verse. The singer's plea for victory in the second verse of "God Save the King" remains in the hymn, but its agent of action has shifted: "Jesus, our Lord, arise, / Scatter our enemies, / Now make them fall!" This transference of faith from human monarch to divine Lord borrows from the language of worship and obedience in the royal anthem to praise a higher authority, thus affirming God's active intercession in worldly affairs and the subservience of monarch and subject alike to divine will.[34]

Whitefield's embrace of the hymn was understandable. He had laid aside his Anglican gowns to minister to Presbyterians, Congregationalists, and other Dissenters. He crossed national and parish boundaries and brought to those who attended or read accounts of his revivals a "translocal consciousness," as Timothy Hall has described it, an awareness of their membership in a community of believers that "transcended geographical and denominational lines." White-

Figure 1.4. The first published version of the melody and line structure of "God Save the King" to appear in America, "Whitefield's" hymn, from Lyon's *Urania.* Courtesy of The Library of Congress.

field, like many others, found the melody of "God Save the King" and the emotions and attitudes associated with its performance easily transferable to other purposes—in this case to support the move from specifically geographical and cultural versions of the nation to sweeping metaphysical and theological versions of God's kingdom. James Lyon's 1761 *Urania* published "Come, Thou Almighty King" under the title "Whitefield's" (see figure 1.4), thus simultaneously appropriating the melody of the British anthem and illustrating for colonists the possibility of adapting its lyrics for other uses. The popularity of both "God Save the King" and Lyon's *Urania* helps explain, then, how "Come, Thou Almighty King" continued to play a subversive role in the American colonies during the Revolution. For example, while British troops occupying Long Island reportedly entered a church during Sunday services and ordered the congregation to sing "God Save the King," congregationists sympathetic to the Revolution responded by singing "Come, Thou Almighty King," thus using the same melody to transform the anthem of occupation into a song of resistance.[35]

Despite the plethora of such poignant stories, historians have long downplayed the role of songs in the revolutionary cause, concluding, as did Philip Davidson, that "songs as a medium of revolutionary sentiment were not extensively used, and those written were not of a very high order." It is now clear that this judgment was mistaken. Indeed, Gillian Anderson has collected 1,455 political and patriotic song lyrics published in colonial American newspapers from 1773 to 1783.[36] Still others have been lost or were published in other forms. Topical songs were a common fixture of military, civic, and family life during the war and were regarded by its leaders as an indispensable resource in the campaign for support among troops and the general public. For example, in a letter to Continental General Anthony Wayne dated 11 July 1779, Richard Perry, secretary to the Board of War, exclaimed that "more can be achieved, by a few occasional simple songs, than by a hundred recommendations of Congress especially considering how few attend to or read them." Perry urged that "ballads [be] dispersed among the soldiery, which, inspiring in them a thirst for glory, patience under their hardships, a love of their General, and submission to their officers, would animate them to a cheerful discharge of their duty, and prompt them to undergo their hardships with a soldierly patience and pleasure." Perry's advice was apparently well heeded, as Frank Moore reports that most companies of the Continental Army had minstrels who lightened the step of soldiers on the march and led them in song in camp and on the field.[37]

On the domestic, nonmilitary front, patriot leaders such as John Adams praised revolutionary songs as an especially effective means of "cultivating the sensations of freedom." Singing in homes and at public meetings was among the most popular forms of entertainment during the wartime suspension of theatrical performances and other amusements.[38] Despite the growing political hostilities between colonists and king, the shared musical, folkloric, and other cultural ties between America and Britain were so strong that of the tunes borrowed and altered for the revolutionary cause, an overwhelming number were originally British. Indeed, Anderson's inventory of political song lyrics in revolutionary-era American newspapers includes dozens of adaptations of British songs, including "Yankee Doodle," "Rule, Britannia!," "To Anacreon in Heaven" (later the musical setting for "The Star-Spangled Banner"), and twenty-one publications of patriot lyrics set to the tune of "God Save the King." Because the melodies used were popular favorites formerly used to promote political and cultural ties between Britain and the colonies, their co-optation by the revolutionaries marked a powerful symbolic shift of affections.

It may seem paradoxical that the American revolutionaries were so musically dependent on British melodies even while striving to promote their political independence from Britain, but borrowed melodies presented both logistical advantages and poignant intertextual resources for the expression of revolutionary principles. On a practical level, new lyrics could be learned more easily by more people if set to familiar tunes; the new songs could thus be sung both by those unable to read music and by audiences presented with the lyrics for the first time. In addition, by using familiar tunes, songwriters avoided the complicating need to publish music along with their lyrics, hence enabling them to maximize the number of songs and song verses printed in newspapers and in inexpensive single-page broadsides. The use of borrowed melodies also permitted more rapid production of patriotic songs during the revolution, as events outstripped the ability of composers to produce memorable tunes. Instead of laboring over new melodies, songwriters could quickly match old tunes with new lyrics tailored in response to specific circumstances, thus producing new topical songs while public excitement about the events was still high. Likewise, revolutionary appropriation of borrowed British melodies made song a medium available to America's foremost political writers, thinkers, and propagandists without requiring skills in musical composition.

Most Americans came very slowly and reluctantly to renounce the king, but when they finally did, they did so utterly, opposing the very institution of monarchy and concluding, as Josiah Quincy wrote in 1774, that "the mystical appellations of loyalty and allegiance" to the king have been "prostituted to that abominable purpose" to "deceive, disunite and enslave the good people of this Continent." Although moderate colonists in 1774 still looked to the king as their protector to overturn the Coercive Acts passed by Parliament, the royal proclamation of rebellion and sedition on 23 August 1775 and other actions soon made it clear that the king himself was leading the suppression of the colonists.[39] The Massachusetts House of Representatives' November 1775 "Proclamation for a Public Thanksgiving" is indicative of this shift in perspective, as it was printed with the exhortation "GOD save the PEOPLE" instead of the customary "God save the King" (see figure 1.5). The Tory Peter Oliver was outraged at the substitution, asking "Will it not suffice your leaders to mock the King but they must mock Heaven also?" Despite Oliver's lament, the monarchy became a focal point of the rebellion. Indeed, in January 1776 Thomas Paine's *Common Sense* denounced George III as "an ass," "the hardened sullen-tempered Pharaoh," "the wretch," and so on, in gloriously raucous prose. That summer, the Declaration of Independence included Jefferson's equally scathing list of the king's egregious behaviors toward the colonies. Both documents framed the Revolution as a battle of republicanism versus monarchism and grounded the colonists' appeals for liberty not in their legally defined and politically limited rights as British subjects but in sweeping claims to "natural rights."[40]

Despite this radical transformation of the bases of political action, all the new revolutionary state governments retained familiar means of enforcing loyalty, as they required their citizens to take public oaths of allegiance and to forswear past loyalty to the king. Loyalists who refused to do so were subject to disenfranchisement, loss of property, imprisonment, exile, and, in some extreme cases, execution. Amid the turmoil of these dangerous times, songs such as "God Save the King," which had once served as a declaration of allegiance to the monarch, were converted into public expressions of American national identity. For example, "A New Song, to the Tune of—GOD SAVE THE KING" (see appendix A), published in the Boston *Independent Chronicle* on 4 December 1777, boldly announces that it is time to "Tell George in vain his Hand / Is raised 'gainst FREEDOM's Band, / When call'd to arms." George's attempt to quell Americans' quest for liberty is futile, the song proclaims, for no one "can resist

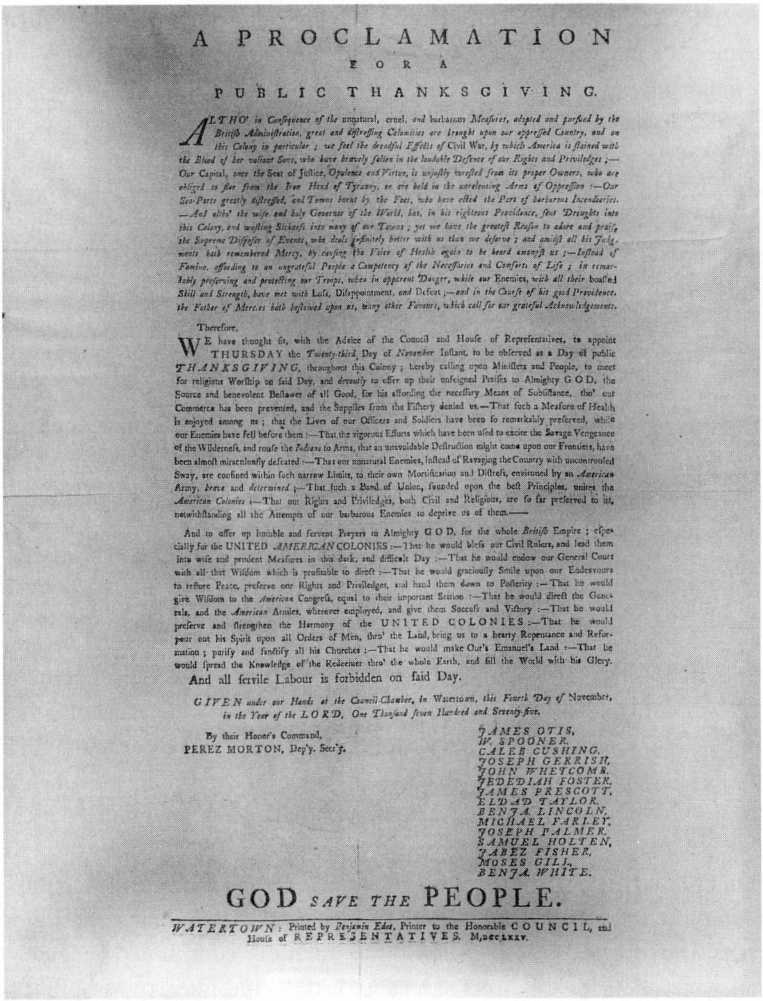

A PROCLAMATION
FOR A
PUBLIC THANKSGIVING.

ALTHO' in Conſequence of the unnatural, cruel, *and* barbarous *Meaſures, adopted and purſued by the Britiſh Adminiſtration, great and diſtreſſing Calamities are brought upon our oppreſſed Country, and on this Colony in particular ; we feel the dreadful Effects of* Civil War, *by which America is ſtained with the Blood of her valiant Sons, who have bravely fallen in the laudable Defence of our Rights and Priviledges ;—* Our Capital, *once the* Seat of Juſtice, *Opulence and Virtue, is unjuſtly wreſted from its proper Owners, who are obliged to flee from the Iron Hand of Tyranny, or are held in the unrelenting Arms of Oppreſſion :—Our Sea-Ports greatly diſtreſſed, and Towns burnt by the Foes, who have acted the Part of barbarous Incendiaries. —And altho' the wiſe and holy Governor of the World, has, in his righteous Providence, ſent Droughts into this Colony, and waſting Sickneſs into many of our Towns ; yet we have the greateſt Reaſon to adore and praiſe the Supreme Diſpoſer of Events, who deals infinitely better with us than we deſerve ; and amidſt all his Judgments hath remembered Mercy, by cauſing the Voice of Health again to be heard amongſt us ;—Inſtead of Famine, affording to an ungrateful People a Competency of the Neceſſaries and Comforts of Life ; in remarkably preſerving and protecting our Troops, when in apparent Danger, while our* Enemies, *with all their* boaſted *Skill and Strength, have met with* Loſs, Diſappointment, *and* Defeat ;—*and in the Courſe of his good Providence, the Father of Mercies hath beſtowed upon us, many other Favours, which call for our grateful Acknowledgements.*

Therefore,

WE have thought fit, with the Advice of the Council and Houſe of Repreſentatives, to appoint THURSDAY the *Twenty-third* Day of *November* Inſtant, to be obſerved as a Day of public *THANKSGIVING*, throughout this Colony ; hereby calling upon Miniſters and People, to meet for religious Worſhip on ſaid Day, and *devoutly* to offer up their unfeigned Praiſes to Almighty GOD, the Source and benevolent Beſtower of all Good, for his affording the neceſſary Means of Subſiſtance, tho' our Commerce has been prevented, and the Supplies from the Fiſhery denied us.—That ſuch a Meaſure of Health is enjoyed among us ; that the Lives of our Officers and Soldiers have been ſo remarkably preſerved, while our Enemies have fell before them :—That the vigorous Efforts which have been uſed to excite the Savage Vengeance of the Wilderneſs, and rouſe the *Indians* to Arms, that an unavoidable Deſtruction might come upon our Frontiers, have been almoſt miraculouſly defeated :—That our unnatural Enemies, inſtead of Ravaging the Country with uncontrouled Sway, are confined within ſuch narrow Limits, to their own Mortification and Diſtreſs, environed by an *American* Army, *brave* and *determined* ;—That ſuch a Band of Union, founded upon the beſt Principles, unites the *American Colonies* ;—That our Rights and Priviledges, both Civil and Religious, are ſo far preſerved to us, notwithſtanding all the Attempts of our barbarous Enemies to deprive us of them.——

And to offer up humble and fervent Prayers to Almighty GOD, for the whole *Britiſh* Empire ; eſpecially for the UNITED *AMERICAN* COLONIES :—That he would bleſs our Civil Rulers, and lead them into wiſe and prudent Meaſures in this dark, and difficult Day :—That he would endow our General Court with all that Wiſdom which is profitable to direct :—That he would graciouſly Smile upon our Endeavours to reſtore Peace, preſerve our Rights and Priviledges, and hand them down to Poſterity :—That he would give Wiſdom to the *American* Congreſs, equal to their important Station :—That he would direct the Generals, and the *American* Armies, wherever employed, and give them Succeſs and Victory :—That he would preſerve and ſtrengthen the Harmony of the UNITED COLONIES :—That he would pour out his Spirit upon all Orders of Men, thro' the Land, bring us to a hearty Repentance and Reformation ; purify and ſanctify all his Churches :—That he would make Our's Emanuel's Land :—That he would ſpread the Knowledge of the Redeemer thro' the whole Earth, and fill the World with his Glory.

And all ſervile Labour is forbidden on ſaid Day.

GIVEN under our Hands at the Council-Chamber, in Watertown, *this Fourth Day of* November, *in the Year of the LORD, One Thouſand ſeven Hundred and Seventy-five.*

By their Honor's Command,
PEREZ MORTON, Dep'y. Secr'y.

JAMES OTIS,
W. SPOONER,
CALEB CUSHING,
JOSEPH GERRISH,
JOHN WHETCOMB,
JEDEDIAH FOSTER,
JAMES PRESCOTT,
ELDAD TAYLOR,
BENJA. LINCOLN,
MICHAEL FARLEY,
JOSEPH PALMER,
SAMUEL HOLTEN,
JABEZ FISHER,
MOSES GILL,
BENJA. WHITE.

GOD *SAVE THE* PEOPLE.

WATERTOWN: Printed by *Benjamin Edes*, Printer to the Honorable COUNCIL, and Houſe of REPRESENTATIVES. M,DCC,LXXV.

Figure 1.5. The Massachusetts House of Representatives, "Proclamation for a Public Thanksgiving," November 1775. Courtesy of The American Antiquarian Society.

our Power, / By FREEDOM fir'd."[41] "Fame, Let Thy Trumpet Sound" adapts a British variation of "God Save the King" that first appeared in the *Gentleman's Magazine* of September 1745 ("Fame let thy trumpet sound, / Tell all the world around, / Great George is King"). The new lyric announces America's independent status to the world ("FAME, let thy Trumpet sound, / Rouse all the World around") and entreats foreign powers to intervene diplomatically on America's behalf. Where "God Save the King" voices the singer's hope that the monarch's forces will be victorious and that divine intercession will "scatter his enemies," "Fame, Let Thy Trumpet Sound" prophesies the inevitable defeat of the king's forces by the American revolutionaries, with "Th' approving Nod of Heaven." In its full thirteen verses, it records the locations, heroes, and circumstances of the early battles of the revolution, thus creating a mythic catechism for the faithful. More important, with one stanza for each colony, the song constitutes an imagined nation, united geographically, bound ideologically, and pledged politically.

Like "God Save the King," "Fame, Let Thy Trumpet Sound" reflexively depicts the act of its own singing, as the prospective achievement of independence by the American colonies—when "Each Island of the Main / Free'd from the Tyrant's Chain, / Shall own our Sway"—is set in a future where those possessing "FREEDOM's Bliss" shall display their happiness through "Loud Songs of Thankfulness" such as this one. In a later verse, the perseverance of the Continental forces through the bitter New Jersey winter is commemorated as a willingness both "To meet the murd'rous Foe!" and to "sing their overthrow." The implied singer here is not a soldier, however, but a civilian whose performance of the song is a sign of his or her support for the troops. The march through New Jersey and its attendant difficulties are claimed by the singer ("To me belong"). In the final verse the singer salutes the soldiers and pledges to remember and reward them. Thus, in addition to its more explicit political claims, "Fame, Let Thy Trumpet Sound" offers a model for the desired response of patriotic citizens who support the struggle for independence, cherish the battlefield sacrifices of those fighting on their behalf, and, in singing, are connected to the cause.

On 1 January 1780 the *Pennsylvania Packet* and *Providence Gazette* each published an alternate version of "God Save the King" entitled "God Save the Thirteen States." Dated 4 July 1779, the version was ostensibly contributed by Dutch citizens sympathetic to the American cause with "a most hearty wish, that they may add fuel to the precious fire which is burning in every true American heart." The attribution of Dutch authorship is significant, for although it is rarely commented on by historians, Americans at the time saw the Dutch as clear forerunners of the fight for freedom. Indeed, Stephen Lucas has recently argued that the *Plakkaat van Verlatinge*, the 26 July 1581 Dutch declaration of independence from Spain (known in English as the Act of Abjuration), may well have served as "a paradigm for the argumentative structure" of the American declaration.[42] Regardless of whether Lucas proves that Jefferson and his colleagues studied the *Plakkaat van Verlatinge*, he demonstrates persuasively that Americans saw the Dutch as fellow rebels against king and colonizer. "God Save the Thirteen States" continues this Dutch/American tradition, as it praises liberty and calls for "No tyrants over us." The song appeared in American newspapers at the height of a diplomatic crisis. Dutch efforts to maintain neutrality in the war between England and France and in the American revolution were severely compromised by the arrival in Amsterdam in October 1779 of American naval captain John Paul Jones and five ships seeking refuge and repair after their stunning victory over the British in battle off Flamborough Head. The Dutch had not recognized the American republic, yet the arrival of Jones with captured ships and crew spurred angry British demands for their seizure, a demand the Dutch resisted. Whether the song was actually written by Dutch citizens or by Americans seeking to bolster the apparent legitimacy and military prospects of their cause, the lyrics proclaim Dutch sympathy and promise military support for the revolution. In a pointed reminder of the deep ideological premises fueling the war, the song ends with the triumphant chant: *"We want* NO KING.*"*[43]

The popular portrayal of the American Revolution as a conflict between monarchists and republicans made "God Save the King" an irresistible vehicle for the conveyance of revolutionary sentiments. The supposedly Dutch version cited here, "God Save the Thirteen States," complicates this political reversal, as it imagines the emerging nation's future in an act of singing ("We'll ever sing") of the past, when revolutionaries "fought for Liberty" not as English subjects but as "one family" struggling for "Independency." Thus the very tune through which the colonists once sang of their loyalty to the crown now proclaimed their rejection of hereditary authority: *"We want* NO KING.*"* Despite the finality of this rejection of British authority, postrevolutionary America could not as easily shed the musical influence of the homeland; hence, moving from the colonial phases of the song's institutionalization through the war period's heated use of alternative versions of the song to contest national identities, the postwar period found Americans appropriating "God Save the King" for use within new cultural and political crises.

Appropriation: "See a New Empire Rise"

After the revolution, "God Save the King" continued to play an important role in American civic life, as more than a dozen lyrical variations of the song were published in the two decades following the war to mark important events in the life of the new nation. Unlike their wartime predecessors, however, postrevolutionary versions of "God Save the King" made few references to the original lyrics. Instead they appropriated the melody and performative traditions of the British anthem to construct public expressions of the new national identity. For example, on 17 June 1786 an estimated twenty thousand people gathered on the slopes of Bunker Hill to celebrate the opening of the new and elegant Charles

River bridge. The crowd crossed the bridge to the accompaniment of drums, fifes, and thirteen cannon fired from Copp's Hill. The opening of the bridge marked the eleventh anniversary of the Battle of Bunker Hill and the burning of Charlestown. After an outdoor dinner, an ode written by Thomas Dawes, Jr., to the tune of "God Save the King" was performed. Thus, in a wonderful example of the political possibilities of appropriation, the anthem of the former colonizer that had burned the town is revised to invest the event with prestige and tradition. The song accordingly links the new structure with the sacrifices of the revolution, when war "water'd Bunker's side / With foreign Blood." As imagined both in the song and the ceremony, then, the new bridge spans past, present, and future, creating a rich, resonant, almost mythical symbol of the nation. This nationalist fervor is explicitly advanced by singing, as the first verse opens with the self-reflexive call to "Now let rich Musick sound / And all the Region round / With Rapture fill."[44]

In his influential 1882 essay "Qu'est-ce qu'une nation?," Ernest Renan wrote that "A heroic past, of great men, of glory (I mean the genuine kind) . . . is the social principle on which the national idea rests." The combination of the opening of a new architectural treasure, the singing of Dawes's ode, and the staging of nationalist pageantry clearly strives to create what Renan called glory, that nationalist sense of the collapsing of past, present, and future into a sense of heroic obligation. Indeed, as Renan describes it, "A nation is a grand solidarity constituted by the sentiment of sacrifices which one has made and those that one is disposed to make again. It supposes a past, it renews itself especially in the present by a tangible deed: the approval, the desire, clearly expressed, to continue the communal life."[45] The Charlestown bridge ceremony fulfilled each of these functions, as the massive gathering at the bridge site was linked by song and symbol to the "grand solidarity" of the nation and was rooted in celebration of both past sacrifices and the future greatness of communal life. In the hyperbole of the moment, Bunker Hill gains a "sky-rapt Brow," Charlestown promises to "strike the astonish'd Eyes / With Glories bright," and the new bridge seems as "Fam'd as the Appian Way" and destined to convey the goods and people of "All Nations . . . From Shore to Shore." Those present therefore celebrate not only the completed structure of the bridge but a vision of an emerging society that will transcend the economic difficulties and political conflicts that beset them in the stormy days before the Constitution consolidated the nation. The bridge ceremony was accordingly hailed by those assembled as an embodiment of the new national spirit, as the celebrants pledged: "With publick Sprit crown'd; / We'll consecrate the Ground / To LIBERTY."[46]

The story of Dawes's appropriation of "God Save the King" for the Charlestown bridge ceremony illustrates nicely the complicated manner in which the rise of romantic nationalism valorized artistic productions, particularly musical compositions, that supposedly reflected the essential character of the nations from which they arose. Within this process of valorizing emergent nationalism via song, "God the Save the King" played an unparalleled role as a transnational as well as national anthem. In fact, its melody was extensively employed by the composers of the anthems of nineteen nations, including Denmark, Bavaria, Sweden, Liechtenstein, Switzerland, Russia, and several German and Italian states.[47] Various explanations have been offered for the remarkable international appeal of "God Save the King." One argument suggests that it was translated and published in continental songbooks during the decades just preceding the rise of nationalism in many cases without clear specification of its nation of origin; thus productively *not* linked directly with any specific movement or nation, the song could be regarded as an indigenous melody in several different countries. Another argument suggests that the remarkable international popularity of "God Save the King" was the result of conscious appropriation, as when in 1833 Alexis Lvof was commissioned to compose "God Save the Czar" for use at Russian state occasions. Still another argument suggests that those nations yet to sanction an official national anthem drew on "God Save the King" as a proven melody that—as it had in England and America—could inspire public devotion and ceremonial majesty.[48]

Many nineteenth-century writers speculated about the peculiar power and appeal of the song, as "God Save the King" was enthusiastically sung by most Britons not only at the ceremonial occasions of state but in public houses, theaters, taverns, and private homes. There are two obvious factors behind this remarkable popularity. First, the melody was popular before its adoption by the state and royal family, hence giving the impression that the anthem of the state was not imposed from above but was a genuine reflection of the peoples' culture. Second, the song's simple construction and limited range (compared, for example, to the vocal gymnastics required to sing "The Star-Spangled Banner") made it possible for even the least musically talented to join in its singing. Writing in 1873, Stephen Salisbury pronounced "God Save the King" the "grandest patriotic song in the English language" and recommended that its musical secrets be explored in order to discover "what our American national song should be":

> The notes are emphatic as a chant, easily learned and distinctly sounded by many, so that the singers hear and are moved by the very words of their companions; and this effect is aided by the shortness of the words. Though the air is simple, it is fitted to rise with the strength of feeling. It appeals with power to loyalty, which in a monarchy is devotion to the king, his crown and dignity. It is suited to all the changes in national life, to joy or grief, to peace or war, to anxiety or triumph. It has enough of the progressive and aggressive character to gratify the Anglo-Saxon temper, and the attractive spice of party spirit is not

wanting. And it is pervaded with an expression of religious trust that is more grateful to the mind of man than our philosophers are willing to admit. A patriotic song equally well adapted to our institutions would be an ornament and a strength to our nation and an untiring enjoyment to our people.[49]

Much like Salisbury's awestruck vision of the ways the song worked on the hearts and minds of singers and listeners alike, so foreign visitors to England in the late eighteenth century, especially composers, were greatly impressed with the popular powers of "God Save the King." Haydn marveled at the political utility of the song during two visits to London in 1791 and 1794, and upon his return to Austria crafted an anthem ("Gott erhalte Franz der Kaiser") based loosely on it. Beethoven declared in his diary the desire to "show the British what a godsend they have in their 'God Save the King'" and accordingly composed both a set of variations on the tune and a battle symphony that quoted it. Carl Maria Weber's *Overture of Jubilation* (1818), composed and performed in celebration of the fiftieth anniversary of the succession of King Frederick Augustus I to the throne of Saxony, featured the melody of "God Save the King" in its climactic conclusion, "which swept the audience off their feet in a frenzy of enthusiasm." "They all heard in this song, which affected them so deeply," writes Nettl, "nothing but the Saxon royal anthem, and no one gave heed to the fact that it was of British origin."[50]

No performer more successfully exploited the transnational appeal of "God Save the Queen" than Louis Moreau Gottschalk (1829–69), the first American composer to establish a significant international reputation. He incorporated variations on the tune in at least three of his best-known works and many of his public performances. Gottschalk sometimes employed the melody in clear reference to Great Britain, as in his lost symphonies, *The Battle of Bunker Hill* and *Grand National Symphony for Ten Pianos*, for which he juxtaposed the tunes of "God Save the Queen," "Hail, Columbia," and "Yankee Doodle" to simulate warfare between Britain and the American revolutionaries. In a concert performance in Martinique in 1859, when he noticed an English major snoring loudly in the audience, Gottschalk launched abruptly into "God Save the Queen," bringing the embarrassed officer to his feet. Like Haydn, Beethoven, and Weber, Gottschalk realized the transnational possibilities of the tune; he therefore featured it prominently in his concert tours through Europe, South America, and the Caribbean. One result of this international touring was the realization that by employing variations of "God Save the King" he could, with a single melody, stir the patriotic passions of audiences in several different countries. For example, when Gottschalk toured Switzerland as a solo piano virtuoso in 1850, his concerts were capped with a sure crowd-pleaser: a set of variations on the melody of "God Save the Queen," which then served as the unofficial Swiss anthem. Gottschalk kept the popular number in his program for concerts in nearby German states as well, where the tune also served as an anthem.[51]

Like many of the new European nations toured by Gottschalk, the United States in 1850 had neither an official flag nor anthem, no common holidays other than the Fourth of July, and little national tradition in literature or the performing arts. Unlike the new European nations, many of which arose in complicated relationships to ancient folk traditions, deep ethnic memories, and longstanding cultural traditions, Americans had little common culture except that gained from their former colonizer. Indeed, partially because the American colonies were historically younger than their European counterparts, they tended to feel themselves tied more closely to Britain than to their fellow colonies. The obvious difficulties in building a common culture, then, something more organic and nationlike than the doctrines of the new state delimited in the Constitution, haunted early American leaders. For example, Bishop James Madison admonished in a 1795 sermon that "Unless a magnanimous spirit of patriotism animates every breast, these superstructures of political wisdom must soon crumble into dust."[52] Given the obvious lack of shared indigenous cultural artifacts on which to build such "a magnanimous spirit of patriotism," "God Save the King" remained an all-purpose melody for public ceremonies designed to express and promote patriotism. It is no surprise, then, to find that the first truly national symbols of American nationhood, the heroes of the Revolution, were soon celebrated in variations of "God Save the King." Chief among them was George Washington.

Indeed, despite profound disagreements in the early republic about the precise character and mission of the nation, there was little doubt as to who best exemplified American nationalism, as Washington was popularly portrayed as the embodiment of the new nation, a leader both flawless in character and brilliant in promise. Gustave de Beaumont thus observed in 1835 that "Washington, in America, is not a man but a god."[53] Prior to Beaumont's gushing appraisal and from as early as the Revolution, observances of Washington's birthday and celebrations of his character in toasts, speeches, and song provided the basis for a nascent American civic culture. In fact, "God Save the King" was adapted many times to honor him. The *New-Jersey Journal* of 26 December 1781 printed a boisterous version asking fellow patriots "From the Americ shore, / The vast Atlantic o'er / Shout—"WASHINGTON!" Washington is thus the name by which America announces itself to Europe; his glory becomes our glory, honoring him the task in which "Americans all unite." As the unquestioned leader of the revolutionary forces, Washington's birthday was celebrated as a public holiday beginning as early as 1781. At a February 1784 observance in New York, a new version of "God Save the King," titled "God Bless America," announced that "'Tis Washington's birth day, / Let joy abound." Much like Dawes's Charlestown

Bridge version, "God Bless America" self-reflexively sings about singing, as the first verse describes how "AMERICANS rejoice, / While songs employ each voice."[54]

Like the British anthem's focus on the king, "God Bless America" metonymically collapses the intangible vastness of the nation into the heroic figure of "great Washington." Singing his praises is layered within images of patriotic flags and streamers ("The thirteen stripes display / In flags and streamers gay"); he has won and represents "our cause"; it is as "AMERICANS" that citizens join in singing of his greatness. Washington's praises are thus sung as an assertion of national identity, which, not coincidentally, is celebrated in the social act of drinking ("Fill the glass to the brink"). "Tuneful pow'rs" also enabled the singing of Washington's "worth from ev'ry tongue" in a 1786 version entitled "God Save Great Washington." Singing toasts to Washington became a kind of public loyalty oath joined by "each true Whig. . . / Whose heart did ne'r re-sign / The glorious cause." On Washington's birthday in 1788, celebrants again turned to the melody of "God Save the King" for an ode of virtual deification: "Hail Godlike Washington! / Fair Freedom's chosen son, / Born to command."[55] In the new versions of the song, Washington's name was substituted for that of the forsaken George and invoked with the reverence due a king. Thus Washington was hailed in song as a hero and protector whose military exploits had secured independence and whose political leadership would guide the new nation toward its destined greatness.

Considering his glorification in the song from as early as 1784, it is fitting that yet another variation of "God Save the King" welcomed Washington to New York for his inauguration as president in 1789. His long route from Mt. Vernon was frequently lined with cheering crowds to whom Washington waved from his carriage, and for whom he frequently abandoned his ride to shake hundreds of hands. In larger towns he switched to horseback to lead the raucous parades arrayed in his honor. From Elizabethtown Point, New Jersey, Washington traveled the last fifteen miles of his journey by water aboard an elaborately decorated barge constructed for the occasion (see figure 1.6). As the barge neared Bedloe's Island, a sloop drew up alongside the starboard bow; twenty male and female singers aboard sang an ode set to the tune of "God Save the King." Published as a broadside with the title "Ode, To Be Sung on the Arrival of the PRESIDENT of the UNITED STATES" (see figure 1.7 and appendix A) and featuring new lyrics penned for the occasion by Samuel Low, the song asks: "Let ev'ry heart expand / For WASHINGTON's at hand / With Glory crowned!" The singers then observed, both visually with their own eyes and musically with their words, the formal transition from monarchy to republic represented by Washington's inauguration as a president "Unsully'd by a throne." One may glimpse the excitement of the moment by noting that the

Figure 1.6. L. M. Cooke, *Salute to General Washington in New York Harbor* (1901; depicting Washington's arrival for his 1789 inauguration). Courtesy of The National Gallery of Art; gift of Edgar William and Bernice Chrysler Garbisch.

song features nine exclamation points, indicating the song's use less as a sung tribute than as a shouted declaration of joyous national arrival.[56] Despite the fourth verse's curious suggestion that "Our leader now no more, / But Ruler thou," Washington's stern rebuke of those who "made to him certain Monarchical Propositions" near the end of the war became a defining anecdote in his public legend. On the other hand, however, the supposed monarchical tendencies displayed in his opulent lifestyle, including his famously lavish entertainment of guests, produced what little public criticism there was of Washington during his presidency.[57]

It is wonderfully ironic, then, to learn that American antimonarchism was expressed so powerfully through the use of the best-known monarchical anthem. For example, "A New Song, To the Tune of 'God Save the King'" was published in the *Providence Gazette* of 25 May 1793, with the first line asking: "God save—THE RIGHTS OF MAN." The song is clearly a reference to Thomas Paine's pamphlet *The Rights of Man* (1791–92), which vindicated the French Revolution, denounced the British monarchy, and sold an astonishing two hundred thousand copies in its first six months of publication. Paine's argument was considered so radical that he was charged with seditious libel and forced to flee from England. In the United States, however, as "A New Song" illustrates, his pamphlet's antimonarchism was praised as an extension of the principles of the

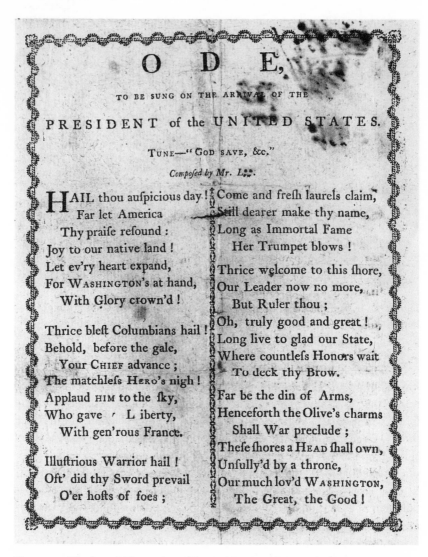

Figure 1.7. The broadside version of Samuel Lowe, "Ode to be Sung on the Arrival of the President" (1789). Courtesy of the Collection of The New-York Historical Society.

American Revolution: "Reason and truth appear, / Freedom advances near, / Monarchs with terror hear, / See how they quake!"[58]

Eighteenth-century performances of such political songs often included theatrical sketches designed to inspire "true love of country and ardor for the American cause." A New York performance of "Hail, Columbia" in 1798, for example, included a sketch in which actors costumed as soldiers protected the American flag from attack, culminating in the featured song. The theater, the tavern, and other public venues thus became reconstituted as patriotic assemblies in which all loyal citizens were expected to join in singing. What is striking about this merging of song and politics, of public and private, is how consciously some songs merged references to singing, patriotism, antimonarchical tendencies, and the rapidly rising American urge for empire. For example, a 1798 "Ode for the Fourth of July," set to the tune of "God Save the King," urged: "Come, all ye sons of Song, / Pull the full sound along / In joyful strains."[59] The patriotic faithful are "sons of song." While this song is the expression of their joyful loyalty, it also claims that the United States, having burst the "tyrannic chains" of British oppression, will "a new empire rise." Hence, in a classic example of appropriation, Americans wrote songs set to the former colonial anthem while imagining their own glorious future as a world power.

Because the "existence of a nation," as Renan describes it, is an "everyday plebiscite," it requires constant reaffirmation through symbols and ceremonies. As discussed earlier, "God Save the King" provided an easily adaptable melody for constructing the collective myths necessary for such constant reaffirmation. In fact, the song was so useful that several new lyrical adaptations were included in popular song collections of the late 1790s.[60] These later versions use the anthem of the former colonizer to attempt to define, if only by negation, what it means to be an American. For example, a 1796 version published in Philadelphia opens by comparing British and American characters through their differing lyrics and uses of the song:

> While others sing of Kings,
> And *suchlike titled things;*
>   To praise in songs,
> HEROES, in battle slain,
> STATESMEN, who still remain,
> Our glory to maintain,
>   To us belongs.[61]

The performance of the song itself is offered as evidence of distinctive national character, as true Americans do not sing of monarchs and aristocrats but rather "praise in song" their martyred war heroes and democratically elected representatives. Their glory, the song reasons, is ours—we are what we sing.

THE institutionalization, contestation, and appropriation of national songs are three distinct but interrelated rhetorical processes. All three are ways of (re)defining the nation and the relationships between singers and nation; all three are integral both to the ceremonies of legitimacy and affiliation that sustain the state and to the organization of resistance and dissent. "The effect of popular songs and airs, especially in times of alarm and danger, has long been known," the *United States Gazette* editorialized in 1805, "and they have often been employed, both by patriot and traitor, to inspire resolution, and to rouse heroism."[62] Indeed, as we have shown, "God Save the King" was used from roughly 1744 up through 1798 to celebrate allegiance to established authorities, to assert alternative national identities, and to honor acts of personal and collective sacrifice. Addressing the multiple variations of "God Save the King" thus enables the rhetorical historian to observe the transformation of American national identities from colonial subjects of a revered king to rebels and embattled loyalists and, later, to citizens of an emerging reconstituted nation. The following chapter accordingly traces how "God Save the King" slowly but surely became known simply as "America" and, eventually, "My Country 'Tis of Thee." Recounting this slow shift from a monarchical "God Save the King" to a democratic "America" in turn enables us, picking up the thread of American nationalism circa 1830, to address the tireless reform efforts of evangelists, educators, and temperance reformers and the many uses they made of "My Country 'Tis of Thee."

TWO

"The Subordination of the Different Parts and Voices"

Popularizing "America" through Grassroots Activism, 1826–1850

D ESPITE the regional differences she observed during her travels through the United States in 1827, Frances Trollope wrote in *Domestic Manners of the Americans* that there were

> some points certainly on which all agree—namely, that the American government is the best in the world. That America has produced the greatest men that ever existed. That all the nations of the earth look upon them with a mixture of wonder and envy and that in time they will all follow their great example and have a president. This, or something like it, I heard everywhere.[1]

Trollope's lament indicates how American superpatriotism of the Jackson era was amusing to many European visitors, to whom Americans seemed too eager to proclaim the arrival of the United States among the world's great nations. Such annoyance was not unfounded, for patriotic speakers from pulpit and platform imagined America as "God's New Israel," a "shining city upon a hill" whose freedom was a beacon to the world. Europe's revolutions and upheavals in the early nineteenth century confirmed for such patriots the comparative wonder of American republicanism.

Nonetheless, some European observers were skeptical regarding the grand pronouncements they heard from so many boisterous Americans. For example, Alexis de Tocqueville, who began his nine-month tour of the United States in May 1831, quickly realized that America was riven by sectionalism and that Americans' apparent superpatriotism was qualified by widespread anxiety about dissolution and vice, immigration and industrialism, wealth and poverty, and heterogeneity and multiculturalism. On the one hand, Tocqueville observed that patriotism was so strong among Americans that it approached "a kind of religion" that "does not reason, but acts from the impulse of faith and sentiment." On the other hand, he realized that such "patriotism . . . is frequently an extension of individual selfishness." Patriotism, then, even the well-nigh religious version found in the frantic, self-righteous, bustling America of Jackson, was tempered by the immediacy of self-interest, which, given the precarious state of both politics and capitalist markets in the new nation, shifted from day to day, wavering like the wind. Like Trollope, Tocqueville was accordingly skeptical of Americans' frequent statements of their desire to preserve the federal system and constitution. In fact, in a passage that eerily foreshadows one of the key issues of the Civil War, Tocqueville ventured the prediction: "If the sovereignty of the Union were to engage in a struggle with that of the states at the present day, its defeat may be confidently predicted."[2]

Thus, some thirty odd years before the epochal dissolution of the nation in the Civil War, Tocqueville realized that the sheer vastness and diversity of the Union mitigated against patriotism, as individual states, he argued, were far more likely than the federal union to represent distinct "objects that are familiar to the citizens and dear to them all." Many Americans shared Tocqueville's concerns about the lack of an overarching national civic culture. The tumultuous 1830s were in fact marked by numerous and competing efforts to establish a sense of national identity, especially through the promotion of patriotic ceremonies, flags, symbols, and songs. The premiere of "America" at Boston's Park Street Church two months after Tocqueville's arrival in the United States was emblematic of these efforts to construct a civic culture. Indeed, the writing, public performance, and popularization of "America" resulted not so much from an isolated moment of inspiration for a solitary writer as from a remarkable conjunction of efforts by several determined reformers, including educator William C. Woodbridge, evangelist and temperance activist Lyman Beecher, and musical pioneer Lowell Mason. All three campaigned for children's musical instruction as a key to the development of an American national culture; their efforts prompted both the writing of "America" and its inaugural performance. Mason's subsequent work in public school music education, along with lyricist Samuel Smith's later leadership in the American missionary movement, promoted the song's rapid popularization and institutionalization. Following upon this first stage of popularization and institutionalization, "America" quickly became one of the signature songs—employing a wide variety of alternative lyrics—of the temperance and women's suffrage movements.

In the following pages we accordingly demonstrate two central points. First, that "America" was rooted in the political controversies, religious revivals, and educational, moral, and suffrage movements of antebellum America. Second, that like its predecessor, "God Save the King," "America" was a focal point for competing visions of identity, citizenship, and nationhood, particularly as expressed in the grassroots activist movements that sprang from the so-called Second Great Awakening. As Perry Miller has observed, "The burning of the Revival, sometimes smoldering, now blazing into flame, [was] never quite extinguished" in the nation until after the Civil War and "was a central mode of this culture's search for national identity."[3] That search included, to an extent almost unimaginable to Americans today, singing about one's politics, one's religion, and one's sense of belonging to a dynamic nation.

"The Soul of Eloquence": Music and Reform in Lowell Mason's Boston

"America" was commissioned and promoted by the leaders of Boston's school music movement. It was first performed by a children's choir and used to demonstrate both the viability and civic virtue of children's choral instruction on a mass scale. Later, "America" was popularized in large part by its use in the public school singing programs that its early performances had helped to create. Vocal music performances by children were a great novelty in 1830s America and became institutionalized, in part, through the efforts of Lowell Mason (see figure 2.1). Born in 1792 in Medfield, Massachusetts, at the age of twenty Mason moved to Savannah, Georgia, to assist in the building of a church organ. After experiencing religious conversion at a revival meeting, Mason joined the Independent Presbyterian Church and directed its choir and Sabbath School singing group. While in Savannah, he studied music with German immigrant Frederich Abel, writing original hymns and reharmonizing works by Mozart, Handel, Beethoven, and others. In 1822 Mason published *The Boston Handel & Haydn Society Collection of Church Music,* a collection of hymns, anthems, and psalm-tunes mostly derived from the work of European composers. Boosted by the prestige of the Society, which had sponsored the first American performances of both Handel's *Messiah* and Haydn's *Creation,* the collection sold over fifty thousand copies in eighteen editions, thus cementing Mason's reputation among Boston's musical and religious elites.[4]

On 7 October 1826, during a visit to Boston, Mason delivered an "Address on Church Music" in the vestry of Hanover Church; he repeated this "Address" two nights later at the Third Baptist Church (see figure 2.2). The clergy in attendance that night included Lyman Beecher and Benjamin Wisner, who were so impressed by Mason's ideas that they jointly commissioned the lecture's publication as a pamphlet and testified in the preface to their belief that it would "awaken interest and promote correct views." Such evangelical and pedagogical enthusiasms were prompted by the fact that Mason's "Address on Church

Figure 2.1. H. Wright Smith, engraving of Lowell Mason (circa 1840). Courtesy of The Trustees of The Boston Public Library.

Music" aspired to be nothing less than a manifesto on the proper role of music in Presbyterian churches, which were forced by the successes of the revivals then sweeping the nation to pursue a more aggressively evangelical mission. Faced with the threat of rising alternative religions, many of which made much more effective use of music than traditionally conservative churches did, Mason argued that music was the medium by which "truth is presented to the heart in the most forcible manner" and that it thus embodied "the very soul of eloquence itself." Furthermore, "There is a strong analogy between the art of oratory and that of music," he observed, for both "can move, or melt, or rouse, an audience."[5]

Rather than moving, melting, or rousing performances, Mason lamented the fact that the sentimental, evangelizing, and "most forcible" potential of church

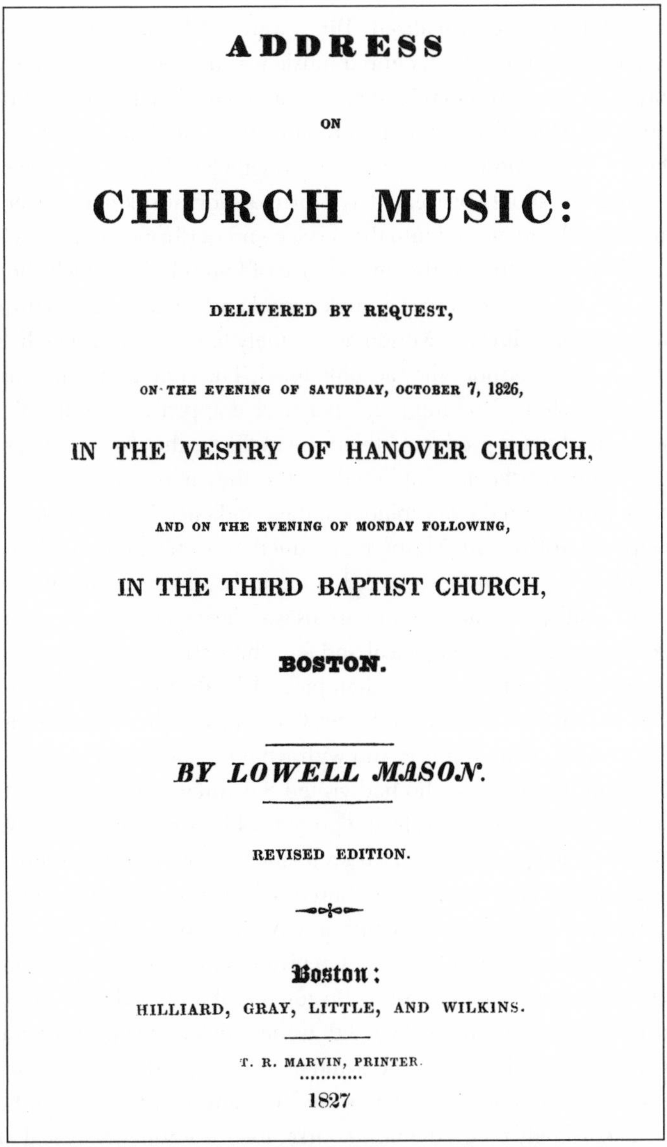

ADDRESS

ON

CHURCH MUSIC:

DELIVERED BY REQUEST,

ON THE EVENING OF SATURDAY, OCTOBER 7, 1826,

IN THE VESTRY OF HANOVER CHURCH,

AND ON THE EVENING OF MONDAY FOLLOWING,

IN THE THIRD BAPTIST CHURCH,

BOSTON.

BY LOWELL MASON.

REVISED EDITION.

Boston:

HILLIARD, GRAY, LITTLE, AND WILKINS.

T. R. MARVIN, PRINTER.

1827

Figure 2.2. The title-plate of Lowell Mason, *Address on Church Music* (1827). Courtesy of The Special Collections of The University of Illinois Music Library.

music was far from being realized. Tunes were inadequate, training was insufficient, and, most important, church music was treated as "affording a kind of interlude to religious worship" rather than as a devotional exercise in itself. One may question Mason's arguments here, for music had long been incorporated into the services of most denominations. Nonetheless, Mason and others argued that vocal music should be treated as a form of worship akin to prayer and that it should be fully integrated into the service and performed both by choirs and congregations. He stressed the importance of hymn lyrics, which should complement the music to "enforce" a single mood and message. In his own work as organist and choir director, Mason accordingly linked appropriate hymns with the subjects of the sermons they accompanied. The choir and its hymns thus became an extension of the minister's persuasive appeals: "A well trained choir have every facility for producing the proper effect—the *rhetorical effect* of church music . . . and like the accomplished orator, they may bring their art to bear with all its force upon the sensibilities of their audience." The proper training of this rhetorical instrument, Mason maintained, must begin in childhood, or else "much progress·cannot be expected afterwards." This first public announcement of Mason's principles and intentions was daring at a time when music was not widely considered pedagogical and few children received choral training.[6]

Mason and his reforms were championed in Boston by Reverend Lyman Beecher, pastor of the Bowdoin Street Church. Beecher was impressed with Mason's ideas on church music and with what he had heard of Mason's musicianship from Bostonians who had visited Savannah's Independent Presbyterian Church. A graduate of Yale and protégé of its president, Timothy Dwight, Beecher was a leading defender and reformer of Calvinism at a time when its Congregational and Presbyterian churches were rapidly losing souls to other denominations. Indeed, while Baptist and Methodist membership skyrocketed between 1790 and 1820 (propelled by revivalists and circuit-riding preachers), Harvard College and many leading Bostonians abandoned Calvinism for Unitarianism. Aghast, Beecher believed that these defections were attributable to doctrinal (or theological) differences and preaching (or rhetorical) practices and that both must be modified to win souls in a new age. Beecher and other reformers accordingly charted a new course, incorporating theatrical and theological elements of the revivals. The success of this strategy was phenomenal, as membership in all major American religious sects soared in the Second Great Awakening between 1820 and 1830 and increased nearly tenfold over the first half of the nineteenth century. Whereas one of every fifteen Americans belonged to a Protestant church in 1800, by 1835, largely as a result of revivals, the ratio had risen to one of eight. In Boston alone, between 1820 and 1840, over two dozen new evangelical churches were established, with most of the members drawn from the burgeoning middle class.[7]

Revivals also spurred social activism, as Beecher and others organized believers in moral reform, thus downplaying Calvinist doctrines of predestination and irremediable human depravity. By placing their theological emphasis on human agency and the possibility of individual and social redemption, Beecher and his fellow reformers encouraged membership in activist, middle-class, evangelical organizations.[8] Beecher's life exemplified this righteous, activist spirit. Indeed, as early as 1803 he had published (and preached on) *The Practicability of Suppressing Vice*; in 1816 he was among the founders of the American Bible Society; for over thirty years he led campaigns against dueling, intemperance, gambling, and Catholicism; his sermons were well attended and widely distributed in pamphlet form. In short, he was a veritable factory of cultural activism.

Furthermore, Lyman Beecher had a keen understanding of the rhetorical dimensions of the ministry and moral reform organizations. For example, in his 1803 sermon/pamphlet, he argued: "Public opinion, has in society a singular influence; if vice can enlist that opinion on its side, it triumphs. But let the weight of that opinion be laid upon any vicious practice, and it will most inevitably sink under it. Hence it becomes a matter of great importance, that public opinion should in all cases be correct; and be arranged with its whole influence on the side of virtue."[9] In order to pursue such correct, arranged, and virtuous opinions, Beecher incorporated strategies of advertising, theatricality, and the rhetoric of conversion that had proven enormously successful in the eastern urban revivals of Charles Grandison Finney. Beecher had initially disapproved of Finney, promising in 1827 when Finney planned a revival in Boston that he would fight him "every inch of the way to Boston and then I'll fight you there."[14] But by August 1831, one month after the premiere of "America," by which time Beecher had adopted many of Finney's ideas and methods, Finney began a seven-month revival in Boston's Park Street Church at Beecher's invitation. Finney insisted that a successful revival was no miracle but rather the rhetorically calculated "result of the right use of constituted means," the product of a systematic and replicable approach to persuasion.[10] Given this premise, music was no longer to be understood as an interlude or break within the otherwise carefully orchestrated rituals of church services but as a powerful means through which revivalists could appeal to worshipers and enlist their enthusiastic participation. Finney and most major American revivalists who followed him (including Dwight Moody, Billy Sunday, and Billy Graham) hired special musical assistants to perform and to organize singing at meetings.[11] Beecher, then, like Finney, endorsed Mason's views regarding music's potential for winning souls. In fact, after attending Mason's 1826 "Address on Church Music," Beecher campaigned among local clergy to hire Mason for the task of transforming the role and practice of church music in Boston.

In 1827 Mason was thus hired as choir director of three Boston churches, including Beecher's Bowdoin Street Church, and was named president of the Handel and Haydn Society. The next year he began conducting free classes in the basement of the Park Street Church and later at the Bowdoin Street Church. Lyman Beecher approvingly observed that Mason's children's choirs "drew in the unconverted, and were instrumental in their conversion." The child singers were not simply vehicles for the effective conveyance of ideas to others but were also themselves the targets of religious appeals. Mason's "influence was not secular," Beecher insisted, "but as efficacious as preaching," with the result that "almost all who went to his classes, instead of being decoyed by it and made frivolous, were converted." As a demonstration of his "efficacious" methods, Mason's Sabbath School choir offered a concert at the Park Street Church on 4 July 1830. By that time Mason had over 150 pupils who were taught to sing and read music without charge in exchange for their pledge to continue the classes for one year. The group's public concerts, including the initial performance of "America," offered strong support for Mason's claims that any child could be taught to sing and that such instruction could be morally uplifting.[12]

Mason's influence extended far beyond his own pupils and touched the hundreds of music teachers and choir directors he trained as well as a general public influenced by his numerous writings and song books. In fact, he published thirty-eight collections of church music, fourteen books of children's songs, and dozens of other collections of songs for glee clubs and singing schools. From among this Herculean outpouring of energy, Mason and Elam Ives's 1831 collection *The Juvenile Lyre* is the earliest known American music book published specifically for the use of primary school students. Two of his collections, *Carmina Sacra* (1841) and *The New Carmina Sacra* (1850), sold more than eight hundred thousand copies combined—an astonishing number for a culture yet to dive completely into the mass production and distribution techniques that arose during and then especially after the Civil War.[13] Several of Mason's own hymns, including "From Greenland's Icy Mountains" and "Nearer, My God, to Thee" (1852) became standards. It is no exaggeration, then, to observe that Mason's concepts, lesson plans, and songbooks for music instruction reshaped nineteenth-century musical performance and education.

Given the scope of such prodigious production, it is not surprising to learn that Mason both translated foreign songs and adapted established melodies to new lyrics (as did his fellow musical activists). In one such case, seeking songs appropriately simple and elevating for his purposes, Mason turned in 1830 to Boston editor and educational reformer William Channing Woodbridge (1794–1845), who had recently returned from Europe with a supply of school songbooks. After graduating from Yale in 1811, Woodbridge served as a principal at Burlington Academy in New Jersey and later taught at Gallaudet's Institute for the education of the deaf and mute in Hartford, Connecticut. Plagued by poor health, he embarked on two prolonged tours of Europe, in 1820 and from 1825 to 1829. While abroad, Woodbridge became fascinated by the revolutionary educational ideas of Johann Heinrich Pestalozzi (1746–1827) and other Swiss reformers who replaced conventional rote-memorization approaches to elementary education with collaborative and creative activities, including singing. In the wake of Napoleon's invasion and subsequent Swiss political conflicts, Pestalozzi sought to improve social harmony and order through an educational system that nurtured the moral, mental, and physical development of children. Prussia's Frederick William III embraced Pestalozzian principles and methods in the new state educational system of 1808, which was explicitly designed to promote social stability and build patriotic support for the government. Intrigued by the pedagogical and nationalist possibilities of this approach, Woodbridge visited many Prussian schools, including Pestalozzi's own institute at Yverdon, and spoke extensively with educators who employed the new techniques. Woodbridge was deeply impressed, as he found pedagogues arguing that singing was "among the essential branches of education." He thus quoted approvingly from the *Prussian Official Gazette* of Cologne, which observed that the "principal object" of music education "in these schools is to cultivate feeling, and exert an influence in forming the habits and strengthening the powers of the will. . . . From its very nature, it accustoms pupils to conform to general rules, and to act in concert with others."[14]

Woodbridge was so taken with this disciplinary sensibility that, upon his return to the United States, he became an influential popularizer of Pestalozzi's theories and practices. Lowell Mason was among those whom Woodbridge persuaded to experiment with Pestalozzian instructional techniques, as he lent Pestalozzian treatises to Mason and described to him the techniques he had observed in practice.[15] Woodbridge then founded and became the first editor of the *American Journal of Education and Instruction,* where he published a series of essays that promoted school music programs and the Pestalozzian approach to instruction. Indeed, drawing on the Prussian experience, he promoted vocal music instruction as a disciplinary method for building patriotic affiliation with the state and for instilling proper habits of order and submission. Like Mason, Woodbridge also explicitly praised the rhetorical instrumentality of vocal music, calling it "eloquence in its most attractive and fascinating form." Echoing again the period's driving concerns with sentiment, pathos, and persuasion, Woodbridge argued that vocal music could be "one of the most powerful engines for influencing the minds of the masses of men." Unlike most oratory, "which is

heard but once, and dies upon the ear," the eloquence of vocal music encourages its listeners to repeat and imitate what has impressed them "and thus re-
doubles its influence, until it forms a part of the current of our own thoughts
and feelings." Woodbridge thus acknowledged that song was indispensable to
the efforts of both political agitators and revolutionaries *and* to the bacchanalian
and sensualist seeking "to encourage himself and his companions in their brutal revelry."[16]

Not surprisingly, considering his influence at the hands of Pestalozzi, Mason,
and other middle-class reformers, Woodbridge argued that society has a substantial interest in directing the mighty force of vocal music toward the cultivation of virtue. Woodbridge made a significant step toward popularizing this thesis on 19 August 1830 when (following quickly on the heels of the first issue of the
American Journal of Education and Instruction) he delivered a widely publicized lecture on "Vocal Music as a Branch of Common Education" at the Boston State
House before a convention of teachers assembled to form the American Institute of Education. Indeed, speaking before his fellow educators, moralists, and
nationalists, Woodbridge maintained that singing was best taught in the public
schools and that vocal music instruction would cultivate moral development
and "habits of order and obedience and union."[17] His talk was accompanied by
suitable songs performed by Lowell Mason's well-drilled child singers, who had
been trained using Pestalozzian methods.

The various efforts and interests of Woodbridge, Mason, and Beecher inter-
sected in 1830, a few months before the writing of "America," as all three—each
of whom viewed music instruction as a means to inculcate proper beliefs and attitudes among children and thereby to improve society as a whole—worked to
institutionalize children's vocal music programs. Armed with a perfectionist zeal
and a genuine love of nation, they sought public occasions and songs through
which their instructional methods might best be exhibited. The campaign for
school-based instruction in vocal music was, as musicologist David Kushner has
written, "directly related to the proposition that appropriate texts, edifying to
the young, could be introduced in a musical context." Songs of musical merit
capable of conveying what the reformers believed were the proper messages to
the child singers and their audiences were consequently of great importance.
Indeed, Woodbridge introduced his lecture to the American Lyceum, "On
Vocal Music As a Branch of Common Education," by expressing the anxiety of
school music advocates "to see a store of suitable materials prepared for young
musicians," which might prevent the fledgling school programs from being
"misdirected."[18] This quest for "suitable materials" led directly to the writing
of "America."

Figure 2.3. Engraving of Samuel F. Smith (circa 1832). Courtesy of The American Antiquarian Society.

Writing "America": Samuel Smith's Fortuitous Inspiration

Unable to read German, Mason in late 1830 or early 1831 brought Woodbridge's Prussian songbooks to Samuel Francis Smith, a friend at Andover Theological Seminary who could translate them (see figure 2.3). Smith was born in 1808 at 37 Sheafe Street in Boston's North End, a block from the Old North Church, where the lanterns were hung that spurred Paul Revere's ride. He spent three years at the Eliot School in Boston and in 1820 entered the Boston Latin School, where he won the prestigious Franklin Medal. After his father, a cooper with a shop on Lewis Wharf, died in 1822 at age forty, Smith worked to support his mother and sister. He entered Harvard in the fall of 1825 along with nineteen classmates, including Oliver Wendell Holmes, George T. Bigelow (later chief justice of the Massachusetts Supreme Court), Francis Crowninshield (later speaker of the Massachusetts House of Representatives), George T. Davis (later member of the U.S. House of Representatives), Benjamin R. Curtis (later associate justice of the Supreme Court, 1851–57), the author and poet James Freeman Clark, the abolitionist Samuel May, and the noted astronomer and mathematician Benjamin Pierce. Charles Sumner and Wendell Phillips were in the two subsequent classes and well known to Smith. Members of the famous class of 1829 held annual dinners (until 1893) at which Holmes occasionally toasted his classmates in execrable verse like this passage from "The Boys": "And there's a nice youngster of excellent pith. / Fate tried to conceal him by naming him Smith! / But he chanted a song for the brave and the free, / Just read on his medal—'My Country of Thee.'"[19]

Holmes's playful rhyming stands in stark contrast to the heavy seriousness of the training he and his Harvard "Boys" received. Indeed, during their years at Harvard, Holmes, Smith, and their classmates were required to attend daily prayers morning and evening in the unheated college chapel. On Sundays, the president of the college preached the sermon. Students wore black uniforms and square caps "to guard against extravagant habits in dress." As a budding young scholar with lofty ambitions, Smith devoted himself to the study of modern and classical languages, adding tutorials in Hebrew so that he might read the several chapters of Genesis required for entrance into leading theological seminaries. Smith was successful in his studies, as he was admitted in 1830 to Andover Theological Seminary. A Congregationalist school twenty miles from Boston, Andover was then America's largest and most prestigious theological seminary and offered a demanding three-year curriculum. It was founded in 1808 "in opposition not only to atheists and infidels," according to the pledge all professors were required to take every five years, "but to Jews, Papists, Mahommetans, Arians, Pelagians, Antinomians, Arminians, Socinians, Sabellians, Unitarians, and Universalists, and to all other heresies and errors, ancient and modern, which may be opposed to the gospel of Christ or hazardous to the souls of men." Unlike most seminaries, it generally required a B.A. and knowledge of Greek, Latin, and Hebrew for entrance.[20] Hence, by 1830, Smith was working amid the nation's most elite intellectuals and conservative theologians.

While at the seminary Smith supported himself by translating articles from the German encyclopedia *Conversations-Lexicons* for the *Cyclopedia Americana*, edited by Francis Lieber, and by translating German songs for Lowell Mason. In fact, in his preface to the landmark 1831 collection *Juvenile Lyre*, Mason acknowledged that most of its song lyrics had been "translated by Mr. S. F. Smith (of the Theological Seminary, Andover), in such a manner as to preserve the music as originally written. The same gentleman has also furnished several beautiful original songs." Mason and Smith also collaborated on a few original songs (with Smith writing the lyrics and Mason the music), including their "Hymn for the Fatherless and Widow Society" (1832). Mostly, however, their joint work consisted of adapting European songs for American purposes. For example, when Mason visited Andover with a collection of Woodbridge's German songbooks in late 1830 or early 1831, Smith later recalled him saying, "Here, I can't read these, but they contain good music, which I should be glad to use. Turn over the leaves, and, if you find anything particularly good, give me a translation or imitation of it, or write a wholly original song—any thing, so I can use it."[21]

Smith worked with the songs in the German collections, "sometimes putting the German songs into English verse, sometimes making songs of his own of the same rhythm and accent as the songs in the foreign dialect." Among these songs was a German version of "God Save the King," which by 1831 had been adapted as the anthem of several German states. Standing before the parlor window at his boarding house on Main Street, Smith discovered the tune and drafted new lyrics suitable for Mason's children's choir. "Falling in with the tune of one of them, now called 'America,' and being pleased with its simple and easy movement," he later recalled, "I glanced at the German words, and seeing that they were patriotic, instantly felt the impulse to write a patriotic hymn of my own, to the same tune." Speaking at a massive gathering held in Boston in April 1895 to honor Smith and his song, Representative John D. Long of Massachusetts elevated the humble moment of its composition to mythic proportions befitting its place in American civic life. Long described Smith as a young theological student at Andover Seminary who sat "in his lonely chamber" in February 1831 while winter storm clouds gathered outside, warmed only by the fire of patriotism and "the glow of American youth." "Were we to use the quaint language of ancient Scripture," Long intoned, "we should say that an angel came down from heaven and breathed upon his lips, or that a vision came to him and the Lord in visible form stood before him and bade him write on tablets of stone."[22] Despite Smith's own description of his relatively effortless appropriation of a "simple and easy" German tune, Long invests "America" with the authority of divine revelation and imagines its patriotic sentiments as latter-day commandments.

The actual circumstances, as Smith himself was always quick to point out, were far more mundane. Smith drafted the new lyrics on a piece of scrap paper in half an hour. "It was struck out at a sitting, without the slightest idea that it would ever attain the popularity it has since enjoyed," he wrote to Captain George Henry Preble of the U.S. navy in 1872. "If I had anticipated the future of it," he mused, "I would have taken more pains with it." Nor was Smith's song entirely a product of the moment. In writing "America," he drew on the lyrics of an earlier song, "The Children's Independence Day," which he had written for Mason's July Fourth celebration the previous year, including the phrases "Freedom's holy light" and "Let music float on every breeze." As in his earlier song, Smith's new lyrics (see appendix A) blended patriotism with religious devotion and reflexively stipulated within the text of the song the significance of its singing. Indeed, the famous opening lines celebrate "My country! 'tis of thee, / Sweet land of liberty, / Of thee I sing."[23] Although Smith's lyrics contain no explicit intertextual reference to "God Save the King," a later-suppressed third verse originally defined American national identity in part by its opposition to the British. In 1914, Reverend D. A. W. Smith, son of Samuel F. Smith, presented the "original manuscript" of "America," containing four verses, to Harvard University. It was evident, however, that the handwritten document had been cut in the middle, a portion excised, and then glued back together on a paper backing. In 1919 Smith released a photograph of the original, uncut manuscript, including five verses, rather than the four traditionally published. The original third verse was performed at the premiere of "America" at Park Street Church on 4 July 1831 (see figure 2.5) and was included in the song as published in Lowell Mason's 1832 hymn collection *The Choir*. It was omitted from the 1833 edition of *The Choir* and from all subsequent printings of the song for nearly a century.[24] The pointed lost verse sings

> No more shall tyrants here
> With haughty steps appear
>   And soldier-bands;
> No more shall tyrants tread
> Above the patriot dead;
> No more our blood be shed
>   By alien hands.

During the early stages of the Revolutionary War, colonial residents of Boston's North End were compelled to provide quarters for British troops. The tread of the tyrants "above the patriot dead" refers to the British occupation of the famous Copp's Hill Burying Ground, two blocks from Smith's birthplace, which contains the graves of the Mathers, Hutchinsons, and other prominent Bostonians. In fact, in a display of hauteur remarkable even for the British, His Majesty's troops used the gravestones of patriots, including that of Captain Daniel Malcolm of the Sons of Liberty, for target practice. The musketball marks are still visible in Malcolm's slate tombstone today. Anti-British sentiment was strong, then, in the North End during Smith's boyhood and especially during the War of 1812, when he often visited the sites of British occupation.[25] "America" was written at a time of renewed tension between the United States and Great Britain, yet as tensions subsided and as Smith considered the children he anticipated singing "America," the aggressive stanza seemed inappropriate, so he excised it.

Smith sent signed copies of the revised lyrics, written in his own hand, to many correspondents. He recounted in letters and public speeches the story of his writing of "America" "over and over again," he confessed near the end of his life, "until it seems threadbare to me."[26] These recountings were inaccurate in certain respects, including his misremembering the year in which the song was written. Smith said, though usually with some explicit uncertainty, that the song was written and first performed in 1832. Its "One Hundredth Anniversary" was celebrated at Park Street Church and nationally in 1932. Printed broadsides of the program at which "America" was first performed survive, however, and bear the date 4 July 1831.

Smith's story of the writing of "America" varied in other respects in different tellings. Sometimes he said that he had not recognized the tune as "God Save the King" when he found it in the German songbook. Interviewed in 1894, Smith explained that it was only afterward that he discovered the tune to be that of "the English national hymn, 'God Save the King.'" "I did not know this at the time," he confessed; rather, he said he put patriotic lyrics to it because a note at the foot of the German songbook page designated it as "patriotic." On other occasions, Smith suggested that his use of the British melody was a conscious act of appropriation. "Finding 'God Save the King'" in a group of German songbooks, he wrote in a letter of 11 June 1861, "I proceeded to give it the ring of American republican patriotism." On still other occasions, such as 3 April 1895, when Smith offered an extended account of the song's origins for a crowd of several thousand in Boston, he downplayed the issue of appropriation by speaking of the tune as one "which England claims as hers because she has so long sung it to the words 'God Save the Queen,' but which the Danes claim as theirs, and which the Germans claim as original with them, and of the real origin of which I believe no one is certain."[27]

One constant element in Smith's recountings of the song's origins is that after writing the song, "the whole matter passed out of my mind"—and, we should add, out of his hands. For example, while he passed the lyrics of his song, along with other poems and some translations of German hymns, on to Lowell Mason in 1831, he was soon surprised to learn that Mason had included the song in an Independence Day program to be held at Boston's famous Park Street Church on July Fourth.[28] Thereafter, Smith's song, originally written for a children's' choir and adopted from a German songbook that had no doubt adopted the tune from earlier British versions, would assume a colorful, well-nigh mythical life of its own as America's unofficial national anthem.

First Performance and Popularization: "To Correct the Habits of the Rising Generation"

Designed by English architect Peter Banner and built on the edge of the Boston Common in 1809–10, on what Bostonians came to call "Brimstone Corner," the Park Street Church was described by Henry James as "the most interesting mass of brick and mortar in America" (see figure 2.4).[29] But the site's importance goes far beyond its architectural beauty. The church was built on the site of the colonial Granary, once the largest structure in Boston, where grain was stored for times of scarcity and where the sails for the revolutionary frigate *Constitution* were made. While the church was built over the old Granary, it adjoined the Granary's burial ground, which contains the graves of revolutionary heroes John Hancock, Samuel Adams, and Paul Revere. Hence, following from both its central geographic location and its historical importance, the church was frequently a focal point for the city's Fourth of July and other mass celebrations. In addition to this rich political significance, the Park Street Church was among the most important religious institutions in nineteenth-century Boston and was noted particularly for the excellence of its music. It was also a significant venue for the meetings of emergent antebellum reform movements such as the American Temperance Society, which was founded there in 1826. On 4 July 1829, two years to the day before the premiere of "America," the twenty-three-year-old abolitionist William Lloyd Garrison entered the church to make his first public speech against slavery. Thus, by the time "America" was first performed there, on 4 July 1831, Park Street Church was well established as a cultural "memory site" of historical, political, artistic, and religious significance and as one of the focal points of cutting-edge local activism.[30] Observances of occasions such as Independence Day in the Park Street Church therefore linked the patriotic and the sacred, past and present, established power and upstart reform.

The Fourth of July was the most widely celebrated civic holiday in nineteenth-century America. Much like today, most American communities observed the occasion in oratory and songs that recalled their revolutionary heritage. Independence Day was also popular among dissenters and social reformers who used the Fourth to protest rather than praise national policies and to appeal to the accepted premises of the Declaration of Independence to argue for social change. In fact, appropriating the Fourth soon became a central component of many of the reform movements in the 1830s, all of which were based on what must surely strike more cynical readers as an improbable, remarkably enthusiastic, even utopian confidence in the possibility of moral suasion and social change. "In this era, perhaps more than at any other time in our history," writes Daniel Feller, "citizens believed in their ability to mold and direct their

Figure 2.4. Engraving of Boston's Park Street Church (circa 1830s). Courtesy of The American Antiquarian Society.

own destiny and that of the world."[31] The Fourth, then, was not only a memorializing, history-celebrating occasion but also an opportunity for demonstrating that the promises of the Declaration were still contested, still unfolding, still the subject of intense debate.

The Fourth of July observance at Park Street Church in 1831, for example, was no simple celebration but rather a complex expression of the anxieties and hopes of its organizers and participants. Most important, the rapid growth of Baptism, Methodism, Unitarianism, and especially Catholicism greatly alarmed Lyman Beecher and other conservative clergy. In fact, Beecher and his fellow Protestant orators frequently used July Fourth programs first to proclaim themselves "100% Americans" and then to attack Catholics as a threat to Republican institutions. They feared that large-scale immigration and the broad extension of the franchise to the uneducated masses could lead to mob rule, as in the French Revolution, or to the corruption of American institutions. For example, the separate schools, churches, newspapers, and social institutions established by Irish immigrants in Boston and other eastern cities were seized upon by Protestants as proof of the Catholics' threat to the social order. In the face of what was then hailed as "Popery" and as a "Papal Plot" against democracy, Lyman Beecher began in January 1831 a series of lectures in which he denounced Catholicism and warned his listeners of Rome's attempts to undermine American liberties.[32] Later that year, in his sermon "The Necessity of Revivals of Religion to the Perpetuity of Our Civil and Religious Institutions," Beecher warned that "the dangers which threaten these United States, and the free institutions here established, are numerous and appalling." Similarly, in his 1831 essay "The Perfect Life," Beecher's Unitarian rival, William Ellery Channing, pastor of Boston's Federal Street Church, marveled apprehensively at the "mighty movement of the civilized world," in which "Thrones are tottering, and the firmest establishments of former ages seem about to be swept away by the torrent of revolution."[33] Beecher, Channing, and their fellow evangelical reformers sought to build a national civic culture and moral foundation capable of withstanding these torrents.

The 1831 Independence Day gathering staged by the Boston Sabbath School Union at Park Street Church exhibited the pillars of this civic edifice as conceived by Beecher: patriotism, Protestantism, and temperance, inculcated both in and by youth through song and sermon. Since January, newsletters had disseminated a national call for Sabbath school celebrations of Independence Day in order "to persuade all to unite in celebrating this most important event in our nation's history, by meeting together to praise and adore the God of armies, rather than go with the thoughtless multitude to worship before the altar of the god of *wine*." Over twenty-four hundred Bostonians responded to the call for a chaste, Protestant, and properly patriotic celebration that would set a righteous counterexample to the drunken July Fourth revelries of their neighbors. Among the good celebrants, Mason's children's choir opened the ceremonies, singing "This is the youthful choir that sings, / When all the town is gay; / That praises God with gratitude / On Independence day."[34] In his 1893 memoir, *A New England Boyhood*, Edward Everett Hale recalled his surprise when he wandered past the Park Street Church on that Independence Day, for "to see a church open on a week-day was itself extraordinary. To see children going in procession into church was more extraordinary." After Mason's children's choir had performed three songs, including the first-ever performance of Smith's "America," interspersed with readings from the scriptures and a prayer, Reverend Dr. Benjamin B. Wisner, pastor of the Old South Church, offered an "Address to the Children." Children were not only the featured performers, then, but also the primary audience for the event. Indeed, the Sabbath School Independence Day gathering, as explained by the editor of the *Sabbath School Treasury*, was intended to "correct the habits of the rising generation, and bring all the children and youth in the land to feel and act right in reference to this national anniversary."[35] Thus the broadsheet announcing the event is topped by an injunction to "Tell your CHILDREN of it, and let your CHILDREN tell their CHILDREN, and their CHILDREN another generation" (see figure 2.5).

Despite such exaggerated emphases on children, it is clear that they were not the only intended audience for the performance, as Woodbridge and Mason had both written of children as particularly effective vehicles for the transmission of sentiments to adult listeners. "We ourselves," Woodbridge testified to the American Lyceum in 1833, "often see the stout heart melt, and the rigid countenance relax, and even a tear tremble in the eye, at the plaintive tones or the more plaintive song of a child, when the simple words, without the accompanying tones, would scarcely have moved a feeling." This is a remarkable statement, for it demonstrates that Woodbridge and Mason and their followers believed that the apparent innocence and sincerity of the child singer, along with the seductive beauty of music, would disarm jaded adult listeners and succeed where oratory, sermon, or tract would fail. This hunch regarding the unparalleled propagandistic powers of singing children had previously been confirmed by a reporter for the *Liberator*, who described the children's singing at the 4 July 1831 performance as "eminently harmonious and soul-subduing, sweeter than the warbling of birds." Indeed, according to the *Sabbath School Treasury*'s review of the same performance, the hymns were sung by Mason's juvenile choir "with manifest effect upon all present."[36]

The children who performed at Park Street Church on 4 July 1831 thus demonstrated for the assembled educators, clergy, and civic leaders both the success of Mason's instructional methods and the potential value of such instruction in the cultivation of civic virtue. In the same year that "America" premiered, Mason published *The Juvenile Lyre*, the first American songbook for public school children, where he maintained that every child, not merely the rare and gifted, could be taught to perform and enjoy music. In order to prove the effectiveness of his approach, he offered free singing classes for children. Furthermore, Mason's Sabbath School Union choir, which first performed "America," represented in its members precisely the redeeming potential of music to unite a fractured and debased citizenry, as it combined voices from the nineteen Boston Congregational Sabbath schools operated by area churches and the Boston City Missionary Society.[37] Formed in 1817 at Park Street Church, the Sabbath schools originally gathered children "from the streets and wharves" who might otherwise be "engaged in play and mischief."[67] Each of the numbers performed that July Fourth by Masons' previously mischief-prone youths, in-

CELEBRATION
OF
AMERICAN INDEPENDENCE,
BY THE
BOSTON SABBATH SCHOOL UNION,
AT PARK STREET CHURCH, JULY 4, 1831.

ORDER OF EXERCISES.

1. SINGING.
[By the Juvenile Choir.]

This is the youthful choir that comes,
　All dressed so neat and gay;
As bright as birds that soar and sing,
　And warble all the day.

This is the youthful choir that loves
　The teacher to obey;
That meets to sing, and pray, and learn,
　On every Sabbath day.

This is the youthful choir that goes
　Through wind and storm away,
From peaceful home to Sabbath school,
　To learn salvation's way.

This is the youthful choir that sings,
　When all the town is gay;
That praises God with gratitude
　On Independent day.

2. READING THE SCRIPTURES.

3. SINGING.
[By the Choir.]

With joy we meet,
With smiles we greet
　Our schoolmates bright and gay:
Be dry each tear
Of sorrow here—
　'Tis Independent day.

'Tis freedom's sound
That rings around,
　And brightens every ray,
On banner floats,
And trumpet-notes:
　On Independent day.

O who from home
Would fail to come
　And join the children's lay—
When praise we bring
To God our king,
　On Independent day.

For liberty,
Great God, to thee
　Our grateful thanks we pay;
For thanks, we know,
To thee, we owe,
　On Independent day.

While thunder breaks,
And music wakes
　Its patriotic lay,
At temple-gate
Our feet shall wait,
　On Independent day.

O Saviour, shine,
With beams divine,
　And take our sins away;
And give us grace
To seek thy face,
　On Independent day.

4. PRAYER.

5. SINGING.
[By the Choir.]

My country! 'tis of thee,
Sweet land of liberty—
　Of thee I sing:
Land, where my fathers died;
Land of the pilgrim's pride;
From every mountain-side,
　Let freedom ring.

My native country! thee—
Land of the noble free—
　Thy name I love:
I love thy rocks and rills,
Thy woods and templed hills;
My heart with rapture thrills,
　Like that above.

No more shall tyrants here
With haughty steps appear,
　And soldier-bands;
No more shall tyrants tread
Above the patriot dead—
No more our blood be shed
　By alien hands.

Let music swell the breeze,
And ring from all the trees
　Sweet freedom's song:
Let mortal tongues awake—
Let all that breathes partake—
Let rocks their silence break—
　The sound prolong.

Our fathers' God! to thee—
Author of liberty!
　To thee we sing;
Long may our land be bright
With freedom's holy light—
Protect us by thy might,
　Great God, our King!

6. ADDRESS TO THE CHILDREN.
By Rev. Dr. Wisner.

7. SINGING.
[By the Choir.]
Hosanna, Hosanna, Hosanna in the highest.

[By the Congregation.]
Tune—DUKE STREET.
What are those soul reviving strains
That echo thus from Salem's plains?
What anthems loud and louder still,
So sweetly sound from Zion's hill?

[By the Choir.]
Hosanna, Hosanna, Hosanna in the highest.

[By the Congregation.]
Behold a youthful chorus sings
Hosanna to the King of kings,
The Saviour comes—and they proclaim
Salvation sent in Jesus' name.

[By the Choir.]
Blessed is he who cometh in the name of the Lord.

[By the Congregation.]
Proclaim hosanhas loud and clear,
See David's Son and Lord appear,
All praise on earth to him be given,
And glory shout through highest heaven.

[By the Choir.]
Hosanna, Hosanna, Hosanna in the highest.

**8. CONCLUDING PRAYER AND BENE-
DICTION.**

Figure 2.5. "Celebration of American Independence," the handbill for the 4 July 1831 premiere of "America" at Boston's Park Street Church. Courtesy of The Chapin Library of Rare Books, Williams College.

cluding "America," reflected textually on the significance of its own performance: "This is the youthful choir that loves / The teacher to obey / That meets to sing, and pray, and learn, / On every Sabbath day."[38] Such performances demonstrated both textually and musically the profound possibilities of children's music as a tool for properly evangelical, deferential, and nationalist socialization. Indeed, such performances were so utterly disarming, so persuasive regarding these ends, that they soon propelled the campaign for public school music into the forefront of reform politics.

It is no coincidence that "America" premiered at a time of revolutionary change in American education. Spurred by the expanding economy's need for educated workers, the abolition of property restrictions on voting, and the Jacksonian rhetoric of egalitarianism, public schooling expanded dramatically in the 1830s. The push for public schools was supported widely by reformers who saw them as a potential solution to the licentiousness and heterogeneity of the rapidly expanding urban masses, who could be shaped, it was hoped, into proper Americans by socializing them in schools. By placing students from different classes and ethnicities together and supplying them with a common base of knowledge, educators sought to create future citizens content with their place in society and committed to its defense. Workingmen's parties and early unions, on the other hand, supported public schools as engines of economic and social advancement, through which the promise of the American Revolution could at last be fulfilled and disparities of wealth and social station narrowed. The explicitly nationalist, socializing function of schools was so ubiquitous that Tocqueville observed that "In the United States, politics are the end and aim of education."[39]

The push for public schooling was launched in Massachusetts, which established a free public school system in 1827. Thereafter, between 1840 and 1865, the number of students enrolled in winter schools in Massachusetts increased by 53.8 percent, the number of schools by 54.5 percent, and the number of teachers by 74.4 percent. Beyond Massachusetts, the growth of public education was equally dramatic, as the time spent in school by the average white American increased from four months in 1800 to twenty-two months in 1850.[40] This remarkable social transformation was fueled in large part by reformers who sought both to provide a free (and compulsory) elementary education for all white children and to establish state control over teacher training and school curricula. It was hoped that the combination of these efforts would promote uniformity in the knowledge, beliefs, and habits of pupils. "America," which became a staple of school songbooks and performances, was popularized through this expansion of public schooling and school music programs. Indeed, the institutional convergence of "America," public schooling, and Mason's pedagogical system was initiated in December 1831, five months after the first performance of the song at Park Street Church, when Mason's friend, the lawyer and Boston school board member George Henry Snelling (1801–92), presented a report to the Boston School Committee on the desirability of incorporating musical instruction in the public schools. On the basis of his subcommittee's observations of Mason's instruction and performances, Snelling argued that all children could benefit from such training. The School Committee responded with a resolution that one school in each district should be selected for systematic instruction in vocal music.

Despite Snelling's glowing report and the Committee's apparent acceptance of its proposals, the resolution to introduce children's music classes into the school system was not acted on. Woodbridge attributed this failure, in the *American Journal of Education and Instruction*, to "the very general and very unreasonable public prejudice in this city against the introduction of vocal music into the public schools." Thus placed on the defensive, Mason and his ally, George Webb, sought to demonstrate the effectiveness of their instructional system and its viability for the school curriculum by staging, in 1832 and 1833, a series of public performances of their children's choir. These performances attracted large audiences curious to see the still-novel phenomenon of a children's chorus and left many who attended the concerts stunned by the results of Mason's training. "Never shall we forget the mingled emotions of wonder, delight, vanquished incredulity, and pleased hope, with which these juvenile concerts were attended," the editors of the *North American Review* reported, concluding: "The coldest heart was touched, and glistening eyes and quivering lips attested the depth and strength of the feelings excited in the bosoms of parents and teachers."[41]

Following the success of these initial concerts, Mason and others formed, in 1833, the Boston Academy of Music, thus establishing a singing school and teacher training program with the expressed purposes of improving church music and establishing music instruction in public schools. Woodbridge, who was already editor of the *American Journal of Education and Instruction*, was named corresponding secretary of the Academy and reported on its activities for a national readership. Within two years, educators in Georgia, Illinois, Maine, Maryland, Missouri, New Hampshire, New York, Ohio, South Carolina, Tennessee, Vermont, and Virginia had corresponded with Mason and the Academy, seeking guidance either on how to establish or to improve music programs. In its second year of operation, the Academy instructed approximately three thousand students, offered classes in several Boston-area private schools, and featured a trained two-hundred-voice choir and amateur orchestra in numerous public concerts. In addition, Mason's *Manual of the Boston Academy of Music*, published in eight editions before the Civil War, presented a comprehensive program of instruction that eventually came to influence a generation of American music teachers.[42]

On the basis of these successes, Mason's supporters petitioned the Boston School Committee on 10 August 1836 to again consider establishing a music curriculum in the public schools. The Committee formed a subcommittee to study the matter and to report its findings. On 24 August 1837, the subcommittee, headed by T. Kemper Davis, enthusiastically recommended that the Boston Academy of Music be authorized to introduce a school music curriculum. This report was approved but not funded. Nonetheless, seizing the moment, Mason volunteered to teach for one year at a public school without compensation and to provide all necessary materials and equipment at his own expense. The Boston School Committee accepted his offer in November 1837 and assigned him to the Hawes School in South Boston, where he would work under the supervision of the schoolmaster and observers from the Committee. Mason taught at the school for one hour a day, two days a week. The Hawes schoolmaster, Joseph Harrington, closely observed Mason's efforts and reported to the Committee that school attendance increased on days of the lessons and that students seemed to prefer their musical activities to any outdoor sports or other forms of play. Students had begun singing spontaneously in groups outside of class, he marveled, and songs incorporated in regular classes sparked greater interest and participation. Most important, he concluded: "of the great *moral* effect of vocal music, there can be no question."[43]

On 14 August 1838, Mason and two hundred of his Hawes School pupils offered a dramatic public demonstration of what public school music instruction could achieve. A large audience, including most of the School Committee members, attended the concert at Boston's South Baptist Church. The well-received performance consisted of eight songs, most drawn from Mason and Webb's 1837 collection *The Juvenile Singing School.* Two weeks later, on 28 August 1838, the Boston School Committee approved and funded music instruction in the public schools, according it a place in the curriculum equal in importance to other traditional subjects. Mason was named the nation's first school Superintendent of Music and was authorized to develop a music curriculum, hire instructional assistants, and purchase needed books and supplies. The 1838 Boston School Committee report that authorized these momentous transformations, hopefully dubbed the "Magna Charta of Music Education in the United States" in the 1839 annual report of the Boston Academy of Music, supported music instruction as a singularly effective instrument with which to impart civic virtue and to preserve democratic liberties. Bostonians were suddenly saying "Amoris patriae nutric carmen" — "Song is the nourisher of patriotism." Pronouncing it far more important "to feel rightly than to think profoundly," the members of the School Committee argued that "through vocal music you set in motion a mighty power which silently, but surely, in the end will humanize, refine, and elevate a whole community." After the "unutterable energies" of the three musical "engines"—"Church Music, National Airs, and Fireside Melodies"—were set in motion through school instruction, they promised, in "two generations we should be changed into a musical people."[44] Thus illustrating the complicated interweaving of religious morals, political aspirations, early nationalism, and liberal reform based on rigid social control, the School Committee concluded that a new generation of children would absorb the noble sentiments of the carefully selected songs in their curriculum and then transmit these sentiments to their families, communities, and future generations.

By 1841, vocal music was taught in all of Boston's grammar schools. Approximately three thousand pupils, nearly half of all students enrolled, attended two half-hour music lessons weekly under Mason's direction. The editors of the popular *North American Review* pronounced that the introduction of organized singing in the public schools was fueling "a great revolution in the musical character of the American people." Following closely the vision outlined by Mason and Woodbridge, the editors argued that school music instruction offered a model of the orderly society through which children learned "the necessity of discipline, strict conformity to rules, the subordination of the different parts and voices, and the distinctiveness of each department." Lamenting that proper submission to authority was long forgotten in the world beyond school, they recommended singing instruction as a palliative for social instability. Music was suited for this disciplinary role, they wrote, because participants in choirs learned to accept their assigned roles, to submit to authority, and to work in concert for "the production of great effects." "America" and the school music movement need to be understood, then, as central to the larger antebellum drive to subdue youthful and "foreign-born" tendencies to barbarism and thus to cultivate proper respect for God, nation, and traditional elites.[45]

Members of the Boston School Committee promoted their school music program as a model for other communities. Their 1838 report expresses the hope that "from this place . . . may the example, in this country, first go forth" and eventually "compasseth round a nation." In fact, Woodbridge and other school music advocates pledged not to cease their reform efforts until a music curriculum was implemented in every American public school. They were remarkably successful in meeting this objective. Indeed, musicologist Michael Broyles has observed that "no other musical development was as directly traceable to a geographic area as the spread of music education nationwide was to Boston."[46] The National Education Association's 1889 national survey of public school music instruction found that music was systematically taught in more than half of the 621 cities and towns studied. By 1900, the Music Teachers National Association estimated that more than one thousand American towns and cities offered music instruction in their public schools. Throughout this period of dramatic growth, the overriding mission of the public schools was the moral and civic development of their pupils, in whom teachers sought to forge a "National Character" both by imparting knowledge of national principles and promoting allegiance to them. Whatever the subject, as Ruth Miller Elson's survey of nineteenth-century textbooks reveals, "the first duty of school-book authors in their own eyes was to attach the child's loyalty to the state and nation."[47]

The incorporation of patriotic songs such as "America" into the classroom not only identified national principles for pupils but compelled them to memorize and voice these sentiments. Children who learned "America" and other national songs, it was reasoned, would embrace the patriotic sentiments as their own. The popularization of "America," then, according to its author Samuel Smith, was largely attributable to Mason's school music initiatives: "Dr. Mason," he explained in 1894, "after considerable effort, succeeded in getting music introduced in our public schools in Massachusetts, and as 'America' was in the collections furnished the schools for use of the scholars it was not long before it was sung everywhere." Before this institutionalization of "America" as a staple element of the nation's hymnals and school song books, however, it was first distributed to a national audience in 1832 in Lowell Mason's collection *The Choir*. Shortly after its publication, Mason submitted the collection to the board of censors at Andover Theological Seminary, where Smith was still a student, and to other prominent religious and educational leaders for endorsements that could be used in sales promotions. The Andover board pronounced its melodies "unequalled in any collection adapted to the use of choirs in general" and recommended its purchase to "all lovers of music." Incorporating simplified arrangements of hymns and anthems, many adapted from the works of European composers, *The Choir* was thus expressly marketed "to singing schools, singing societies and choirs, throughout the United States."[48] The Andover Theological Seminary's praise, along with other such endorsements, was then used in advertisements for the collection, which, as Mason had anticipated, found an eager and rapidly expanding market.

Mason's ambitions were blessed with the good luck of arising at a fortuitous moment in the history of music in America, as the period between 1825 and the Civil War witnessed a tremendous proliferation of community singing groups and home musical performance. For example, while nine thousand pianos were manufactured in the United States in 1852, most for home use, just eight years later, nearly twenty-two thousand (along with 245 church organs and over twelve thousand melodeons) were produced.[49] Furthermore, and following the general trend of the so-called print-capitalism revolution, music publishing exploded, thus enabling "America" to be distributed widely in sheet music form and in song collections. The popularity of "America" derived then from a complicated and overlapping series of personal, economic, and technical factors, not the least of which was Mason and Woodbridge's tireless work to promote music as a means of educating the masses.

Another key factor in the success of "America" is that its author never tired of celebrating the song. Indeed, in the sixty-four years between his writing "America" in 1831 and his death in 1895, Samuel Smith played a significant role in promoting the song's popularity. In 1833, Smith became a professor of modern languages at Waterville (now Colby) College in Maine; the following year he was ordained as a Baptist minister. From the time Smith left the faculty of Waterville College in late 1841 until his death in 1895, he was employed primarily in church-related activities. He was a minister, a popular author and collector of hymns, and a leader in the international missionary work of the Baptist Church. In January 1842 Smith assumed the pastorate of the First Baptist Church in Newton Center, Massachusetts, where he lived for the rest of his life. He published several works, including a massive *History of Newton*, and many poems. Smith understood himself to be a patriot, educator, artist, minister, and missionary, roles he saw as interrelated and mutually reinforcing. In an autobiographical sketch published in his collected *Poems of Home and Country* in 1895, Smith explains that he "courted the Muse . . . Chiefly from an earnest desire to promote patriotic sentiment and Christian living." Smith wrote many hymns, including the well-known song "The Morning Light Is Breaking," and with Baron Stow edited *The Psalmist* (1843), which for over thirty years was the most widely used Baptist hymnal in the United States. Smith included "America" in the hymnal, which both contributed to the song's popularization and reinforced its performative fusion of the secular and sacred. In fact, "America" was frequently accorded the status of a hymn sung by congregations as an act of religious and civic devotion. Thus, following the lead of *The Psalmist*, "America" appeared in most leading northeastern hymnals published in the period, including the General Association of Connecticut's *Psalms and Hymns for Christian Use and Worship* (1845) and Henry Ward Beecher's influential *Plymouth Collection of Hymns for the Use of Christian Congregations* (1855), where it is included among the hymns of "Church Missions and Reform."[50]

Between the premiere of "America" and the start of the Civil War, the United States added over one million square miles of territory and its population increased by 150 percent. Spread westward in part by the massive migration of New Englanders on the canals, turnpikes, and railroads of the early Industrial Revolution, "America" and other sacred national texts were elements of an ostensibly unifying civic culture that transcended the vast distances and differences of the nation. As the new settlers established churches, schools, and civic cultures, "America" became a staple of the cultural repertoire, linking pioneers with their New England pasts and the "imagined community" of the rapidly expanding nation. This is not the place to engage in an analysis of the complex questions of how such nationalizing fervor destroyed local cultures, how it contributed to the unchecked spread of capitalism and industry, how it strained traditional political affiliations, or how it led, ultimately, to both a Civil War and the genocide of hundreds of thousands of indigenous peoples. For now, our point is simply to demonstrate that Mason's hunch and Smith's claim were both correct: musical education in general and "America" in particular played significant and much-celebrated roles in socializing citizens of heterogeneous backgrounds, religions, and classes into "patriotic sentiment and Christian living." As we demonstrate hereafter, both the temperance and women's suffrage movements soon became important factors in continuing the popularization of "America" by employing it as a means of moral reform and political persuasion.

Temperance: "Roll Back That Hellish Wave"

Groups organized in opposition to alcohol consumption wielded a powerful influence in America from the earliest days of the nation. Unlike the late-twentieth-century's "War on Drugs," an unpopular and unprecedented bureaucratic disaster, the temperance movement was a genuinely popular grassroots upsurge of moral (and moralizing) activism in which millions of Americans attended temperance meetings and events, sang temperance songs, took the temperance pledge, and worked to convert individual drinkers and to promote legal restrictions on the sale of alcohol.[51] Like Mason and Smith and Woodbridge and their fellow antebellum social reformers, temperance activists portrayed themselves as redeemers not only of individuals but of the nation. Because alcohol was a threat to the republic, they argued, America could only fulfill its shining destiny by curbing its consumption of spirits. Temperance activists thus identified their cause with the nation's sacred texts and principles, including the song "America." However, while Americans had previously used the melody of "God Save the King" to toast the health of George III and later George Washington ("Fill the glass to the brink, / WASHINGTON's health we'll drink, / 'Tis his birth-day"), "America" was a temperance song from the outset.[52] Indeed, Samuel Smith, its author, was an influential temperance advocate, and, as already mentioned, "America" was first performed at a Sabbath school observance on 4 July 1831 that was advertised as an alternative to the drunken celebrations of Independence Day by other Bostonians. Thus, while "America" was institutionalized in public schools, churches, and civic ceremonies as an expression of national identity, it was first performed in the midst of and gained added significance from its use by the temperance movement. Almost from the moment the song premiered in July 1831 it was reprinted in temperance songbooks, sung in temperance meetings, and adapted in dozens of alternative temperance versions true to the cause. "America" held an important place in the movement not only because of its recognizable melody and the prominent temperance stand of its author and chief supporters but also—and perhaps most important—because it spoke to issues of liberty and nationhood, enabling temperance activists to speak not as factional or interest-specific organizers but as the supposed conscience of the nation.

While the temperance movement exploded during the revivalism of the Second Great Awakening, its historical roots in a sense of national peril extend back as far as the American Revolution. For example, Dr. Benjamin Rush, a signer of the Declaration of Independence, an early abolitionist, and one of the leading figures of the revolutionary era, was among the earliest and most influential American temperance activists and warned in his influential 1784 *Inquiry into the Effects of Ardent Spirits on the Human Mind and Body* that alcohol was a dire threat to the new nation. "Intemperate and corrupted voters" would undermine democratic principles and betray the Revolution, Rush predicted, and the crime, violence, and dissipation associated with excessive drinking would rend the social fabric and risk America's loss of God's favor. Following Rush's lead, later temperance orators and songwriters portrayed their cause not only as evangelical in nature but also as essential for national survival. Given these nationalistic and evangelical premises, it was understood by temperance activists that the saved were both politically and morally obligated to secure the blessings of liberty for all Americans, even those unaware of their need to be saved. "Intemperance is a national sin," Lyman Beecher preached in 1825, "carrying destruction from the centre to every extremity of the empire, and calling upon the nation to array itself, *en masse*, against it."[53]

Despite the sweeping moral claims and cataclysmic visions of reformers such as Rush and Beecher (not to mention Beecher's curious reference to the young America as an "empire," which in 1825 was more national fantasy than reality), the fact of the matter is that drinking was an integral part of American politics and national celebrations. Taverns had been the meeting houses of the American Revolution; drinking whiskey was celebrated as a patriotic rebellion against imported rum and tea. Virtually all civic functions and political meetings in the late eighteenth and early nineteenth centuries involved drinking. Early politicians (including Washington, Jefferson, and Jackson) provided free liquor to attract voters, and alcohol was served liberally, even lavishly, at polling places. National holidays and patriotic events, such as the Fourth of July, were celebrated in many communities by drunken revelries. The temperance movement thus faced the daunting challenge not only of transforming everyday drinking practices but of dramatically recreating how Americans participated in many of the nation's most celebrated occasions.[54]

The Second Great Awakening provided new opportunities for reconsidering these entrenched cultural norms, for by the 1820s millions of Americans were attending camp meetings and other gatherings where emotional sermons and musical performers emphasized new doctrines of individual redemption and salvation couched in a discourse of national perfectionism. But even before the world-changing energy of these revivals hit the nation, the temperance movement was highly organized and enjoyed powerful institutional support, as Protestant denominations throughout New England and the middle atlantic states formed temperance societies. In 1813 the Society for the Promotion of Morals was founded to combat the evils of drinking, Sabbath-breaking, and profanity. The first national temperance organization, the American Society for the Promotion of Temperance (later renamed the American Temperance Society) was formed in 1826. By 1829 there were an estimated one thousand temperance societies in the United States, with a combined membership of approximately one hundred thousand. By 1834 there were five thousand societies with over one million members.[55]

Despite these impressive numbers, temperance organizations had their work cut out for them. Drinking had been deeply ingrained in American life since the arrival of the first European settlers, including the Pilgrims, whose first great crisis in the New World was a shortage of beer. Like most Europeans of the time, they regarded water as life threatening and considered daily consumption of alcohol an essential component of health and productivity. Adults drank rum, whiskey, and other liquors *beginning at breakfast* and administered hygienic spoonfuls of liquor to their children. Most farmers took liquor into the fields to lighten their labors; community work and group labor, such as harvesting, barn-raising, and quilting, usually involved drinking. In urban areas, many shop and factory owners provided drinking breaks (and sometimes the alcohol itself) twice a day, usually at eleven and four. The city hall bell in Portland, Maine, as in many other communities, was rung each day at those times. By the 1790s, it is estimated that the average American over fifteen years old consumed approximately six gallons of absolute alcohol each year, about twice modern levels. These levels further increased during the early nineteenth century, as a glut of cheap whiskey from bountiful western corn production and the social anxieties associated with expansion and industrialization produced what W. R. Rohrabaugh has called a "national binge." Average annual consumption increased between 1810 and 1830 to more than seven gallons, the highest rate in the nation's history. The attendant medical and social problems of this binge—including delerium tremens, poverty, and domestic violence—were alarming, as was the noticeable effect on worker productivity. The Secretary of War estimated in 1829 that three-quarters of the nation's laborers consumed over four ounces of distilled spirits daily.[56]

In the face of these longstanding cultural practices, temperance activism, combined with other social and economic changes of the 1830s, had a dramatic effect on American consumption patterns. Average annual per capita consumption of absolute alcohol fell to around three gallons in 1840, the largest ten-year decrease in American history. Hundreds of distilleries went out of business. The drop in consumption was attributable in part to the millions who had taken the pledge and joined temperance organizations and to the influence of the movement in moderating the behavior even of those drinkers who did not join. Thus, while temperance leaders recognized that they faced tremendous resistance, they stressed the possibilities of modifying public opinion and behavior through sophisticated mass persuasion campaigns designed to stigmatize alcohol use. For example, in an 1825 sermon Lyman Beecher reassured temperance workers that victory was possible: "Because the public mind is now unenlightened, and unawakened, and unconcentrated, does it follow that it cannot be enlightened, and aroused, and concentrated in one simultaneous and successful effort?" Beecher then relies on dramatic hyperbole when he prophesies: "*Our all is at stake*—we shall perish if we do not effect it." Like a properly scowling Calvinist minister he then castigates his audience as a mob in need of moral uplift because they are "unenlightened, and unawakened, and unconcentrated." Finally, Beecher argues that the cause of the moment, temperance, is in fact the cause to end all causes, for "no nation [has] ever [been] called upon to attempt it [reformation] by motives of such imperious necessity." These exaggerated rhetorical maneuvers were employed consistently in a variety of widely distributed media, including pamphlets, newspapers, speeches, theater, poetry, fiction, and song. The success (or at least the popularity) of this persuasive campaign may be seen in the fact that two million copies of Reverend Eli Merrill's temperance "ox sermon" were reportedly sold in a single year.[57]

Along with such printed efforts at persuasion, temperance activists trained speakers and singers, providing them with materials and techniques designed to persuade the unconvinced and to reinforce the faithful. Songs were an essential part of this process. For example, in his 1853 preface to *The Temperance Musician*, A. D. Fillmore underscored the centrality of music in his instructions for establishing a temperance society. Every neighborhood should first establish a "Temperance Music Band," he instructed, and meet as a singing society to practice. Only after the singing group has mastered a few songs should a temperance meeting be attempted. When short speeches are interspersed with "appropriate songs," Fillmore assured his readers, "you will soon be astonished at the grand result of your labors." Good singing, he reasoned, would inspire members to make better speeches and make even the lesser speeches more bearable. Speaking and singing were regarded as integrally related rhetorical activities; temperance elocution trainers accordingly advertised their vocal instruction programs as equally suited for either form of expression. The layering together of singing and speaking was thus present at virtually every temperance meeting and function, particularly in the form of interwoven songs and prayers. "The Crusade," Senator Henry Blair recalled in 1888, "was half song." Some temperance activists went so far, in fact, as to argue that song was a persuasive tool *superior to speech and writing*. For example, Robert Potter prefaced his 1842 *Boston Temperance Songster* by noting that "in many instances, where every other means have failed, the electrifying influence of song has aroused the individual to a sense of his danger, and sent conviction to his heart."[58]

The growth of the temperance movement and its high demand for music created a booming market for topical songbooks. In fact, hundreds of different temperance songbooks were published in the late nineteenth century, and hundreds of thousands of copies were sold. The Massachusetts Temperance Union, for example, sold and distributed over thirty-two thousand copies of its *Temperance Hymns and Songs* (1840) in two years and ten thousand copies of its *Song Book* in 1842 alone. The functions and occasions of songs in particular temperance organizations may be surmised by examining such song collections. The American Temperance Union, for example, published its *Temperance Hymn Book and Minstrel* in 1842 for use in "temperance meetings and festivals." Founded in 1833 as an umbrella association of state and local temperance organizations, by 1835 it included eight thousand societies and over one million members throughout the United States and Canada.[59] The Union's *Hymn Book and Minstrel* opens with a section of hymns expressing both the "perfections of God" and the activists' "confidence in works of Moral Reform." "Come thou Almighty King," written in the meter of "America," opens the collection. The next two sections outline the purposes for which the songs were intended, including describing "the power and promises of the Gospel to reform and save" and cataloging the "Woes of Intemperance." The fourth section consists of songs on the "Object and end of the Temperance Reformation" and imagines a future nation remade by the triumph of the temperance cause. The fifth section offers "Praises and thanksgivings for encouragement and results," through which movement members could celebrate victories small and large. The seventh and ninth sections contain songs targeted to children and sailors, while the eighth section features "Odes and songs for meetings and festivals," including alternate versions of several national songs. An "Ode for the Fourth of July," for example, set to the tune of "America" and included in this section, draws on traditional July Fourth themes and symbolism to promote the temperance cause. "On this her natal day," temperance workers are enjoined to "Roll back that hellish wave / Which sweeps the land!"[60]

Much of the burden for rolling back the hellish wave of drinking was placed firmly on the shoulders of converted ex-drinkers. Indeed, the temperance movement accorded a singularly important place to conversion narratives of former drinkers who had been reclaimed from "Rum's long reign of night." For example, some of the most popular temperance lecturers, including John Hawkins, John B. Gough, and John G. Wooley, were recovering alcoholics who told the tale of their redemption thousands of times in public appearances. Gough is estimated to have given over three thousand public lectures from 1842 to 1852 alone and to have induced more than 140,000 of his listeners to sign pledges of abstinence. Early temperance organizations such as the Washingtonian Society, founded around 1840 by six heavy drinkers in a Baltimore tavern, relied primarily on former drunkards to persuade current ones to pledge abstention. Converts were particularly persuasive activists, as they could both speak with authority about the devastation wreaked upon their former lives by alcohol and identify with the complex resistances and rationalizations of the drinkers in the audience. Most important, the living example of the orator/convert's own recovery provided hope to others that they too might be saved.[61] It is no surprise, then, to note that many temperance songs expressed the possibility of conversion. For example, John Pierpont's 1842 "Fourth of July Ode" for the Washingtonian Society, set to the tune of "America," voiced the celebrants' confidence that their efforts to reform drinkers would be successful:

> Through this most blessed breach
> The drunkard we can reach!
>   Oh! joyful sound!
> The Washingtonians strive —
> The wife's crushed hopes revive;
> The drunkard's children thrive;
>   The lost are found![62]

Whereas Pierpont's song sings in the righteous voice of reformers confident of their eventual triumph over the "drunkard," bringing joy to forlorn wives and children, other songs appealed directly to drunkards themselves. When performed at public meetings, such songs encouraged those present to come forward and accept the guidance of God and the group and thus to pledge themselves to reform. For example, an 1856 song set to the tune of "America" urges:

> Slave of the cup, arise!
> And raise your weeping eyes,
>   To God above,
> He'll give you strength to break
> Your iron yoke, and wake,
> True courage to partake,
>   Of heavenly love.[63]

The conversion song thus illustrates the curious manner in which temperance activists blended together and claimed authority over theological and secular power, for while "Slaves of the Cup" were urged to redeem themselves "to God above," they were also pressured to make this metaphysical pledge earthly and material by signing official temperance "pledges." Indeed, much as revivalists urged sinners to come forward and accept Christ in public conversion performances, so temperance meetings culminated in the signing of pledges to abstain from the consumption of "ardent spirits." And while the pledge was considered an oath "sworn before God" in a quasi-religious ceremony, the pledge also served much more explicitly political and functional purposes, as temperance orators and organizations measured their success by the number of pledges (however briefly observed) they obtained. Songs were performed during the pledge ceremony, entreating the wayward to come forward and repent. A. D. Fillmore's 1853 *Temperance Musician,* for example, supplies a song in the meter of "America" that opens with this invitation: "As we are gathered here, / Let us, with souls sincere, / Our pledge renew." The closing verse is particularly interesting, as it would appear to suggest that such pledges were indeed hard to keep: "We make that pledge our choice, / Let us, with heart and voice, / In every hour rejoice, / To hold it true."[64]

While holding true to one's personal pledge may have required both prayer and singing, such pledges were also complicated by the fact that the question of what it meant for temperance activists "To hold it true" changed over time. Most early temperance activists encouraged moderation, not teetotalism. They saw "ardent spirits" as the problem, not wine, beer, or hard cider, which many temperance activists themselves continued to imbibe and even encouraged as less debilitating alternatives. The Hutchinson Family Singers, for example, noted for their temperance songs, made one hundred gallons of hard cider annually for household consumption at their New Hampshire farm. Nonetheless, by the 1840s the movement had largely shifted to the promotion of total abstinence, as moderate drinking came to be regarded as a habit that would lead inexorably to immoderate drinking. An 1853 song, "Overthrow of Alcohol," set to the tune of "America," thus urged: "And moderate drinkers too, / The voice addresses you, / Come, go along." The term "temperance" eventually fell out of favor, as antialcohol organizations refashioned themselves "Cold Water Armies." This shift was reflected in song, as temperance activists sang the glories of water. For example, "Praise of Water," an 1845 song set to the tune of "America" and included in a tiny three- by four-and-a-half-inch pocketbook entitled *The Temperance Songster* (see figure 2.6), sings of the healing "circuit of the waters." Whereas alcohol is nothing less than bodily and spiritual poison, "cold water" "Floats the gay barge of pleasure, / And without stint or measure, / Wafts on that heavenly treasure / True wisdom's health."[65]

In addition to this shift away from the attempt to moderate drinking habits toward a push for total abstinence, the temperance movement soon realized

Figure 2.6. Title page of *The Temperance Songster* (1845). Courtesy of The Special Collections of The University of Illinois Music Library.

that its cause could be advanced by using children as both the objects of moral reform and as the subjects of heartwrenching tales. The American Temperance Union's 1842 *Temperance Hymn Book and Minstrel* accordingly included a separate section of "juvenile temperance hymns." Following the leads of Mason and Woodbridge, temperance strategists believed children would absorb and retain the moral lessons inscribed in the song lyrics they memorized and repeatedly performed. "In that way," one temperance activist observed, "we shall convey important truths to the mind, and stamp them as with a pen of iron, lasting as time."[66] John Pierpont's "Children's Temperance Hymn" even concludes by having its young performers testify to this hope:

> So let each faithful child
> Drink of this fountain mild,
>   From early youth;
> Then shall the song we raise
> Be heard in future days—
> Ours be the pleasant ways
> Of peace and truth.[67]

Temperance activists clearly believed that songs learned in childhood would shape future adults committed to the pleasant ways of peace and truth and cold water. While they accordingly pursued the mass indoctrination of children through songs learned in both Sabbath schools and public schools, temperance activists also valued children as effective intermediaries for reaching adult audiences. Indeed, temperance activists hoped that children's innocent and sincere appeals would touch the hearts of the most jaded adults and thus move them to moral contemplation and action. This effect was felt to be especially profound in the cause of temperance, in which child singers might appeal to their own parents to abstain. The child (typically tousle-haired, tearful, and clothed in rags) pleading with a parent to come home from the saloon thus became a staple image in temperance illustrations, songs, and dramatic productions. For example, John Hawkins, the most popular national temperance speaker of the late 1830s, told audiences of how his young daughter Hannah had rescued him from alcoholism. Her plaintive cry to him one hung-over morning, "Father, don't send me after whiskey today," had led him to pledge sobriety. Hannah's image was featured for years on temperance banners and pamphlets, stamping to death the hydra-headed beast of Intemperance.[68]

Such examples of persuasion through family-based shame led temperance leaders to train children to convert their parents, in part through song. Most families could be expected to attend their children's musical performances, which sometimes produced enormous audiences. For example, a mass choir of more than two thousand children performed at a Juvenile Temperance celebration in Boston's Marlboro chapel on 24 February 1841. The "childlike simplicity and grandeur" of the performance, a correspondent for the *Singer* reported, moved all who attended, for "The influence of such a scene is beyond all calculation." Temperance activists also expected children to bring their antidrinking songs home. I. F. Shepard's 1842 "Thanksgiving Hymn," set to the tune of "America," depicts the "happy hearth" of the temperance household. Thanks are offered by wives who "this hour may sing" of the redemption of their husbands from the "damning chains" of drink. Shepard credits children's songs, in part, for these conversions, as "From crowding children break / Anthems that raptures wake, / For parents found."[69] Thus, through the emotional work of "Anthems that raptures wake," temperance reformers undertook the mass persuasion of both children and adults in order to redeem as many sinners as possible.

Like Mason and Woodbridge using July Fourth as an opportune occasion for persuasion, so temperance activists also saw the Fourth as among the most important opportunities to air their arguments before large crowds. For example, on 4 July 1829, in Boston's Park Street Church, speaking two years prior to the premiere of "America," William Lloyd Garrison voiced his disgust at the drinking with which the Fourth was generally observed: "Liberty has gone hand in hand with licentiousness—her gait unsteady, her face bloated, her robe bedraggled in the dust. The love of country has been tested by the exact number of libations poured forth, the most guns fired, the greatest number of toasts swallowed, and the loudest professions of loyalty to the Union, uttered over the wine-cup."[70] Following Garrison's typically aggressive stance, temperance activists sought to reclaim the Fourth of July as a symbolic step toward reclaiming the nation. Reclaiming the Fourth enabled temperance activists, much like abolitionists (to whom we turn in Chapter 3), to emphasize the national character of their proposed reforms by appropriating national songs and symbols. Temperance activists thus held separate and often religious observances on July Fourth and used the holiday as an annual meeting date and for public concerts and sermons.

Indeed, as detailed earlier, "America" premiered in 1831 at a Fourth of July gathering convened by the Sabbath School Union specifically as an alternative to the popular drunken celebrations. On such simultaneously nationalist and temperance occasions, activists borrowed the language of the Fourth to draw parallels between the urgency prompting their own "Cold Water Armies" and the original life-and-death struggle for American independence, to compare British tyranny with the tyranny of King Alcohol, and to read declarations of independence from drinking. For example, the appropriation of revolutionary symbols for the temperance cause is crucial to John Pierpont's 1842 "Fourth of July Ode" (see appendix A). Set to the tune of "America," Pierpont's version interlaces the holiday and its historical associations with the temperance cause. However, in a move that must have struck some listeners as nothing less than audacious, Pierpont suggested that whereas

> Our fathers, when they broke
> Proud Britain's galling yoke,
>   Fought *one* good fight!
> A *better* one fight they
> Who "cast the bowl away,"
> And toast this glorious day
>   In water bright.[71]

The triumphalist tone, hyperbolic claims, and grand appropriation of historical symbols indicate how completely and righteously temperance activists saw themselves as both heirs to the Revolution and saviors of the nation.

Despite the apparent success of such appeals, by the 1850s many antialcohol organizations had shifted focus from the mass reformation of individual drinkers through "moral suasion" to support for "legal suasion." The push for legislation to prohibit the manufacture and sale of intoxicating beverages indicated a belief that those who could not be persuaded would need to be saved from themselves. Gilbert Seldes observes that this shift in focus demonstrates how for temperance activists, as with most other nineteenth-century reform movements, "self-improvement turned to uplift and uplift to prohibition." The sense that sober temperance activists would have to save the nation from the drunken masses had been prevalent in temperance literature from as early as the Revolution, however, and had gained popular credence during the Second Great Awakening. For example, Lyman Beecher's influential 1826 *Six Sermons on the Nature, Occasions, Signs, Evils and Remedy of Intemperance* warned that "unless you intend to resign your liberty forever, and come under a despotism of the most cruel and inexorable character, you must abandon the morning bitters, the noontide stimulant, and the evening bowl."[72] In this sense, because alcohol leads to violence and other antisocial behavior—including a disposition toward "despotism"—the personal liberty to use it was overshadowed by the infringements its use created on the personal liberties of others. Along the same lines, William Whipper in his presidential address to the Colored Temperance Society of Philadelphia on 8 January 1834 spoke of the need for legislation to restrict the "uncontrollable liberty" to drink ardent spirits.[73] Disciplining others, then, whether through moral threat or legal injunction, amounted for temperance activists to a salvational rescue mission of those either too drunk or simply too obtuse to save themselves. One result of such thinking was the prohibitive "Maine Law" of 1851, which was implemented in a dozen other states over the next four years (although several of these laws were soon overturned).

Given the premise that drinking alcohol impedes one's ability to exercise free will, it comes as no surprise that temperance activists compared dependence on alcohol to slavery. This metaphorical argument was, in part, an appeal to the overlapping membership the temperance movement shared with the antislavery movement, as most abolitionists, especially African American abolitionists, were also supporters of temperance. Indeed, Frederick Douglass, Frances E. Watkins Harper, William Wells Brown, and other prominent African American abolitionists were active in the temperance cause, with Harper serving as national president of the "Colored Auxiliary" of the post–Civil War Women's Christian Temperance Union. Support for temperance was so strong in this community that every African American national convention from the first in 1830 issued resolutions in favor of temperance or abstinence (as well as against slavery). The second national convention authorized the formation of the Coloured American Conventional Temperance Society; by 1840 most free African American communities had some form of temperance organization. In fact, some African American abolitionists, including Whipper, argued that because it imprisoned the mind and soul as well as the body, alcoholism was worse in some ways even than chattel slavery. Thus Frederick Douglass wrote in *My Bondage and My Freedom* (1855) that "It was about as well to be a slave to *master*, as to be a slave to *rum* and *whiskey*."[74]

Following such provocative claims, temperance meetings confronted drinkers with songs depicting alcohol dependency as slavery. For example, in the 1853 "Slave of the Cup," set to the tune of "America," the enslaved drinker is told of his or her bondage: "Strong are your fetters bound, / And all is dark around, / No lasting joys are found / Where'er you go." In the face of such horror, "Slave of the Cup" offers the support of "freemen" who "around thee sing," thus encouraging drinkers to join the sober fellowship of free men by stepping forward to take the temperance pledge.[75] Slavery functions in this song, then, as both the material reality against which abolitionists struggle and as the metaphorical condition against which temperance activists fight. Despite such nods toward the work of abolitionists, the ideal nation imagined in most temperance songs was white, Protestant, and nativist. Indeed, beginning in the 1820s, temperance activists exploited public anxieties about immigration and Catholicism and were politically and rhetorically intertwined with nativist groups such as the Know-Nothings. Irish and Germans in particular were stereotyped as problem drinkers and associated with the production of alcohol. These charges were not completely absurd, as most major American breweries had German names and drinking was an important part of many immigrant cultures. Immigrant communities were also among the strongest opponents of temperance and prohibitionist activities, which further fueled nativist ire. The leap from these simple observations to the sweeping claim that Irish and German drinkers were a threat to democracy, however, seems in retrospect to tell us more about Protestant middle-class and nativist fears than about the supposed monsters temperance sought to discipline.[76]

The tide of prohibition was temporarily reversed under the shadow of the coming conflict—nothing like a battle to make one need a stiff drink!—but, as detailed in chapter 5, antidrinking organizations regrouped after the Civil War and became increasingly national in scope and ambition. Before turning to the work of abolitionists in chapter 3, however, it is important to explore the work of yet another antebellum reform movement that relied heavily on "America": the women's suffrage movement.

Suffrage: "Woman . . . Assert Thy Due!"

Women were active participants in the temperance, antislavery, and other major nineteenth-century moral reform campaigns, through which they entered the public sphere as speakers and political activists, sometimes in organizations under their own leadership.[77] Although the struggle for women's rights predated the reform movements of the 1830s, women's experiences in these movements strongly influenced the organization and rhetorical strategies of the suffrage campaign. Indeed, like their contemporaries in the education reform and temperance movements, women suffragists sought to arouse public interest and to galvanize supporters by advocating legal reform, and by publicizing their cause through public events, "moral suasion" campaigns, and songs. Despite the sense that songs supporting women's rights are perhaps less well known today than songs of other eighteenth- and nineteenth-century movements, songs were an essential part of most suffrage meetings.[78] And while women's rights advocates used songs to organize members and to disseminate beliefs, songs were also an important medium for political expression by individual women writers who, long before the formation of organizations for women's rights, published lyrics they hoped would find voice among like-minded Americans. In fact, women's rights songs have appeared in newspapers and songbooks from the earliest days of the republic. These include several variations on "America" and "God Save the King" in which women's rights advocates used the popular melody to question whether America was in fact a "sweet land of liberty." Liberty, they argued, depends on political status, but those denied the vote, restricted from education and employment, and limited in property rights cannot be said to be free. Suffragists thus used Smith's song to assert their own claims of belonging and entitlement, often with explicit intertextual reference to the original. In doing so, they offered a competing, reformed vision of the nation in which liberty was no longer the sole privilege of their fathers, husbands, and sons.

There is a tendency to think of organized women's rights campaigns in the United States as beginning with the Seneca Falls convention of 1848, but American women actively asserted their rights long before it and used song to do so. In fact, women were an important publishing market after the Revolution, when pamphlets and magazines created a forum for communication among women that sometimes included discussions of women's property rights and civil liberties. Philadelphia produced several of the best-selling women's magazines of the period, including the *Philadelphia Minerva*, published from February 1795 to July 1798. Its male editor promised "the most admired and sentimental pieces in prose and verse, entertaining anecdotes, and affecting narratives." These included fiction, such as "Beauty in Distress," and advice columns touted as a "Valuable Guide to Correct Conduct."[79] Songs and poetry were published in a special section called the "Court of Apollo," which on 17 October 1795 included a remarkable piece entitled "Rights of Woman," by "A Lady" (see appendix A). Set to the tune of "God Save America," the fourth verse boldly asserted:

> O Let the sacred fire
> Of Freedom's voice inspire
> A Female too, —
> Man makes his cause his own,
> And Fame his acts renown, —
> Woman thy fears disown,
> Assert thy due.[80]

Published fifty-three years before the Seneca Falls Convention and thirty-six years before the first public performance of Smith's "America," this revision of the monarchical "God Save the King" into a feminist anthem is a truly revolutionary document. The lyrics pay tribute both to Mary Wollstonecraft, whose *Vindication of the Rights of Woman* was first published in 1792, and to Thomas Paine's *Rights of Man* (1791–92), the stirring defense of the French Revolution and republicanism that prompted his banishment from England. Paine's pamphlet sold over two hundred thousand copies in its first six months and was widely read and discussed in the United States. Paine had written of women's oppression in "An Occasional Letter on the Female Sex" in *Pennsylvania Magazine* in August 1775; his later antimonarchical essays became touchstones for women's rights advocates. Led by figures such as Paine, the 1790s were a period of intense discussion among Americans about the meanings of citizenship and the extent of liberty, including the political rights of women. In fact, women voted in New Jersey from 1790 to 1807 and were sometimes a powerful force in state electoral politics during this period. Women's political activities of the 1790s thus proved inspirational to later activists, such as Elizabeth Cady Stanton, who explained: "our struggle is not for the attainment of a new right, but for the restitution of one our foremothers possessed and exercised."[81]

Written during this turbulent period of debate regarding both democracy in general and women's rights in particular, "Rights of Woman" encourages other women to become activists. Six of its ten stanzas are explicitly directed to female readers who are urged to "disown" their fears, "assert thy due," and "endure no more the pain / Of slavery." The last three stanzas imply not only women readers but also women singers, who perform the song both as individuals committing themselves to the cause ("their maxims I disown, / Their ways detest") and collectively in organized protest. When one woman sings to assert her rights ("Woman aloud rejoice, / Exalt thy feeble voice"), the song imagines a chorus of other women who join in to form "A voice re-echoing round," all proclaiming that "Woman is Free!" Indeed, the final stanza closes the song with a subtle but important transition from the hope that "Woman be Free" to the assertion that "Woman *is* Free." This radical appropriation of "God Save America" thus associates feminist and national principles and illustrates nicely Elizabeth Sanders's argument that suffragists used "America" and other patriotic tunes to claim "the vote as a right consistent with the fundamental ideals of the U.S. governmental system."[82]

MUCH like the temperance and school music reform movements of the antebellum era, the women's suffrage movement was also slowed by the accelerating pace of and escalated stakes involved in the period's crises over slavery and national unity. Hence, before returning to the post–Civil War struggles of temperance, women's suffrage, and labor activists, we turn in chapter 3 to the uses abolitionists made of "America" and in chapter 4 to its uses during the Civil War and Reconstruction.

THREE

"Bombast, Fraud, Deception, Impiety, and Hypocrisy" in the "Dark Land of Slavery," 1830–1859

W HEN Smith's song first proclaimed America a "sweet land of liberty" and a "land of the noble free" at Boston's Park Street Church on 4 July 1831, over two million Americans were in bondage. In fact, a majority of the nation's residents, including Native Americans, slaves, and women, were denied the franchise and other legal rights. Then-president Andrew Jackson was a slaveholder who wagered his human property on horse races and championed the removal of all Native Americans from lands east of the Mississippi. In 1831, Ohio disqualified African Americans from jury duty, Indiana required all African Americans entering the state to post bond, Mississippi made it illegal for free African Americans to remain in the state, and the white citizens of New Haven, Connecticut, voted seven hundred to four to prevent the construction of a college for African Americans.[1] Thus, despite Smith's nationalist and evangelical fervor, not all (or even most) Americans could embrace "America"'s promises without raising serious questions about the state of the union. Even in Boston, where "America" premiered and Smith's fellow reformers held positions of high privilege, public transportation, schools, lecture halls, housing, churches, and public entertainment were divided along the color line. When an African American came to own a pew on the "whites only" lower floor of Boston's Park Street Church one year before "America" was first performed there, he was prevented from occupying it. The *Liberator* reported that at the Sabbath school singers' premiere performance of "America," "the colored boys were permitted to occupy pews one-fourth the way up the side aisle," while "the colored girls took their seats by the door, as usual."[2] For many Americans, then, singing of a "sweet land of liberty" meant denying the reality of their own experience.

While the Jacksonian era was marked by this stunning contradiction between the utopian rhetoric of liberty and the brutal reality of inequality, it was also marked by the rise of abolitionism as a mass movement that, beginning around 1830, increasingly supported immediate emancipation. The abolitionists, although organized primarily in the northern states, viewed slavery as a national problem and accordingly encouraged national reform by reference to national principles that they argued were at odds with the practice of slavery. "America" was particularly useful for illustrating the country's hypocrisies and for providing familiar, poignant melodies for antislavery lyrics. Much as with the temperance movement and the reform activities of Mason and Beecher and Woodbridge, the Fourth of July was one of the most important annual occasions for abolitionists to engage in such musical politics. Thus, on the same day when communities across the country gathered to sing patriotic songs and to listen to speakers laud national achievements, abolitionists met to consider and sing about the failure of the American Revolution to secure "liberty for all." Because "America" was strongly associated with the Fourth of July, it was frequently derided, parodied, or reconstructed at abolitionist observances on that date. In fact, the abolitionists crafted dozens of alternate versions of "America" (some designed specifically for use on July Fourth) that distinguished between national boasts and realities while envisioning a nation redeemed from the sin of slavery and true to its promise of liberty.[3]

"America" and Abolition: "Oppression's Dirge Be Sung!"

"America" was first performed at a time of dramatic change in the antislavery movement. Prior to 1830, organized antislavery societies were concentrated in the South and their membership was largely elite, white, and male; after 1830, antislavery societies were concentrated in the northern and border states and their new leadership and mass membership included many African Americans and women. Before 1830, most local antislavery societies and national organizations were supportive of colonization and gradual emancipation and were conciliatory toward southern states and slaveholders (supporting compensation of slaveholders, for example); after 1830, many antislavery societies became more radical, as they favored immediate and uncompensated emancipation and excoriated southern states and slaveholders, who controlled the presidency, vice-presidency, and Congress. There were some immediate abolitionists prior to 1830, particularly among African Americans, yet it was not until after 1830 that abolitionism gained substantial numbers of new adherents and organizational strength. In short, "Post-1830 abolitionists," writes Ronald Walters, "were

generally more strident, and bolder in rhetoric and in deed than most early antislavery men and women had been."[4]

The dramatic turn in American antislavery efforts was fueled in part by developments in Britain. Until 1826, the British Anti-Slavery Society had advocated gradual emancipation of slaves in the colonies yet met with little success
in Parliament, concluding finally that gradualism meant "half-way between
now and never." Beginning in 1826, British abolitionists began petitioning Parliament in favor of immediate emancipation and produced a torrent of pamphlets, newspaper articles, and speeches in support of their cause. Parliament
began debating the question of immediate emancipation in July 1830; by the
end of the year its imminent passage was apparent both in Britain and America,
where newspapers reported the deliberations of the British Parliament in excited and anxious detail. Based on this coverage, antislavery activists decided,
as the *New York Whig* editorialized on 23 September 1831, "that this kind of
reform needs to begin in our country." American antislavery activists thus
adopted many ideas from their British counterparts, mining British antislavery
propaganda for facts, arguments, and rhetorical strategies that might be used in
the American campaign.[5]

The tone for the new abolitionism was set by William Lloyd Garrison in the
first issue of the *Liberator* on 1 January 1831, one month before Smith wrote the
lyrics to "America" in nearby Andover. The offices of the *Liberator* were located
in the African Meeting House on Joy Street, three blocks from Park Street
Church. In his inaugural issue, Garrison made "a full and unequivocal recan-
tation" of his former views favoring colonization, instead endorsing immediate
emancipation in language that was bold and uncompromising:

> I *will* be as harsh as truth, and as uncompromising as justice. On this subject,
> I do not wish to think, or speak, or write, with moderation. No! No! Tell a man
> whose house is on fire, to give a moderate alarm; tell him to moderately rescue
> his wife from the hands of the ravisher; tell the mother to gradually extricate
> her babe from the fire into which it has fallen—but urge me not to use mod-
> eration in a cause like the present. I am in earnest—I will not equivocate—I
> will not excuse—I will not retreat a single inch—AND I WILL BE HEARD.[6]

Following Garrison's audacious lead, new organizations emerged to support
immediate emancipation and related reforms (including temperance and, in
some instances, civil rights for women and free African Americans). For example, the New England Anti-Slavery Society was founded in 1832; the American
Anti-Slavery Society began the following year; states and towns soon formed
their own antislavery societies and sent delegates to regional and national conventions. The network of organized antislavery activities thus expanded with
great rapidity, from forty-seven societies in 1833 to more than one thousand in

1836. The new abolitionist movement—*I will not equivocate*—drew on the religious fervor of the revivals that had swept America during the Second Great Awakening of the 1820s. Indeed, in much the same manner as Mason, Smith, Woodbridge, and their colleagues viewed their socializing, nationalizing, music education movement in evangelical terms, and much as temperance activists understood their political work as essentially moral reform, so most abolitionists regarded slavery *as a sin*. Abolitionism thus became a form of evangelism in which proselytizers sought to spread the word through publications, revival-style meetings, and songs. Taking full advantage of the new means of travel afforded by turnpikes, canals, roadways, and rail lines, abolitionist lecturers, like evangelical circuit-riders and temperance activists, crossed great distances to speak to uncommitted and hostile audiences in an effort to convert them. In addition, the development of the steam-powered printing press made it possible to mass-produce and distribute inexpensive antislavery materials. Abolitionists were so successful in harnessing these new means of communication that many of their less savvy contemporaries suspected foul play, surmising that only massive foreign assistance could enable such awesome blanketing of the nation with information.[7]

While utilizing many of the revolutionary, modern means of mass politicking made possible by new technologies of transportation and communication, the abolitionists simultaneously borrowed heavily from the more familiar practices of revivalism. Indeed, they adapted the revivalists' techniques of advertising and promotion to secure audiences, and their conventions, local society meetings, fairs, bazaars, picnics, and other gatherings featured fiery speeches, personal testimonies, and heartwrenching music. In formal meetings and occasions, as in a church service, abolitionist programs alternated between preacher and congregation, one voice and many, as speeches were preceded and followed by songs combining individual voices in a unified chorus of shared sentiment and commitment. George Clark's hymn "We Are Come, All Come," even has the participants sing about their own act of vocal performance: "We are come, all come, with the crowded throng, / To join our notes in a plaintive song." By joining together in song, the lyric explains, abolitionists demonstrate their power and commitment, "For the bond man sighs, and the scalding tear / Runs down his cheek while we mingle here." The song thus both sings of and embodies the collective expression of abolitionist ideas. Clark articulated this sense of music as both an activating force and communal occasion in the preface to the 1844 collection that included "We Are All Come," *The Liberty Minstrel*, where he argued that music could "subserve every righteous cause—to aid every humane effort for the promotion of man's social, civil and religious well-being."[8]

Hence, like Mason, Smith, Woodbridge, and Beecher, Garrison and Clark recognized the remarkable force of music both to reach the uncommitted and to rally the faithful. "Righteous sentiment, joined to appropriate music," Garrison observed, "move mankind to action." In fact, many abolitionists viewed song as the most persuasive medium for propagating their beliefs. Whatever the power of abolitionist oratory, they believed, music was even more important to the cause. For example, a correspondent who attended the New England Anti-Slavery Convention in 1843 reported to the *Practical Christian* that "speechifying, even of the better sort, did less to interest, purify and subdue minds, than this irresistible anti-slavery music."[9] The availability of song as a medium also broadened opportunities for participation in the movement. As Jairus Lincoln observed in the preface to his *Anti-Slavery Melodies*, "There are many who have not the gift of *speech-making*, but who can, by *song-singing*, make strong appeals, in behalf of the slave, to every community and to every heart." Furthermore, many abolitionists saw songs fulfilling the traditional religious function of sanctifying daily life, of bringing worship into daily practice. Hence, in an 1840 ode set to the tune of "America," Maria Weston Chapman pleads with her fellow songsters "Wake with a song, my soul! / Free from all base control, / Wake with a song."[10] It is clear, then, that antislavery activists held much the same opinions regarding music as both the reformers and civic leaders who institutionalized "America" in the 1830s and the temperance activists who helped make the song so popular. Indeed, in all three movements (school music, temperance, and abolitionism), music was seen as: (1) a powerful *evangelical* instrument capable of producing "moral uplift" among those who performed and listened to it; (2) an equally powerful *disciplinary* instrument capable of structuring a properly righteous life among those who sang it; and (3) perhaps the most pragmatic *proselytizing* instrument capable — even more than "speechifying" — of converting new masses to the movement.

Evangelical focus, disciplinary rigor, proselytizing fervor — the music education, temperance, and abolitionist movements' uses of "America" were driven by these three principles. For example, the children who first sang "America" at Park Street Church were meant to function as *proselytizing performers of* persuasive music, as *disciplined objects in* a rigorous musical regime, and as *evangelical searchers* literally singing their way to a higher, more righteous consciousness. Impressed by what they saw in those first early years of organized children's choirs, activists came to believe that by memorizing and performing songs with virtuous sentiments, child singers would themselves become more virtuous. Antislavery activists thus emphasized the musical instruction of children as a means by which to "impress upon their minds the beauty of freedom, and the impolicy and wickedness of slavery."[11] The proselytizing function of music was also central to abolitionist thinking regarding children, as they were seen as ideal performers for converting adult audiences whose hearts the children would melt with sweet voices and innocent sincerity. In fact, children's choirs performed at innumerable antislavery meetings, and at least two antislavery songbooks were compiled expressly for use by children. Some of these antislavery versions of popular songs, including an antislavery version of "America," were sung by the Garrison Juvenile Choir, an African American children's choir, under the direction of Susan Paul. In a performance in Boston's Columbian Hall on 4 February 1834 the children sang to

> Ye who in bondage pine,
> Shut out from light divine,
> > Bereft of hope;
> Whose limbs are worn with chains,
> Whose tears bedew our plains,
> Whose blood our glory stains,
> > In gloom who grope.

Thus, only three years after the utopian yet segregated premiere of Samuel Smith's "America," an all-black juvenile choir sang hopefully of an end to slavery, when "Liberty's sweet song / Be sung by all," while simultaneously (and realistically) indicating the horror of those "In gloom who grope" for freedom.[12]

As demonstrated by the Garrison Juvenile Choir, antislavery activists generated lyrics that were specific to the concerns of the movement. In fact, the proliferation of antislavery societies helped to produce a new market for published song collections that could be used in meetings and at home. Antislavery songwriting thus exploded in the 1840s, as antislavery activists wrote more than seven hundred songs, with and without music, and published fourteen song collections, several of which enjoyed significant sales.[13] George W. Clark was one of the central figures in this abolitionist music publishing boom as he compiled three popular collections of antislavery songs, including *The Liberty Minstrel*, which went through seven editions. Like Mason and Smith before him, he both wrote original music and set poems (including some of his own) to well-known hymns and other melodies. Appropriating already established tunes made pragmatic economic and political sense, for songs set to familiar melodies were cheaper to distribute, as they did not require printed music, and could be performed more easily by more people, even by those unable to read music. Recognizable melodies were also used in some instances—such as the Garrison Juvenile Choir's 1834 abolitionist version of "America"—to create counterpoint between the movements' lyrics and those they supplanted.

Indeed, as the unofficial "national hymn," the song most widely performed in civic ceremonies, and the lyric in which the boast of liberty was most pronounced, "America" became an important rhetorical touchstone for abolitionists—and particularly for African American abolitionists such as Nathaniel

Paul, James Madison Bell, and Robert Purvis. For example, in the "land of liberty," Nathaniel Paul explained from London in 1833, "the laws are so exceedingly liberal that they give to man the liberty of purchasing as many negroes as he can find means to pay for, and also the liberty to sell them again." Paul thus transforms "liberty" into the sign of barbarism, into a botched promise corrupted by the "free" exercise of oppression. At the Ohio State Negro Convention of 1850, following the passage of the Fugitive Slave Act, a resolution was passed that reaffirmed the "doctrine of urging the slave to leave immediately with his hoe on his shoulder, for a land of liberty"—that land was not America. Indeed, on the anniversary of emancipation in the West Indies, James Madison Bell wrote "'Tis *not* of thee my native land." Bell later left the United States for Canada, where he helped John Brown plan armed insurrection and a new black nation.[14] The African American abolitionist strategy of disputing traditional American claims to liberty by subverting the sacred texts through which the claims were advanced is particularly evident in the writings of Robert Purvis, who characterizes America as "a country with a sublimity of impudence that knows no parallel." In the wake of the 1857 *Dred Scott* decision, Purvis exploded in a tirade of flabbergasted sarcasm regarding America's "setting itself up before the world as a *free country*, a *'land of liberty'!*, 'the *land of the free*, and the *home of the brave*,' the *'freest country in all the world'!*" Purvis continues:

> Gracious God! and yet here are millions of men and women groaning under a bondage the like of which the world has never seen—bought and sold, whipped, manacled, killed all the day long. Yet this is a *free country*! The people have the assurance to talk of their *free institutions*. How can I speak of such a country and use language of moderation? How can I, who, every day, feel the grinding hoof of this despotism, and who am myself identified with its victims?[15]

For black abolitionists such as Paul, Bell, Purvis, and others, then, the contrast between the principles of "America" and the social reality of America was stark, damning. Nonetheless, some abolitionists placed great faith in Smith's original lyrics and accordingly sang "America" at meetings and events. For example, Cincinnati African Americans honored Salmon P. Chase in 1845 for his legal defense of Samuel Watson, who had been seized as a fugitive slave, by singing "America" "with great taste and dignity." But generally, abolitionists wrote new and explicitly antislavery lyrics set to the melody of "America." Indeed, the remarkable popularity of the song created ample opportunities for producing counterdiscourses in which the song was used to criticize, rather than praise, the nation. "A new language, if it is to be political, cannot possibly be 'invented,'" writes Herbert Marcuse; "it will necessarily depend on the subversion of traditional material." The examples offered here demonstrate that "America" was among the traditional material most often subverted by antebellum dissidents and reformers. In fact, abolitionists, temperance activists, women's suffragists, labor organizers, and other grassroots activists drafted over two hundred alternate versions of "America." Antislavery activists in particular adapted the melody of "America" more than any other song.[16] For example, in 1839 a pseudonymous contributor to the *Liberator* (named "Theta") remarked on the already enormous popularity of "America" and suggested an alternative version:

> In the popular little hymn, entitled "America," written by S. F. Smith, and often sung with such great eclat, there is such a manifest unlikeness to our true condition as a nation, which it was the author's design to depict, that if it were divested of its caption and the author's signature, it would be difficult to guess the original. In order to bring out some great and *shameful* truths in relation to our national character and condition, which are concealed by this otherwise beautiful production, I send you for publication the following parody.

Theta's "Parody" (see figure 3.1 and appendix A) opens with these compelling lines: "My country! 'tis of thee, / Stronghold of Slavery— / Of thee I sing." The song thus works intertextually with Smith's original, as each of the following verses is constructed around the corresponding verse in Smith's version. Each verse, except for the third verse, begins with the same line as in "America" (the third substitutes "wailing" for "music": "Let *wailing* swell the breeze"). The entire fourth verse is virtually the same as in Smith's version, except for the substitution of a single word: "Long may our land be bright" becomes "*Soon* may our land be bright," emphasizing that "Freedom's holy light" does not yet shine here. The implied singer of "America—A Parody" shares many of the beliefs of Smith's implied singer: a sense of belonging to the nation by ancestry, a love of its physical beauty, a desire to awaken the populace through song, and a belief in God as actively intervening to protect and guide America in its quest for liberty. Yet each of these beliefs is qualified or differentiated from that proclaimed in Smith's original, as the implied singer believes the country is not, as it stands, a "sweet land of liberty" but a "stronghold of slavery." It is not freedom, then, but infamy that rings "from every mountainside." As in Smith's version, the singer of this parody addresses the nation, but in reproach, not worship. The author's preliminary statement of purpose laments the extent to which Smith's version has come to define the "national character and condition" for many Americans. It also, however, invests some hope in the prospect that the song, when properly reconstructed, might reveal the "great and *shameful* truths" of American society, as "Thy deeds shall ring." Along with those of Paul, Bell, and Purvis, "Theta"'s variations on "America" designate the song as an arena of struggle, as a cultural icon subject to dispute and refiguration, parody and irony.

LITERARY.

For the Liberator.

'AMERICA!'—A PARODY.

FRIEND GARRISON :

It must be matter of regret to every true philanthropist, that there is such obvious want of *fidelity* on the part of some of the most popular writers of the age, in presenting the truth *undisguised* upon the subjects which they treat. In the popular little hymn, entitled ' America,' written by S. F. Smith, and often sung with great eclat, there is such a manifest unlikeness to our true condition as a nation, which it was the author's design to depict, that if it were divested of its caption and the author's signature, it would be difficult to guess the original. In order to bring out some great and *shameful* truths in relation to our national character and condition, which are concealed by this otherwise beautiful production, I send you for publication the following parody.

> My country ! 'tis of thee,
> Strong hold of Slavery—
> Of thee I sing :
> Land, where my fathers died ;
> Where men *man's* rights *deride ;*
> From every mountain-side,
> Thy deeds shall ring.
>
> My native country ! thee—
> Where all men are born free,
> If *white* their skin :
> I love thy hills and dales,
> Thy mounts and pleasant vales ;
> But hate thy *negro* sales,
> As foulest sin.
>
> Let *wailing* swell the breeze,
> And ring from all the trees
> The *black* man's wrong :
> Let every tongue awake,
> Let *bond* and free partake,
> Let rocks their silence break,
> The sound prolong.
>
> Our fathers God ! to thee—
> Author of *Liberty !*
> To thee we sing ;
> *Soon* may our land be bright,—
> With *holy Freedom's* light—
> Protect us by thy might,
> Great God, our King.

THETA.

NON-RE

INFIDELITY—JAC

Vincit (

It is a matter of sor
state of public opinion r
straining and overcomir
the inferences drawn fr
tance. It reminds one c
their apologists against
olition. ' Levelling,' '
tal or divine ;' ' infidel
' bloodshed.' The sam
Tracy and others agair
against it by the Purit:
innocent Quakers, Wm
phenson and Mary Dye
was raised against it wl
land, as George Fox pre
it was preached by the *I*
it was preached by the *I*
and in Judea, when it w
Jews said Christ was di:
tion, a leveller, an enemy
because he called himsel
because, they said, he sp
holy place. So the Apo:
mies to Cæsar, as oppo
they preached the king
Christ to be King of ki
' jacobins,' infidels,' ' ath
resentations of those wh(
kingdoms of this world.
many, those who think
system is not binding or
to be the Christian's only
whom they are to leave
doers in his own time a
as advocating doctrines
delity and anarchy.

I am reminded of the
our puritan ancestors ex
ligious *toleration* as hel(
Hutchinson and the Qua

' Toleration would :
Sodom. Toleration is tl
the sure way to destroy :

Another, N. E. War(
Ipswich, says :

Figure 3.1. "America," by "Theta," from the *Liberator* (3 May 1839). Courtesy of The Library of Congress.

Indeed, "like many other American reform movements," writes Ronald Walters, "antislavery achieved its effect by pulling new implications out of words, phrases, and images that were ancient and widely shared." Paul's, Bell's, Purvis', and "Theta"'s alternative versions of "America" therefore function as part of a counterdiscourse designed to subvert official language and dominant ideology through parody and irony.[17]

Dozens of such antislavery versions of "America" were created during the antebellum period, and some were widely reprinted and performed. The activist and poet John Pierpont (1785–1866) alone composed at least five alternate sets of lyrics to the tune of "America." From 1829, when one of his songs accompanied the first public antislavery speech of William Lloyd Garrison, through the Civil War, Pierpont repeatedly used the melody to support various reform causes. Pierpont, grandfather of J. P. Morgan and a Unitarian minister in Boston, was active in the antislavery, peace, and temperance movements and frequently composed poems or songs for reform meetings and special occasions. On 17 September 1842 a song by Pierpont set to the tune of "America" was sung by a crowd of John Quincy Adams's supporters upon his return from Congress after battling the "gag rule." The second half of one verse announces that "from a sterner fight, / In the defense of Right, / Clothed in a conquerer's might, / We hail him home." In addition to this "Ode" to Adams, Pierpont used "America" to prepare a song for the funeral service for abolitionist Asa Wing in 1855 and general versions of more diffuse appeal, such as "Prayer of the Christian" (1829) and "National Hymn" (1863), both of which were widely reprinted and performed for decades.[18]

Jairus Lincoln included six separate lyrical variations of "America" (along with two alternate hymn melodies) in his 1843 *Anti-Slavery Melodies*. George Clark included three antislavery songs set to the tune of "America" in the seventh edition of *The Liberty Minstrel*. Printed on facing pages were "My Country" ("My country, 'tis for thee, / Dark land of slavery, / For thee I weep"), "Spirit of Freemen, Awake," and "The Liberty Army," which proclaimed: "Let slavery's knell be rung! / Oppression's dirge be sung! / And every bondman's tongue / Of *freedom* sing." Playing on Smith's lines ("from every mountainside / let freedom ring"), the lyrics imagine an abolitionist future, in which all might join in singing songs of freedom. William Wells Brown included another version of "Spirit of Freemen, Awake" in the 1848 *Anti-Slavery Harp; A Collection of Songs for Anti-Slavery Meetings* (see figure 3.2). The implied singers use Smith's melody to rally sympathizers to action ("Sons of the Free! we call / On you, in field and hall, / To rise as one") and sound the patriotic sentiments of Smith's version to dramatize the evil of slavery: "What lover of her fame / Feels not his country's shame, / In this dark hour?"[19]

Noted African American abolitionist songwriter Joshua McCarter Simpson

THE

ANTI-SLAVERY HARP:

A

COLLECTION OF SONGS.

BY

WILLIAM W. BROWN.

Figure 3.2. The front cover of William Wells Brown, *The Anti-Slavery Harp* (1848).
Courtesy of The Library of Congress.

composed two alternate versions of "America," both of which worked intertextually with Smith's lyrics. Simpson was born in Windsor, Ohio, around 1820. Bound out as a laborer until age twenty-one, he attended preparatory school at Oberlin College and became a respected herbalist and conductor on the underground railroad. Simpson wrote fifty-five antislavery songs, most of which were collected in 1854 in *The Emancipation Car*; the only known antislavery collection in which all the songs were written by one person, it stands among the earliest published collections of verse by an African American. Among its two alternate versions of "America," "Song of the 'Aliened American'" bemoans:

"My country, 'tis of thee / Dark land of Slavery, / In thee we groan." Simpson thus recharacterizes the nation as one in which slavery, not liberty, is the definitive property, hence recasting the "national hymn" as a lamentation. Indeed, for Simpson, America is a land of tyranny and oppression, not liberty and freedom: "The white man rules the day— / He holds despotic sway, / O'er all the land." Simpson again samples Smith's lyrics in the final verse but finds "sweet freedom's song" in African American pleas for justice rather than in patriotic paeans to past achievements:

> No! no! the time has come,
> When we must not be dumb,
>   *We must awake.*
> We now "Eight Millions Strong,"
> Must strike sweet freedom's song
> And plead ourselves, our wrong—
>   Our chains must break.[20]

Simpson thus offers critical commentary on Smith's "America" by blending elements of the original with new words that cast doubt on its claims. The intended result is what Stuart Hall has termed a "negotiated version of the dominant ideology" that is "shot through with contradictions."[21] These contradictions were most effectively revealed on the Fourth of July, the annual ritualistic celebration of national identity. As the Fourth of July presented the best recurring opportunity to contest American national policies by reference to national principles, by the 1850s counterobservances of the Fourth had become the largest annual antislavery gatherings. As demonstrated hereafter, abolitionist versions of "America," some specially crafted for the Fourth of July, played a vital role in efforts to reconstruct the occasion.

Independence Day: "This Fourth of July Is Yours, Not Mine"

The Fourth of July, writes Howard Martin, was "the most important national ceremonial during the last century." In many American communities, July Fourth was (and still is) the largest gathering of the year and was celebrated with picnics, ceremonies, fireworks, songs, and speeches, as citizens reveled in the mythic past and glorious prospects of the nation. However, unlike our currently saturated culture, so overloaded with both institutional and symbolic markers of our nationality, antebellum America bore few institutionalized expressions of its (then increasingly fragile) unity: there was no official flag or anthem, and holidays were largely local or state rather than national observances. The Fourth of July was therefore a unique national ritual. Initially, during the American Revolution, July Fourth celebrations supplanted traditional colonial celebrations of the monarchy (such as the king's birthday) through which the colonists declared both their loyalty to the king and their identity as British subjects. In contrast to such promonarchical celebrations, the Fourth of July expressed new and explicitly American national identities rooted in independence. In 1778, Congress gave its official sanction to the celebrations and the following year ordered that "the chaplains of Congress be requested to prepare sermons suitable to the occasion."[22] By the War of 1812, organized Fourth of July celebrations had spread from urban areas to settlements across the United States, in effect creating the first *national* ceremony in the new nation.

Formal Fourth of July observances were devoted to the consideration of American national identity. To celebrate the nation's independence was to justify its separate status and distinctive character; doing so on July Fourth located the nation in the founding principles of the Declaration of Independence. Much like the first performance of "America" at Boston's Park Street Church in 1831, July Fourth observances also had a religious tone, and were "commemorated," as John Adams had hoped, by "solemn acts of devotion." In fact, throughout the early nineteenth century, many July Fourth ceremonies followed the form of a Protestant church service, as they were conducted "by priests appointed," as the editors of the *Liberator* later commented, "under the name of orators." Under the direction of such nationalist priests, the holy text of the Declaration of Independence was read and the sermonic oration was delivered, interspersed with prayers and hymns. "The ubiquitous salute to the day," Martin observes, "had the ring of an invocation, a call to worship." Indeed, the Fourth of July was "the political Sabbath," the highest holy day for an American civil religion in which the United States was envisioned as "God's New Israel," a divinely favored nation with a distinctive mission in the world. Given this simultaneously nationalist and religious context, it is not surprising to learn that "America," the unofficial "national hymn," was accorded a prominent place in most Fourth of July celebrations (especially in the North), where it was used to open or close the program with what was generally full and rousing audience participation.[23]

Municipalities sometimes staged spectacular fireworks displays for the Fourth of July. In multicolored explosions and national symbols, these displays asserted grand, heroic national identities. For example, in 1852 a massive "National Tableau," 275 feet long and 80 feet tall and advertised as the "largest pyrotechnical structure ever fired in the United States," was erected on the Boston Common for the Fourth. Its central figure was a colossal statue of the goddess of liberty "trampling upon the broken symbols of despotism"; "liberty" was surrounded by scrolls decorated with the seal of the United States, thirty-one stars, and the word "Liberty." On each side were columns and urns bearing the names of battles and heroes from the American Revolution; each column erupted in "immense jets of flame and variegated stars." Finally, "a discharge of 500 rockets, together with Shells and Mines, forms a grand terminating Bouquet de Feu."[24] Patriotism made for good spectacle.

In addition to the spectacular and religious Fourths already noted, the visions of the nation expressed in local Fourth of July ceremonies were generally diverse, frequently partisan, and sometimes militaristic, as local militias marched in parades while battles were commemorated and reenacted. Some celebrations were riotous and drunken, while others were deadly, such as when eight persons were killed and dozens more injured in racially motivated riots surrounding the Fourth in 1857 in New York City. In his sermon that day in Jersey City's Unitarian Church, Octavius B. Frothingham reproachfully observed that liberty to most Americans on July Fourth seemed to mean the "freedom to make a noise, and shout huzzah, and burn saltpeter, and eat and drink, and go rollicking about at will, and hear ourselves exalted in grand orations." "Liberty in America seems to mean, popularly," he concluded, "the liberty of the white race to do what it pleases." While elections and public celebrations in America have generally been acknowledged by historians as carnivalesque eruptions of class and racial tensions, clergy at the time nonetheless denounced the drinking and fighting common among Fourth of July celebrants as a defamation of the occasion and as a misunderstanding and misuse of the freedoms commemorated.[25]

Whether drunken or austere, racist or noble, community celebrations of the Fourth were usually capped with speeches that one observer characterized as "the highest form of American oratory." In fact, hundreds of Fourth of July speeches and sermons were published as pamphlets and newspapers, and some were widely distributed and reviewed in literary journals. To be selected as a community's Fourth of July speaker was an honor, yet while it was an occasion when such honored speakers strove for eloquence, it was also a time of formulaic, grandiloquent, and clichéd blather. The term "Fourth of July oratory" came to be, as Ohio senator Stanley Matthews lamented, "a hissing and a byword, a scorn and a reproach" for speeches that made bombastic appeals to patriotism. Indeed, most Fourth of July orations followed a thematic formula and were executed with stock phrases and sentiments. Hence Walt Whitman's 1856 complaint about the "threadbare tediousness of a Fourth-of-July Oration." Such threadbare tediousness could also give way to examples of what many readers will no doubt see as rank hypocrisy. For example, in slaveholding Charleston, South Carolina, John J. Mauger's oration on the Fourth in 1817 celebrated the day as one on which "millions of freemen assemble in commemoration" of the "Birth Day of American Freedom." Speaking in the same city on the same day in 1820—just two years before Denmark Vesey would plot the armed revolt of Charleston's slaves—William Lance could say without blushing that his country countenanced "no *distinctions* of rank, no *degrees* of right, to tarnish the *natural equality* for which" the nation's founders "fought and conquered." Even when Fourth of July orators decried conditions of tyranny and oppression elsewhere, most portrayed their own country as one in which such conditions had been eradicated by the Revolution. Thus, in his July Fourth oration of 1823 Horace Mann imagines the "Great Being" who, when scanning the globe, finds that there is "one spot alone" where no despot dares lift his hand to pluck a leaf from the tree of liberty" and where every heart thrills to its glories. "That spot," he concludes, "is our country; those hearts our own."[26]

Such Fourth of July boasts of America's status as a beacon of liberty were deeply offensive to many abolitionists. How could America be seen as a "land of the free" when millions were enslaved? Writing about the events of 4 July 1831, when "America" premiered, William Lloyd Garrison condemned such hypocritical national self-congratulation:

> We have lived to see once more our nation's Jubilee! Millions hailed it with exultation! . . . The orators of the day, as usual, recounted the many and great blessings which have been vouchsafed unto us. . . . They eulogized in no measured terms our civil constitution, and indulged, as our predecessors have done, in high anticipations of our future greatness and glory. Who did not partake in the feelings of the occasion? Who did not join heartily in welcoming the day? But there are some, 'tis believed, who rejoiced with trembling. All ought to have done so.

To "rejoice with trembling" is to recognize the fundamental paradox of American history, that "while we have been vaunting our free institutions, and claiming for our country the admiration of the world, as the birth place of liberty, the asylum of the oppressed, we have been holding two millions of our fellow men in the most abject servitude."[27]

While the Fourth of July was invested with a variety of ideological, cultural, and racial meanings, many Americans, black and white, saw it as a "whites only" festivity, as the liberties celebrated on July Fourth were white liberties. In fact, blacks (both free and enslaved) were restricted from both white visions of the nation and from participation in its ceremonial observances. For example, the Reverend Dr. Dalcho, a slaveholding minister from South Carolina, insisted:

> The celebration of the Fourth of July belongs *exclusively* to the white population of the United States. The American Revolution was a *family quarrel among equals*. In this, the NEGROS had no concern; their condition remained, and must remain, unchanged. They have no more to do with the celebration of the day,

than with the landing of the Pilgrims on the rock at Plymouth. It therefore appears to me, to be improper to allow these people to be present on those occasions.[28]

Despite Dalcho's argument, some free African Americans in the North observed the Fourth of July, but southern slaves and free blacks were generally prohibited from participation in July Fourth activities. For example, advertisements for the Independence Day program at Charleston's Vauxhall Gardens in 1799 asserted that there would be "no admittance for people of color."[29] And while such "whites only" celebrations indicate the tendency toward *exclusionary politics*, in which blacks were denied access to public space (both figurally and literally), the period was also marked by even more aggressive practices of *brutalizing politics*, in which white public space was created, both physically and psychically, through violence against blacks. Indeed, by the beginning of the nineteenth century, white mobs in the northern states regularly attacked African Americans on July Fourth. Thus, in dire and deadly contradiction of the promised "Sweet land of liberty," the Fourth of July was anticipated by many African Americans (and later Irish immigrants, who were also the targets of mob violence) with apprehension and fear.

Some African American orators, poets, and songwriters endeavored to depict July Fourth for white audiences from the perspective of one enslaved. William Wells Brown shocked his several thousand listeners in Framingham on July Fourth in 1859 when he began his speech by reading aloud an advertisement from a recent issue of the Winchester (Tennessee) *Journal*. It announced the sale, on 4 July, that very day, of an enslaved African American woman and her children, "together with a top buggy, and several wagons and horses." The Fourth of July, he informed the audience, was "the high-market day for slaves throughout the South . . . the day when more slaves were to be sold under the hammer than any other." To the slave, Brown said, the Fourth of July is "more dreaded than almost any other day of the year."[30] Much like Brown's dramatic rhetorical maneuver, black abolitionist orators addressing predominantly white audiences at Independence Day observances frequently asked their listeners to consider the occasion of July Fourth from the perspective of one enslaved. How would one in chains feel about celebrations and songs proclaiming the nation's freedom? For example, in what is perhaps the most quoted passage of his 1852 address in Rochester, New York, Frederick Douglass describes the Fourth from the perspective of the enslaved:

What, to the American slave, is your Fourth of July? I answer: a day that reveals to him, more than all the other days in the year, the gross injustice and cruelty to which he is the constant victim. To him, your celebration is a sham; your boasted liberty an unholy license; your national greatness swelling vanity; your sounds of rejoicing are empty and heartless; your denunciations of tyrants brass-fronted impudence; your shouts of liberty and equality hollow mockery; your prayers and hymns, your sermons and thanksgivings, with all your religious parade and solemnity, are to Him mere bombast, fraud, deception, impiety and hypocrisy—a thin veil to cover up crimes which would disgrace a nation of savages. There is not a nation on the earth guilty of practices more shocking and bloody than are the people of the United States at this very hour.[31]

Even before Douglass's thundering attack on America's "bombast, fraud, deception, impiety and hypocrisy," early abolitionists, particularly African Americans, condemned conventional observances of the Fourth of July. Religious and political leaders urged people to boycott them. "The festivities of this day," Reverend Peter Williams, Jr., preached on the Fourth in New York, 1830, "serve but to impress upon the minds of reflecting men of colour a deeper sense of the cruelty, the injustice, and oppression, of which they have been the victims." Williams asked his listeners to donate the amount of money they would normally have spent in celebrating the Fourth to support instead the emigration of African Americans driven out of Cincinnati to Canada. Likewise, the national African American convention of 1834 voted to urge African Americans not to participate in public celebrations of the Fourth. In an even more aggressively symbolic gesture, the editors of the *Colored American* in 1838 suggested that instead of the American flag, a slave whip should be unfurled as the national symbol on the Fourth.[32]

Abolitionists did not share the anti-British sentiments expressed in many Fourth of July ceremonies. Whereas British rule was routinely characterized as oppressive and tyrannical, with the American rebellion celebrated as a quest for liberty, abolitionists lamented the loss of what was widely perceived as Britain's progressive stand on slavery. Some African American abolitionists, such as H. Ford Douglass in his July Fourth oration of 1860, went so far as to say that they "would rather curse than bless the day that marked the separation" of the colonies from England, for had they remained British subjects, American slaves would have been freed in 1834 when Britain abolished slavery in its remaining colonies. Indeed, while rejecting what Douglass called the sham of the Fourth, African Americans celebrated instead either 1 August, the date on which British slavery in the West Indies was abolished, or other dates of abolition or slave trade suspension (such as 1 January and "Juneteenth"). Hence, in much the same way that the Fourth was celebrated by whites, many African American communities celebrated 1 August with parades, speeches, and picnics. For example, in yet another reversal of "America," this time away from its borrowed British tune equipped with pro-American lyrics back to the pro-British sentiments originally expressed in "God Save the King," African American poet

James Madison Bell (1826–1902), who migrated from Ohio to Canada and whose home served as John Brown's headquarters in 1858, composed an anti-slavery and pro-British "Song for the First of August" to the tune of "America":

> This is proud Freedom's day!
> Swell, swell the gladsome lay,
>> Till earth and sea.
> Shall echo with the strain,
> Through Britain's vast domain;
> No bondman clanks his chain,
>> All men are free.[33]

It is Britain's love of freedom, not America's, that Bell celebrates in song, and 1 August, not 4 July, that he proclaims "proud Freedom's day." Thus, as demonstrated here by Bell's appropriation of "America," African Americans were more likely to consider Britain or Canada, rather than the United States, a "land of liberty."[34]

African Americans sometimes held parallel ceremonies on the Fourth itself. On 4 July 1827 New York emancipated its slaves, and celebrations were held in African American communities throughout the state and beyond. In Rochester, New York, the emancipation act and a copy of the Declaration of Independence were read aloud, followed by an oration by Austin Steward, who carefully distinguished the proceedings from other Independence Day observances. He had been born in slavery and reminded his audience that while they enjoyed their freedom in New York, "we should remember, in joy and exultation, the thousands of our countrymen who are to-day . . . writhing under the lash and groaning beneath the grinding weight of Slavery's chain." "We will rejoice," he advised, "though sobs interrupt the songs of our rejoicing, and tears mingle in the cup we pledge to Freedom."[35] The following year, Steward emigrated to Canada.

In order to differentiate their celebration of New York's emancipation from the national holiday and to avoid physical attacks from drunken whites, many African Americans held their observances on 5 July rather than 4 July. This postponement symbolically represented the fact that the liberties celebrated by white Americans on the Fourth had not yet been extended to African Americans. Peter Osborne explained to his New Haven audience on 5 July 1832 that "on account of the misfortune of our color, our Fourth of July comes on the fifth." Only when the terms of the Declaration of Independence were "fully executed," he explained, "may we then have our Fourth of July on the fourth." July Fifth thus became a common meeting date for African American antislavery gatherings that featured speeches, music, and sometimes elections. It was an occasion when, as Leonard Sweet writes, African Americans "could symbolically express their alienation from the promises of July 4."[36]

The most famous July Fifth denunciation of the Fourth is undoubtedly Frederick Douglass's brilliant oration "What, to the Slave, Is the Fourth of July?" delivered in Rochester, New York, in 1852. Rochester was an important stop on the underground railroad, and the Douglasses offered many fugitives their last American shelter before crossing the border into Canada. For Douglass and his comrades in Rochester in 1852, then, the stakes were high, even deadly (see figure 3.3). Indeed, the passage of the Fugitive Slave Law in 1850 and its brutal enforcement in northern states the following year made no place within American borders safe for any African American, as bounties and a lack of due process meant that even "free" blacks were falsely charged and sent into slavery. In 1851, Douglass hid three men who had shot and killed the slaveholder who pursued them. Despite the manhunt mounted for them, Douglass personally made the perilous drive with the fugitives to the boat that would take them to Canada. When he accepted an invitation the following year to deliver a Fourth of July oration in Rochester, Douglass accordingly explained his alienation from the occasion in typically brilliant and bitter prose:

> I am not included within the pale of this glorious anniversary! Your high independence only reveals the immeasurable distance between us. The blessings in which you, this day, rejoice, are not enjoyed in common. The rich inheritance of justice, liberty, prosperity, and independence, bequeathed by your fathers, is shared by you, not by me. The sunlight that brought light and healing to you, has brought stripes and death to me. This Fourth of July is *yours*, not *mine*. *You* may rejoice, *I* must mourn.[37]

Like many other abolitionist orators, Douglass voiced particular disdain for the national songs used to celebrate the Fourth, for as "songs of freedom" they were hypocrisies, made worse because all were expected to join in singing them. In his 1830 sermon, Peter Williams asked his listeners to consider how patriotic songs on the Fourth sounded to those who are "slaves in the midst of freedom" and whose chains and voiced wrongs "make a horrid discord in the songs of freedom which resound through the land." In the public ceremonies that celebrate the Fourth, African American abolitionist William Watkins told the Massachusetts legislature in 1853, "our jubilatic anthems roll" across the land, insisting "'We are free, We are free.'" But, like Williams, Watkins pairs chord and discord, hymn and lamentation, "for amid the rapturous symphonies of Freedom's song, I hear a low sepulchral voice; the voice of agony" that "gives the lie to your song of Jubilee." In a similar rhetorical strategy in an 1856 address, Sara G. Stanley of the Delaware (Ohio) Ladies' Anti-Slavery Society compares national hymns with the sounds of human misery they conceal:

> As the song of freedom reverberates through the northern hills, and the lingering symphony quivers on the still air and then sinks away into silence, a low

Figure 3.3. Samuel Miller, half-plate daguerreotype, in closed case, of Frederick Douglass (1852). Courtesy of The Acquisitions Centennial Endowment of The Art Institute of Chicago.

deep wail, heavy with anguish and despair, rises from the southern plains, and the clank of chains on human limbs mingles with the mournful cadence. What to the toiling millions there, is this boasted liberty?

Williams, Watkins, and Stanley each demonstrate how song was a powerful metaphor for freedom and how abolitionists disrupted this metaphor by imagining the sounds of slavery, the clank of chains and the screams of the tortured, alongside those of freedom.[38]

Although free African Americans sometimes joined in singing national songs, many resisted the expectation that they do so. "To drag a man in fetters into the grand illuminated temple of liberty and call upon him to join you in joyous anthems," Frederick Douglass scolded his predominantly white audience in Rochester on 5 July 1852, "were inhuman mockery and sacrilegious irony." Douglass compares the expectation that African Americans would join in the celebration of July Fourth and the singing of patriotic songs that accompany it to the predicament of the ancient Israelites during their exile in Babylon. He quotes Psalm 137: "For there they that carried us away captive required of us a song; and they that wasted us required of us mirth, saying, sing us one of the songs of Zion." Douglass asks, in the words of the Israelites, "How shall we sing the Lord's song in a strange land?" How, he insists, can we sing a song of freedom in a land where we are not free? Whatever song Douglass is to sing on this day, he explains, must pierce the melody of "national, tumultuous joy" with "the mournful wail of millions, whose chains, heavy and grievous yesterday, are today rendered more intolerable by the jubilee shouts that reach them." For him to join in the song of national joy, "to chime in with the popular theme would be scandalous and shocking and would make me a reproach before God and the world." The song he sings in this strange land, then, must itself be strange, distanced from dominant ideology and custom. According to Molefi Asante, this is a recurring predicament for "the African American protest speaker or writer," who "confronts the reality of the possible verbal space with every sentence of rebellion, forced, as it were, to speak a strange tongue." In a nation of slavery, then, as Douglass illustrates, a true song of freedom must *make strange* national claims of freedom and liberty.[39]

Joshua McCarter Simpson composed such a strange protest in "Fourth of July in Alabama," a song set to the tune of "America" and published in *The Emancipation Car* two years after Douglass's speech (see appendix A). Like Douglass, Simpson imagines the holiday from the perspective of one enslaved. He includes a prefatory paragraph, explaining that the song is "the meditation and feelings of the poor Slave, as he toils and sweats over the hoe and cotton hook, while his master, neighbors, and neighbors' children are commemorating that day, which brought life to the whites and death to the poor African." The song opens with a melancholy question addressed to the Fourth of July: "O, thou unwelcome day, / Why hast thou come this way?" For while white Americans greet the day with festive spirits as "cannons loudly roar / And banners highly soar," Simpson wonders: "Where is the happy throng / Of Africa's sons?" who "have got no song." Thus, like Williams and Watkins and Stanley before him, Simpson describes the familiar sounds and customs of July Fourth from the estranged perspective of one enslaved. He sings of his inability to join in the performance of national songs, as "There is no song for me." Instead, for Simpson, and the "four millions slaves" who "remain in living graves," the Fourth celebrates the "jubilee / Which set the white man free / And fetters brought to me." The imaginary national unanimity of the Fourth, as emphasized in Smith's "sweet land of liberty," is here revealed instead as a fractured, tortured, dismal plain of mass-produced misery. Simpson, then, like Douglass and other abolitionists, used the Fourth to interrogate and subvert national conventions and sacred texts such as "America."[40]

Reconstructing the Fourth: "This Holy and Patriotic Work"

Despite such rousing condemnations of the Fourth of July, Douglass and Simpson and most other abolitionists did not abandon the occasion altogether. Instead, they sought to construct a critical observance, rather than celebration, of the holiday. In this regard the abolitionists, even while castigating the nation, were partaking of one of its traditional gestures, for the Fourth of July was always a political occasion. And while conventional Fourth of July ceremonies generally reinforced the legitimacy and power of the state, these celebrations were neither universal in content nor uniform in style. For example, trade unions and political parties held their own Fourth of July gatherings, which were saturated with their own party- or union-specific meanings. In fact, beginning as early as the 1790s, American trade unionists celebrated the Fourth as their day and drank toasts to "The Fourth of July, may it ever prove a memento to the oppressed to rise and assert their rights." Such trade union gatherings used the occasion to draw attention to the oppression of workers, to lament the unfinished business of the Revolution, and sometimes to propose alternative Declarations of Independence. In Boston, the Federalists and Democratic-Republicans held competing Fourth of July celebrations to rally their members. Frances Wright's scandalous Fourth of July orations of 1828 and 1829, in which she combined appeals for a variety of radical reforms, including women's rights, sexual liberty, and abolitionism, denounced patriotism as a sentiment that "surely is not made for America." She argued instead that the Fourth was a day best devoted to "celebrating protests against it." Temperance activists also relied on the Fourth, as already detailed, as one of the most potent opportunities both for attacking what were perceived to be national sins and for proposing the moral reforms necessary to salvage democracy. The Fourth of July was thus used by a variety of political groups to grant legitimacy to their causes, to align their diverse visions of the future with the myths and principles of the Revolutionary past, and to refashion both the meanings of the Fourth and the national texts it celebrates.

It comes as no surprise, then, to learn that the Fourth of July was used to protest slavery at least as early as 1783, when, at a celebration of American independence in Woodbridge, New Jersey, a prominent local physician mounted the platform along with his fourteen slaves and, after citing the principles of the Declaration of Independence, emancipated them on the spot. On 4 July 1791, two years after the ratification of the Constitution, George Buchanon, M.D., a member of the American Philosophical Society, delivered *An Oration Upon the Moral and Political Evil of Slavery* at a public meeting in Baltimore of the Maryland Society for the Abolition of Slavery. Buchanon's speech was dedicated to Thomas Jefferson, invoked the language of the Declaration in support of abolition, was widely circulated in pamphlet form, and was eventually read by President Washington.[42] The universal human rights proclaimed in the Declaration and its justification of resistance to oppression thus made the Fourth of July an irresistible opportunity for antislavery activists to argue for reform on the basis of accepted premises.

Aside from these heroic individual actions, the earliest regional and national efforts to encourage organized anti-slavery observances of July Fourth were undertaken by the American Colonization Society. The American Society for Colonizing the Free People of Color in the United States was founded in 1816 and had many eminent supporters, including James Monroe, Daniel Webster, Henry Clay, and Francis Scott Key, the author of "The Star-Spangled Banner." Its efforts to promote the emigration of free African Americans to Liberia were at first supported by many white antislavery activists and a few African Americans, who despaired of ever gaining equality in America. The Colonization Society's prejudicial rhetoric, however, which urged whites to support the removal of free blacks, who were seen as an inherently inferior and troublesome group, soon produced unified opposition. In the 1820s and 1830s, the Colonization Society sponsored annual Fourth of July meetings, using the occasion to wrap their controversial programs in the garments of patriotism—these were the colonizationists' best-attended and most lucrative fund-raising events. In fact, on July Fourth in 1829, at a ceremony sponsored by the American Colonization Society in Boston's Park Street Church (where Smith's "America" would first be performed two years later), twenty-three-year-old William Lloyd Garrison delivered his first major public address against slavery. Garrison would soon abandon the colonizationists and denounce their schemes as racist and supportive of slavery. In this speech, he was already far more militant than most colonizationists, as he denounced the Fourth of July as "the worst and most disastrous day in the whole three hundred and sixty-five." Garrison nonetheless used the conventions of the Fourth to his rhetorical advantage, as he both found support in the Declaration of Independence for his thesis that slavery was a national sin and contrasted the hypocritical proclamations of national virtue that characterized traditional celebrations of the Fourth with national realities. In one of his most aggressive passages, Garrison argued that the Fourth occasioned "that pompous declamation of vanity, that lying attestation of falsehood, from the lips of tumid orators, which are poisoning our life-blood."[43]

Along with such stark proclamations, the publication of Garrison's *Liberator* in 1831 fueled efforts to organize alternative observances of July Fourth. African American abolitionist Anna Elizabeth of Philadelphia published "A Short Address to Females of Color" in the *Liberator* on 18 June 1831, noting the suggestion "by some of our best friends" (Garrison chief among them) "that the approaching fourth of July be set apart, by us, as a day of humiliation and prayer." She asks African American women to join her in acting accordingly. Thus 4 July 1831, the date on which "America" premiered, was perhaps the first Independence Day on which abolitionists organized counterobservances across localities and states in competition with those of the colonizationists. At an observance on the same day in Lynn, Massachusetts, orator Alonzo Lewis proclaimed the appropriateness of the occasion for antislavery appeals, arguing that "On a day like this, it is highly suitable to speak of whatever has a tendency to advance or retard national honor, happiness and prosperity."[44]

In the next issue of the *Liberator* (9 July 1831), Garrison criticized nonabolitionist observances of the Fourth and denounced the hypocrisy of conventional celebrations, in which "Our love of liberty increases with the multiplication of our slaves." Despite the fact that the American "slave population is larger by SIXTY THOUSAND souls than it was at the last anniversary," Garrison asked, "when have we made so extensive and boisterous a parade of our patriotism?" Garrison voiced particular disdain for the July Fourth sermon by Lyman Beecher in favor of colonization, in which Beecher urged "every man, woman, and child to put their hands into their pockets, and contribute money" for "the removal of the whole colored population to Africa." Following the leads of Elizabeth, Lewis, and Garrison, criticism of conventional and colonizationist observances of the Fourth would soon become a standard feature of abolitionist rhetoric.[45]

Though his paper reported the event, it is not known whether Garrison attended the first performance of "America." In a letter of 29 June 1832 (the year following the song's first performance) to Ebenezer Dole, Garrison seems to draw on the song's lyrics to deride the anticipated celebration of the Fourth:

> The mockery of mockeries is at hand—the Fourth of July! By many, the day will be spent in rioting and intemperate drinking—by others, in political defamation and partisan heat—by others, in boasting of the freedom of the

American people, and unhazardous denunciations of the mother country. The waste of money, and health, and morals, will be immense. Another party will seize the occasion (many of them with the best motives) to extol the merits of the Colonization Society, and increase its funds. Mistaken men! A very small number will spend the day in sadness and supplication, on account of the horrible oppression which is exercised over the bodies and souls of two millions of the rational creatures of God, in this boasted land of liberty.[46]

Garrison mocks the second line of "America," identifying Smith's land of liberty as merely boasted rather than actual. July Fourth, Garrison observes, was a holiday with very different meanings for different groups of Americans. In the *Liberator* three weeks later, Garrison reprinted a column in which the editor of the Lynn *Record* argued that "no day, perhaps is better adapted to urge an appeal" on behalf of those enslaved "than the Fourth of July." Beginning the following year, Garrison and others promoted annual counterobservances of July Fourth. The abolitionists thus sought to make the day their own, to turn the Fourth into an occasion when Americans would contemplate the paradoxical proclamations of freedom amid the continuing practice of slavery.

Following such sentiments, July Fourth was turned, from roughly 1833 through the beginning of the Civil War, into the most important annual meeting day for abolitionists, on which huge gatherings and fund-raising events were held across the nation. The *Liberator* in 1834 carried notices for six antislavery Fourth of July observances in three states and in 1835 listed sixteen. These were largely local affairs, although some invited notable outside speakers and advertised to attract attendance from other communities. The New-England Anti-Slavery Society, for example, on the Fourth in 1834 sponsored a regional antislavery meeting in Boylston, Massachusetts, that was attended by delegates from several states. But the logistical difficulties and expense of travel prevented large-scale regional gatherings until the development of rail lines. In the interim, abolitionist leaders urged the proliferation of local observances "in every place where a society exists for the furtherance of this holy and patriotic work."[47]

As July Fourth became a focal point of abolitionist activism, so it became a focal point of abolitionist rhetoric. For example, Maria Weston Chapman included five antislavery lyrics designed specifically for use on the Fourth of July in her 1836 collection *Songs of the Free and Hymns of Christian Freedom*. As the drumbeat for annexation of Texas sounded, which many Americans saw as but a façade for extending slavery into new lands, Chapman's lyrics (published in the year of the Alamo's fall) denounced the militaristic celebrations of the Fourth held in communities throughout the country: "I hate that noisy drum! It is a sound / That's full of war and bondage." Hence, much as conventional Fourth of July ceremonies linked local communities in the evocation of nationhood, so antislavery gatherings also connected local communities with national issues. For example, at the Plymouth County (Massachusetts) Anti-Slavery Society's July Fourth observance in 1837, a hymn by George Russell, set to the tune of "America," asked:

> Shall Despotism sway,
> Its iron scepter *here*,
>> *Our* lips to close?
> Sons of the pilgrims! Say!
> Will ye proud lords obey,
> And ask *them* when ye may
> The *truth* disclose?[48]

Russell's song asks those gathered to consider the congressional gag rule—the 1836 law that institutionalized the "closing" of abolitionist "lips"—as a restriction on their own speech and to see in their local heritage (as "Sons of the Pilgrims") a national responsibility.

The attempt to build national affiliations was facilitated—for abolitionists, temperance activists, capitalists, and imperialists alike—by the spread of the railroads. Indeed, in the 1840s and 1850s railroads enabled regional consolidation of antislavery Fourth of July observances into rallies that in some cases attracted thousands of participants. In his 1886 memoir of antislavery activities in Maine, Austin Willey recalled that "the fourth of July had been much used" in "the cause of liberty to which it belonged, and with great benefit." On July Fourth in 1847, antislavery meetings were held throughout the state, "in groves and churches, with speeches and music, the women preparing the picnic." By 1852, improved transportation, as well as the impetus to antislavery organizing provided by passage of the Fugitive Slave Act, enabled the Maine societies to stage an enormous July Fourth antislavery rally at which Harriet Beecher Stowe, the author of *Uncle Tom's Cabin*, addressed an estimated "six to ten thousand" people convened in a grove near East Livermore. Normally used for Methodist camp meetings, the grove was festooned with banners bearing mottoes (including "No Compromise With Slavery," "The Daughters of Freedom Opposed to the Nebraska Bill," and "Temperance and Liberty") or pictures, such as Uncle Tom's cabin with Aunt Chloe.[49]

Such mass rallies would have been virtually impossible without both railroads and improved turnpikes. Once these new transportation possibilities proved efficacious in organizing large gatherings of citizens, abolitionists quickly moved toward a new form of mass politics. Thus, from 1852 through 1860, the Massachusetts Anti-Slavery Society sponsored huge annual "Anti-Slavery Celebration[s] of Independence Day" in rural groves. Five thousand people from throughout Massachusetts attended the 5 July 1852 gathering at Abington "to listen to the speeches of freemen, and to sing the songs of freedom." Horses and carriages "stood almost innumerable in the shade of the trees" and "booths well filled with wholesome viands, but containing nothing which could intoxicate, stood all around." African American abolitionist Charles Lenox Remond was elected president of the day's gathering and delivered the principal oration. His speech was followed by an "Original Hymn" written for the occasion by D. S. Whitney and set to the tune of "America." Whitney's version of the song begins with this invocation: "Children of Pilgrim stock, / Firm as your granite rock, / Now stand for Right!" Liberty is understood here as both a blessing and an ob- ligation with both political and religious imperatives, for "It's your good destiny / To help Men to be free, / Whoever they may be / Beneath God's light."[50]

While Remond was speaking in Abington on July Fifth in 1852, the Massachu- setts Anti-Slavery Society was holding the first of what became its annual July Fourth meeting in Framingham. Framington's Harmony Grove was a popular tourist attraction in the 1850s for urban residents who wished to spend a day in the country, rowing on the lake or perhaps playing roundball or cricket on the adjoining field. "The Grove itself," Reverend Elias Nason recalled, "consists of several acres of tall, majestic pine, oak, maple and chestnut trees, whose spread- ing branches form a dense and grateful shade" in which "the squirrel leaps from bough to bough" while "song birds fill the air with melody." The air of Har- mony Grove was also filled with speeches. Antislavery and temperance meet- ings were held in a natural amphitheater, 250 feet long and 150 feet wide, that seated over a thousand people. Special abolitionist trains carried attendees from Boston, Worcester, and other towns and cities for the July Fourth rallies, which were frequently all-day affairs (see figure 3.4). The thousands who attended the Framingham event in 1857, for example, "spent some six hours in the various exercises appointed for the occasion." Speakers included Garrison, Wendell Phillips, Charles L. Remond, William Wells Brown, Frances Ellen Watkins, and Thomas Wentworth Higginson.[51]

The Framingham Anti-Slavery Fourth of July rally gained national attention in 1854 when Garrison began his speech by burning copies of the Fugitive Slave Act and Judge Edward G. Loring's decision approving the seizure of Anthony Burns as a fugitive slave. Finally, in a bravura performance of pyrotechnical pol- itics, he burned a copy of the U.S. Constitution, which he pronounced a proslavery "covenant with death and agreement with hell." The crowd erupted in a mixture of cheers and hisses. As one can easily imagine, given the literally incendiary nature of such spectacles, the Framingham rallies intensified the na- tional debate over slavery. Indeed, as Edgar Potter, curator of the Framingham Historical Society, recalled in 1896, the Framingham rallies "kept the whole country in an uproar."[52]

Like traditional gatherings, then, abolitionist observances of July Fourth fea-

Figure 3.4. Sketch of an abolitionist train arriving in Framington's Harmony Grove, from *Gleason's Pictorial Drawing Room Companion* (12 June 1852). Courtesy of The University of Illinois Rare Book and Special Collections Library.

tured oratory, music, family picnics, political campaigning, banners, and national symbols. Abolitionists thus capitalized on established conventions of the holiday in order to reconstruct its meanings and purposes. "A people yet suffering under oppression," one letter to the *Liberator* explained, "should use all occasions when the word FREEDOM is spoken, to remind themselves and each other they have it not." Considering this call to appropriate "the word FREEDOM," it comes as no surprise to learn that abolitionists used the Fourth to identify their own causes with the American Revolution, to emphasize their own contributions to the Revolution, to draw parallels between the Revolution and their own causes, and to claim that their movement was continuing or completing the Revolution. For example, James Eels of Ohio observed on July Fourth in 1836: "It is peculiarly proper to link together these two American Revolutions, and to celebrate the triumph of one and the progress of the other, at the same Anniversary; for they are intimately allied, and have relations so closely interwoven, that they could not well be separated."[53]

Eels was not alone in forging this historical and rhetorical bond between the first American Revolution and the abolitionist cause, as abolitionist speakers and writers frequently both praised the colonial revolutionaries who took up arms against the British oppressors and emphasized those aspects of their struggle most analogous to the antislavery campaign. Indeed, abolitionists drew parallels between their similar numbers (three million colonists then, three million enslaved now), their shared objective (liberty), their animating principles ("that all men are created equal; that they are endowed by their Creator with certain inalienable rights"), and their willingness to die for their freedom.[54] For example, the declaration of delegates at the 1833 National Anti-Slavery Convention recast the story of the American Revolution as one in which "three millions of people rose up as from the sleep of death, and rushed to the strife of blood; deeming it more glorious to die instantly as freemen, than desirable to live one hour as slaves." By drawing parallels between the Revolution and their cause, abolitionists made use of the mythic structure through which the Fourth had long been conventionally celebrated, yet they recast the roles in the revolutionary morality play. Thus Douglass argues in his 5 July 1852 Rochester address that it is the abolitionists who are most akin to the "agitators and rebels" who led the Revolution of "the oppressed against the oppressor," while those now in power, who hate "any great change (no matter how great the good to be attained, or the wrong to be redressed by it)," are today's tyrants and Tories. The Revolution is thus refashioned as a justification for the radical actions of the abolitionists.[55]

Such rhetorical appropriations and revisions of the American Revolution were woven throughout the speeches and promotional materials for antislavery July Fourth gatherings. A notice for the 1860 event in Framingham was headlined "THE INSURRECTION OF 1776!" and urged "all who hate despotism in the garb of Democracy and Republicanism as well as of Monarchy, and would overthrow it by every weapon that may be legitimately wielded against it" to assemble (see figure 3.5). Linking the Revolution to abolitionism was made easier by the hyperbolic language used to describe the patriot cause. An excited poet wrote in the *Florida Herald* in 1829, for example, that the Fourth of July was "the glorious day / When slavery's clouds were chased away." The Revolution was justified, then, as a response to tyranny, as breaking the chains of British oppression. The metaphoric description of British colonialism as bondage and slavery suggested obvious connections to the abolitionist cause. Such argument by association was also spun in biblical directions, as Fourth of July orations regularly compared the Revolution to the Israelites' providentially guided escape from Egyptian bondage. Given the popularity of such traditional materials, abolitionists made the leap from vague references to figurative and Biblical bondage to explicit debates regarding contemporary slavery. Furthermore, abolitionists argued that their cause was even more noble than that of the American revolutionaries. The grievances of the colonists, delegates to the National Anti-Slavery Convention declared in 1833, "were trifling in comparison with the wrongs and sufferings of those for whom we plead." "Our fathers," they ex-

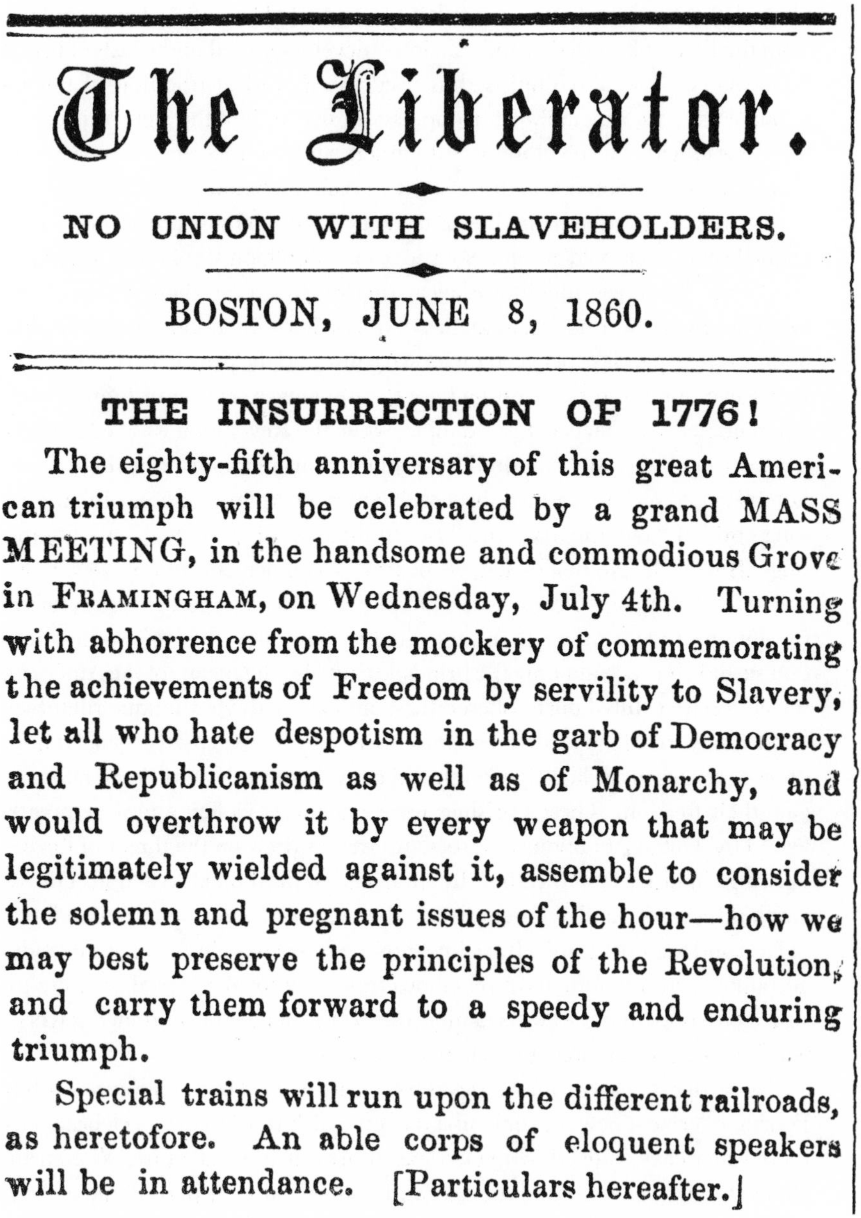

The Liberator.

NO UNION WITH SLAVEHOLDERS.

BOSTON, JUNE 8, 1860.

THE INSURRECTION OF 1776!

The eighty-fifth anniversary of this great American triumph will be celebrated by a grand MASS MEETING, in the handsome and commodious Grove in FRAMINGHAM, on Wednesday, July 4th. Turning with abhorrence from the mockery of commemorating the achievements of Freedom by servility to Slavery, let all who hate despotism in the garb of Democracy and Republicanism as well as of Monarchy, and would overthrow it by every weapon that may be legitimately wielded against it, assemble to consider the solemn and pregnant issues of the hour—how we may best preserve the principles of the Revolution, and carry them forward to a speedy and enduring triumph.

Special trains will run upon the different railroads, as heretofore. An able corps of eloquent speakers will be in attendance. [Particulars hereafter.]

Figure 3.5. Call to celebrate an abolitionist Fourth of July, in the *Liberator* (8 June 1860). Courtesy of The Library of Congress.

plained, "were never slaves—never bought and sold like cattle—never shut out from the light of knowledge and religion—never subjected to the lash of brutal taskmasters." The abolitionists thus used the rhetorical tradition of talking about slavery as a metaphor for oppression, first to link the righteousness of their cause with the revolutionary founders and then to elevate their cause above the Revolution, for their slavery was real, not figural.[56]

Although mainstream abolitionists denied the charge, proslavery forces latched on to such bold comparisons to accuse abolitionists of fomenting slave rebellions. As with so much proslavery rhetoric, however, these charges were more indicative of southern anxieties than northern intentions, for while abolitionists drew parallels between their own cause and the principles of the American Revolution, most (excluding here the obvious exception of John Brown) differentiated their tactics. For example, while the Revolution was "effected by the sword and bayonet," James Eels explained on July Fourth in 1836, abolitionists would succeed instead through "argument and persuasion." In an 1848 song entitled "The Liberty Army" (set to the tune of "America"), abolitionist singers pledged: "No bloody flag we bear; / No implements of war, / Nor carnage red shall mar / Our victory." Despite these pledges to fight a rhetorical revolution of ideas rather than an armed revolution of carnage, some abolitionists did embrace not only the principles but also the means of the American revolutionaries. July Fourth offered these militant activists a unique rhetorical opportunity to defend armed resistance to slavery. Those enslaved staged hundreds of revolts in the late eighteenth and early nineteenth centuries in efforts to gain their freedom. These uprisings were sometimes violent and were greatly feared by whites. Abolitionist orators and writers drew on the threat of further uprisings in order to alarm their listeners and to prod them to action. For example, Reverend La Roy Sunderland's *Anti-Slavery Manual*, a pocket handbook of facts and arguments used by many antislavery speakers in the 1830s, includes accounts of twenty-four slave rebellions from 1712 to 1831. Speakers were instructed to present these "facts demonstrating the danger of continued slavery," which made further violent rebellions inevitable.[57]

The prospect of slave uprisings was routinely invoked by abolitionists on July Fourth, offering a new meaning to a day on which rebellion was celebrated by most Americans. Indeed, conventional Fourth of July celebrations often included military parades and themes, and orators routinely praised the willingness of the revolutionaries "to conquer or die" in armed resistance to British oppression. Some abolitionists, such as Garrison, parodied these traditions, asking: "Do they not fear lest their slaves may one day be as patriotic as themselves?" The Fourth of July, he argued, must not only "embitter and inflame the minds of slaves" but "furnish so many reasons" why "they should obtain their own rights by violence." In an oration delivered in Lynn, Massachusetts, on July

Fourth in 1831, as "America" premiered in nearby Boston, Alonzo Lewis warned his listeners that they must emancipate those enslaved before they "deluge our southern cities with blood." Nat Turner had originally planned to stage his Virginia uprising, the bloodiest in American history, on that same day, before illness forced him to postpone it.[58] In fact, while observed in the North as a contested and generally drunken yet peaceful day of politicking and partying, July Fourth in the South was a common occasion for acts of resistance and retaliation by those enslaved.[59]

Regardless of their disputes over tactics, abolitionists and other reformers agreed that the American Revolution was unfinished and that its promises had to be fulfilled by current and future generations in order to avert catastrophe. Members of the 1833 Anti-Slavery Convention pledged their support "for the achievement of an enterprise, without which, that of our fathers is incomplete." Thus, despite its carefully limited and specifically political function at the time of its production, the Declaration of Independence was regarded by abolitionists as a statement of principle. July Fourth was accordingly understood to be an occasion on which abolitionists, as well as those who attended conventional celebrations, rededicated themselves to the nation's founding principles. For example, "An Appeal to American Freemen" (1859), consisting of four stanzas set to the tune of "America" and designed for use at antislavery July Fourth observances, instructed celebrants to initiate a second American Revolution, to "Light up again the fires / Once kindled by your sires / In Freedom's cause." It would not be long before this call was heeded with a fury unprecedented in American history.[60]

WHILE the most important function of conventional Fourth of July celebrations was, as Len Travers has written, "to mask disturbing ambiguities and contradictions in the new republic, overlaying real social and political conflict with a conceptual veneer of shared ideology and elemental harmony," the primary function of abolitionist Fourth of July observances was to reveal these contradictions and to strip away the veneer of harmony. Some abolitionists even went so far as to equate participation in conventional July Fourth celebrations and the singing of national songs with support for slavery. "We'll meet beneath no gilded arch with pomp and show and pride," the participants in Framingham's 4 July 1860 antislavery meeting declared, refusing "To chant the songs of freedom, while we swell Oppression's tide." Indeed, abolitionist orators, songwriters, and poets sketched scathing portrayals of conventional Independence Day speeches and celebrations, in part to differentiate their own efforts on that date. Garrison praised the July Fourth observance in Fall River, Massachusetts, in 1836 as the most "appropriate" he had seen, in that "not a single banner was unfurled to the breeze . . . no cannon roared— quietude prevailed in the streets—and there seemed to be a general consciousness that, while millions were enslaved in our midst, it would be something worse than mockery to celebrate the day with pomp and show."[61]

The problem with publicly desecrating national symbols and subverting patriotic texts, including "America" and other national songs, however, was that such radical acts further alienated many Americans, who already despised abolitionists as dangerous troublemakers. Nonetheless, in the years leading up to the Civil War, July Fourth rallies were regarded by abolitionists such as William Wells Brown as "the most important meetings held during the year," for they were occasions that drew large crowds and exposed contradictions that "deepened the impression" on those who attended. Perhaps more than any other national song or text, antislavery versions of "America" gave collective voice to these "impressions," offering visions of an America freed from slavery and sectional strife. Indeed, decades before the Gettysburg Address and Reconstruction, abolitionists imagined a nation reconstituted without slavery, a nation worthy of singing "That's my country, that's the land, / I can love with heart and hand." So James Russell Lowell envisioned his commitment to a land freed of slavery, a land so truly democratic that "Of her glories I can sing."[62] Like Lowell, those who attended antislavery gatherings on the Fourth joined together to sing their mutual commitment to creating a "land of liberty" where none yet existed. This commitment would ultimately find expression in civil war.

FOUR

"Teach Us True Liberty"

"America" in the Civil War and Reconstruction, 1861–1869

In the first month of the Civil War, a group of New York businessmen offered a prize of five hundred dollars for the best new national hymn "adapted to the existing condition of the country." After the fall of Fort Sumter, members of the Committee for a National Hymn explained, "indignation flashed through the astonished land; and the loyal citizens of the Republic rose as one man to avenge the wrong and defend the national existence." They observed that public places were crowded with people eager to discuss the war and its implications and that a resurgent patriotism "struck at once its roots to the very centre of the nation's being, and in a single night blossomed into fruitfulness." There was one problem, however: "A national hymn was lacking."[1] Existing American patriotic songs (including "America") were mostly set to borrowed British melodies and rooted in past conflicts. Without a distinctive national song geared to the crisis at hand, the businessmen believed, loyal Americans were unable to express fully either their patriotism or the deeper issues involved in the struggle.

Despite the ridicule of the *Musical World* and *Music Review*, whose editors insisted that great songs could not be composed on demand, the contest received over twelve hundred entries. Most "were consigned to the great rubbish bin (or clothes-basket) after reading the first three lines," selection committee member George Templeton Strong recounted. "A few were put aside as meritorious and worth looking at, and a few others were brilliantly absurd and therefore worth saving." The submissions were winnowed to thirty songs; all were ultimately rejected.[2] Committee member Richard Grant White was commissioned to write a report explaining the decision to award no prize, which he entitled *National Hymns: How They Are Written and How They Are Not Written, A Lyric and National*

Study for the Times (1861). Like Mason, Smith, and Woodbridge before him, White argued that songs are the ultimate medium of patriotic sentiment, and that those who feel deeply about their country yearn to express themselves in song. True national songs, he insisted, grow out of formative national experiences and the common blood ties and heritage of citizens. White accordingly wrote in the preface of his opposition to slavery (while making clear that he was "neither Abolitionist nor 'Black' Republican"), yet he reacted with incredulity to the suggestion of some European writers that "Negro melodies" be considered the national songs of the United States:

> They might as well fasten upon us the songs of the Chinese coolies in California, or the war-whoops of the Cherokee Indians, as our national melodies. They are no more to us as a people, or even as a nation, because they are heard in this country, than the songs of the birds or the howling of the wolves. We have no national melodies; nor has there been either occasion or mode by which we would obtain them. It seems also pretty sure that we shall never have them. For national melodies are the nursery songs of a people, heard in the dimly recollected days of its infancy, lingering in its maturer memory. . . . But this nation was born of full age.[3]

For many Americans, however, the Civil War presented an opportunity, albeit devastating, to remake the nation—literally to begin anew without the baggage that accompanies "full age." It comes as no surprise, then, contrary to White's predictions, that the war produced new and enduring national songs. Indeed, the American Civil War was fought with songs as well as bullets: at home and hospital, battlefield and camp, rally and wake, music accompanied the activities of soldiers and civilians. Songs for North and South identified the stakes of the conflict, expressed both the singers' fealty to their cause and enmity for their foe, and documented the mundane events and emotions of life during wartime. As music historian Vera Brodsky Lawrence has written:

> People on both sides of the battle lines placed great reliance on the songs, finding in them a source of strength, courage, solace, hope, much-needed laughter, and a general escape valve for the unbearable tensions of their lives at a time of fratricidal slaughter. Everybody sang everywhere: at home, at work, in school, in church, at rallies, in camp, on the march, in retreat, in victory, in defeat, in reunion, in sorrow, in jubilation.[4]

The remarkable omnipresence of singing amid almost every aspect of war is explained at least in part by the fact that in the three decades before the Civil War music had become an increasingly popular form of public and home entertainment. Professional singers (such as Jenny Lind), minstrel troupes (such as Dan Emmett and Wood's Minstrels), and touring groups of family singers (including the Hutchinsons, the Rainers, and the Hungarian Brothers) played to large audiences across the United States, including in some communities that had constructed new music halls and concert houses. In part because of the expansion of music instruction in the public schools, community singing groups and musical instrument sales thrived, while newspapers advertised sheet music for new songs. Popular songbooks, such as *The Western Minstrel*, were printed inexpensively on steam-powered presses, thus spreading the latest songs and adaptations of familiar melodies published alongside older favorites. Music was also an important element of home and social life, as Americans gathered to sing around parlor organs or pianos and at quilting bees, parties, and other gatherings.[5]

American musicians and the fledgling music industry adapted swiftly to the needs and opportunities created by the Civil War, as bands and individual musicians played in camp, on the march, on the battlefield, and in hospitals for the wounded. Bands played during the burning of cities and to mark victories or defeats. As Kenneth Olson has written, "it was impossible for the Union or Confederate soldier to escape the sound of music." Soldiers sang under every circumstance of military life, while music was used on the civilian front both to promote enlistment and to demonstrate support for the war. At most of these occasions one was likely to hear any number of popular variations of "America." Generally associated with the Union, the song was a fixture of wartime ceremonies and social gatherings and was included in songbooks published for use by both soldiers and supportive civilians. Indeed, the soldiers of the Civil War were drawn from the first generation of schoolboys to have "America" drilled into their consciousness, which helps to explain why "America" was sung not only at recruitment meetings and after defeats and victories but also by soldiers after their wounds had been dressed in field hospitals. "America" worked its magic on schoolgirls of the era as well, as witnessed in the fact that it was sung by the women who made bandages to send to the front. Regardless of gender, then, by the start of the Civil War Smith's "national hymn" had been turned into a totem of nationalist fervor. As C. A. Browne writes, "America" "nerved" this generation "in the hour of their country's peril."[6]

Nonetheless, as demonstrated in chapters 2 and 3, not all Americans embraced Smith's "America" either before or during the war. Boston's public schools required that all students join in singing "America" at the beginning of each day's classes. When Eli Biddle, a seventeen-year-old African American student, refused to do so in early 1863, he was suspended from school. Later that day, while roaming the streets of Boston, Biddle encountered a recruiter for the newly formed Massachusetts Fifty-fourth Colored Infantry. He enlisted, willing to fight in the attempt to create a country that he had refused to sing of as if it already existed.[7] Like Biddle, many Americans, North and South, black and white, saw the war as an opportunity to remake the nation. Their conflicting visions of the nation were in turn reflected in their complicated relationships to and competing versions of "America."

Battle Songs: "When the Wild Tempests Rave"

Military and civilian leaders on both sides regarded music as an integral part of the war effort. "Good martial, national music is one of the advantages we have over the rebels," editorialized the *New York Herald* on 11 January 1862. "I don't believe we can have an army without music," Robert E. Lee remarked in 1864. A Confederate private recalled that after a stirring band concert, "I felt at the time that I could whip a whole brigade of the enemy." Based on such enthusiasms, both the Union and the Confederacy enlisted thousands of musicians and put them to use in every aspect of wartime operations. In fact, stories of inspirational songs were a regular feature of battlefield reporting and, after the war, of soldiers' memoirs. Along with fulfilling such obviously political and military functions, music also offered soldiers a diversion from the monotony of camp life and the deadly prospect of battle. Because of the dramatic expansion of musical training and performance in the United States during the two decades prior to the war, many soldiers had received some musical training and had some experience in choral groups or bands. Many soldiers brought instruments—guitars, flutes, violins, banjos—with them, and played solo or in small groups. In addition to these individual performers and ad hoc groups, most regiments or brigades had their own bands and glee clubs that provided evening concerts for the entertainment of the troops. The civil war, then, was a distinctly musical affair.[8]

Among the popular forms of musical performance of the period, perhaps none was as ubiquitous as the brass band. Indeed, the mass production of valve instruments after 1840 spawned what Charles Wolfe has described as a "national boom in the popularity of the community brass band." By 1856 brass bands were the most common medium of musical performance in Boston and many other cities and accompanied most public functions and ceremonies. Many bands were associated with local militias and, after the Civil War began, assisted community efforts to recruit soldiers by playing patriotic songs, including "America." Thus the Reverend Elias Nason's recollection that "as these old melodies arose from well-trained bands, the braves came forth from peaceful homes to do battle in the sacred cause of liberty." When the militias were called up for service, many bands affiliated with them also enlisted en masse. Some of these bands, such as the famed thirty-five-piece band of the Seventh New York State Militia, Patrick Gilmore's Twenty-fourth Massachusetts, and P. V. Collis's "Zouaves," were large and of high quality. Furthermore, over one hundred sixteen-piece all-star brigade bands, drawn from the best musicians in the various regimental bands, entertained the troops with twilight concerts when not on the march.[9]

On national holidays, regimental and brigade bands offered concerts of patriotic music. For example, two companies from Charlestown, Massachusetts, camped one mile outside Alexandria, Virginia, observed the occasion of Bunker Hill Day on 17 May 1861 with a drill and concert. In a nearby grove of oaks, long tables were laden with fruits, meats, pastries, berries, and "tea and punch, but no other spiritous liquors." "After the feast came the patriotism," in the form of speeches by several officers and the singing of an ode, "For Bunker Hill," written by George H. Dow to the tune of "America." Dow's song draws strength for a difficult present from the glories of the past, singing: "For, brothers side by side / We stand, in manly pride, / Beneath the shadow wide / Of Bunker Hill." Indeed, "The memory of that spot, / Ne'er by one man forgot, / Protects us here!" "Oh, how grandly it sounded through the woods!" wrote the correspondent for the *Boston Journal*, as the Michigan Regiment's band "took up the harmony when they had finished, and it crashed louder than before." Linking their cause with the American Revolution, the singers entertained an audience including a "crowd of sable sons and daughters of the Old Dominion." Columns of "ten thousand men in review, with their banners waving in the air" marched with the Capitol building and the unfinished Washington Monument visible in the distance. "It was," the reporter observed, "a scene of indescribable beauty and grandeur."[10]

The melody of "America" was also adapted for use in Confederate military ceremonies. For example, a new song, "God Bless Our Southern Land," was "respectfully inscribed" for Major General J. B. Magruder at a public reception and military review held in his honor in Houston on 20 January 1863. The song opens with a line that was popular during the war, "God bless our Southern land," and ends with this verse:

> "O Lord, our God! Arise,
> Scatter our enemies,
>   And make them fall!"
> And when, with peace restor'd,
> Each man lays by the sword,
> May we with joy record
>   Thy mercies all.[11]

"God Bless our Southern Land" thus foregrounds its appropriation of "God Save the King" by placing the first three lines of the last stanza, lifted directly from the British anthem, in quotation marks. And much like the original version of "God Save the King," published in 1744 and then popularized the following year when Bonnie Prince Charlie threatened George II's hold on the kingdom (see chapter 1), so "God Bless our Southern Land," published during similarly dangerous times, musically and spiritually links its singers to an idealized Confederate nation. Indeed, the song expresses the purposes of the war (to secure white "liberty" and "freedom"), praises the battlefield exploits of the assembled troops, celebrates the heroism of the guest of honor, and imagines a postwar nation reconstructed on Confederate terms.

Military music during the Civil War was not restricted to the camp and parade ground, however, as musicians quickened the step of marching troops and propelled them into battle. A band played during the war's initial engagement at Fort Sumter, and bands were on the field during every other major battle of the war, including Gettysburg, where ten bands took the field only to have some members lay aside their instruments in the midst of the battle to take up arms. In some divisions of the Union army, soldiers were ordered to sing "The Battle-Cry of Freedom" as they engaged the enemy. Duryea's Zouaves, dressed in their signature crimson uniforms, charged the batteries at Shiloh after singing a choral arrangement of "The Star-Spangled Banner." While virtually every regiment had its own band at the start of the war, this seemed like a luxury as the carnage progressed; most regiment bands were thus dissolved by 1862. In fact, in a chilling turn of events that demonstrates the rapid shift from a heroic, music-enhanced war of glory to a horrific, death-laden march of suicide, many of the remaining bandsmen served in battle as stretcher-bearers and assistants to field surgeons, while the remaining regimental bands played hospital concerts for the wounded and dying. "America," which expressed the high purpose of the wounded soldier's sacrifice, was among the most commonly played songs in those Union hospital concerts. In a fit of improbable enthusiasm, the abolitionist poet John Greenleaf Whittier wrote to Samuel Smith that "the sick and wounded have forgotten their pain in listening to it."[12]

Most songs played by camp bands were popular and sentimental rather than patriotic or rousing. Soldiers' favorites included Root's "Just before the Battle, Mother," "Home, Sweet Home," "Somebody's Darling," "The Yellow Rose of Texas," and the best-selling song of the war, "When This Cruel War Is Over." Soldiers generally preferred popular songs from before the war to those newly crafted for the conflict, as these songs expressed the common sentiments of soldiers who yearned for home and loved ones while imagining the resumption of life after war. Many soldiers wrote of the importance of popular songs in relieving the drudgery and terror of military life: "We boys used to yell at the band for music to cheer us up when we were tramping along so tired that we could hardly drag one foot after the other," recalled one veteran. The soldiers themselves performed most music in camp and on the march, where they sang as individuals, in small groups and glee clubs, and occasionally in large-scale "musical sprees" or "jubilees" in which many soldiers joined voices. Informal singing around the campfire was a favorite diversion for the troops of both sides.[13]

In yet another example of how war creates economic opportunities, music publishers sold inexpensively printed songs and songbooks specifically for the use of soldiers. Single songs were printed on broadsides and in folding illustrated cards; collections were published in sheet folios and pocket books; anthologies, such as *The Camp Fire Songster* and *The Flag of Our Union Songster*, were specifically advertised for the use of soldiers. Most of these collections included a variety of popular and patriotic songs, traditional hymns, and new songs about the war. For example, *The Soldier's Companion*, published in 1863, was among the most popular of the Civil War pocket-songbooks and appeared in many editions. "Dedicated to the Defenders of their Country in the Field, by their friends at home," *The Soldier's Companion* included eighty songs and a series of "selections from the scriptures" designed to serve the different dimensions of military life, including mourning, camp entertainment, ceremonies, recruitment, marching, and worship services. In the preface of *The Soldier's Companion*, the compilers express the hope that their collection will "make the camp-fire more cheerful, and the solitary watch less lonely."

Eleven of the eighty songs in *The Soldier's Companion* are set to the tune of "America." In fact, Smith's song, listed as the "National Hymn," is the first song in *The Soldier's Companion*, with four alternate sets of lyrics printed on the facing page. The alternate lyrical versions cover a remarkable range of topics and perspectives appropriate to various concerns and occasions in the life of the soldier. For example, "Praise to the God of Harvest" was designed for use in thanksgiving observances in which soldiers away from their farms could sing of the cycles of planting and harvesting:

> The God of harvest praise;
> Hands, hearts, and voices raise
> With sweet accord;
> From field to garner throng,
> Bearing your sheaves along,
> And in your harvest-song
> Bless ye the Lord.

In contrast to "Praise to the God of Harvest," which spoke of the rural concerns of farmers, not soldiers, several versions of "America" included in *The Soldier's Companion* speak to the specific needs and circumstances of soldiers, who, as the implied singers of the songs, reflect on the purposes of their sacrifices. "The Soldier's Prayer," for example, by Robert Nicoll, asks:

> Lord, from thy blessed throne,
> Soldiers look down upon:
>   God save the land!
> Teach us true liberty;
> Make us from tyrants free;
> Let our homes happy be;
>   God save the land!

Other versions of "America" emphasize that the fate of the nation depends on the courage of its soldiers, yet in a nod to an issue that clearly occupied elites fearful of disorderly mobs of wayward ruffians and drunken soldiers, some songs urge unity through sobriety. Thus the moralizing tone of John Pierpont's "Temperance Hymn." Most alternate versions of "America" in *The Soldier's Companion*, however, like Smith's original, include prayerful requests for divine protection. For example, whereas Smith's "America" asks God to "protect us by thy might," "A Prayer for our Country" adapts this request to the specific needs of the Civil War:

> God bless our native land!
> Firm may she ever stand
>   Through storm and night!
> When the wild tempests rave,
> Ruler of wind and wave,
> Do thou our country save
>   By thy great might.

John Pierpont's "National Hymn," also set to the tune of "America," is less oblique. Instead of veiling the war in meteorological metaphors, Pierpont asks for God's direct intervention on the battlefield against the sinful, traitorous foe:

> Should treason's bloody hand
> Be lifted, and the land
>   Quake with alarm,
> Then clothe her with thy might,—
> The strength that robes the Right,—
> And let thy lightning smite
>   The traitor's arm.[14]

The alternate versions of "America" quoted here sought to link soldiers' actions to national purposes and traditions, to portray their efforts as blessed with (or at least as deserving of) God's support, and even to sing their praises as righteous agents of God, whose "lightning," through them, will "smite the traitor's arm." Most of the lyrical variations on "America" in *The Soldier's Companion* thus promoted military service and spoke to the ceremonial and spiritual needs of military life. Indeed, soldiers used the national patriotic songs in *The Soldier's*

Companion to express the causes for which they fought, to proclaim in song the distinctive virtues of their side, and to denounce their opponent. As in most earlier versions of "America," the chief purpose of the versions in *The Soldier's Companion* was to enable a sense of patriotism. For example, on the eve of the second battle of Bull Run, Union soldiers sang "America" in camp. One of these singing soldiers, Colonel E. H. Haskell, later testified to "how much this glorious hymn had to do with stimulating that patriotic spirit which welded together the Grand Army and Navy of the Union."[15]

Confederate soldiers also sang "America." As demonstrated on the cover of the broadside version of "God Save the Southern Land," Southerners too invoked both the melody of "America" and the original phrasing of "God Save the King" to appeal for divine blessings, to honor the "soldier's friend," and to "benefit Soldiers and Needy Families" (see figure 4.1). The popular *Soldier's Hymn Book*, published by the South Carolina Tract Society in 1862 and reprinted several times, includes five sets of lyrics to the tune of "America." In one untitled version Smith's four popular stanzas are reprinted with only one modification: instead of "land of the Pilgrim's Pride," which is clearly identified with New England, the untitled Confederate version reads "Land of the Southron's pride, / From every mountain side / Let freedom ring." By using Smith's lyrics, the song claims elements of the former national identity while establishing a new nation. The Confederate "America" thus proclaims the slaveholding South to be the true "sweet land of liberty," where freedom rings "from every mountainside," and for which the soldier prays: "still may our land be bright / with freedom's holy light." Hence, in a reversal of Pierpont's appeal to God to protect northern troops "with thy might," this alternate version of "America" hopes that the Confederate army will be "protected by thy might, / Great God, our King!" Of the remaining four versions of "America" in *The Soldier's Hymn Book*, three are generally apolitical religious hymns, but one ("Our land, with mercies crowned") clearly expresses the ambitions of white Southern nationalism. Like "America," "Our Land" invokes divine blessings on the nation and its military efforts:

> Still, Lord defend the right,
> In freedom's fearful fight,
>   From all its foes.
> A nation now create,
> And lead its marches great,
> And build its pillared state
>   And grand[t?] repose.

While the lyrics are specific to the conflict at hand, they simultaneously imagine a future Confederate nation architecturally embodied in its "pillared state."

Figure 4.1. The cover of *God Save the Southern Land*, an 1864 song sheet. Courtesy of Emory University Special Collections.

"Our Land" thus asserts a new national identity sung to the melody of the old national hymn.[16]

Two additional sets of alternative lyrics to the tune of "America" were published in the second edition of *The Soldier's Hymn Book*, which was printed in 1863 in a run of thirty thousand copies. Both of the 1863 versions are explicit expressions of Confederate nationalism ("Our loved Confederacy," "May we a Nation be") that acknowledge the current crisis.[17] Much like their northern enemies, southern soldiers sang such songs both as appeals to God's blessing and protection and as pledges of loyalty to a new nation. That they sang such appeals and pledges with the same melody by which they had once sung the praises of the now forsaken Union indicates again how powerfully appropriation functions as a means of cultural production. Indeed, the alternative versions of "America" in *The Soldier's Hymn Book* and other Confederate songbooks reflect the conflicting nationalist impulses of a South that is rooted in sentimental attachments to a forsaken Union (and its most cherished melodies) yet fired with the separatist imagination of a new white nation.

Early in the war, some supporters of the Confederacy believed that instead of creating its own flag and national songs, the South should claim those of the United States. A Louisiana correspondent explained in *Dwight's Journal of Music* in 1861 that these songs have been "admired and loved" by Southerners "from earliest boyhood to the present moment." "These tunes and anthems of right belong to the South," the anonymous writer insisted; "instead of abandoning, let us claim them as our own legitimate property." Likewise, a Charleston correspondent to the *Richmond Examiner* maintained in 1861 that "The Star-Spangled Banner" should never be surrendered to the Yankees because it is "Southern in its origin, in sentiments, poetry and song; in its association with chivalrous deeds, it is ours." The honorable and gentlemanly South, it was argued, maintained the principles represented in these national emblems and anthems, while the money-grubbing industrialists of the North had abandoned them. Other commentators insisted that the songs and symbols of the Confederacy should express a distinct national identity. For example, much as early American nationalists had denounced reliance on British arts and literature, so A. J. Bloch of Mobile prefaced his *Southern Flowers* sheet music series with the admonition that "the South must not only fight her own battles but sing her own songs & dance to music composed by her own children."[18]

"America"'s employment by both sides during the Civil War was not unique—many songs crossed the lines. In fact, Bell Irwin Wiley's studies of soldiers' letters and diaries reveal considerable overlap in the songs popular among Union and Confederate soldiers, including especially sentimental songs that had been popular before the war. Regional provenance and symbolism was sometimes overlooked in such popular wartime songs. Julia Ward Howe's "Battle Hymn of the Republic," for example, borrowed its melody from the abolitionist song "John Brown's Body," which in turn derived from a Southern Methodist camp-meeting hymn. "Dixie's Land," which premiered as the finale in a New York minstrel show in 1859, spread rapidly through the South after a New Orleans production and its subsequent publication in 1860. By 1861 "Dixie" had become the Confederate battle hymn and national anthem. Yet in a deliciously ironic twist indicative of the blurred lines of association and allegiance of both the period and popular music in general, the song was composed by an African American and popularized by Dan Emmett, the son of an Ohio abolitionist. The white supremacist's national anthem, a song written by an African American and popularized by the son of an abolitionist, was thus played at the inauguration of Confederate president Jefferson Davis. Despite the South's claiming "Dixie" as its own, the song remained a favorite of northern troops and their political leaders, including President Lincoln. In fact, the popularity of "Dixie" among northern troops and citizens drove some to devise alternate lyrics more suitable to the Union cause. For example, T. M. Cooley's version, published in the *Ann Arbor News* of 4 June 1861, used the melody and some of the original lyrics of "Dixie" to scold the South as traitors to the Revolution: "And men with rebel shouts and thunder, / Tear our good old flag asunder, / Far away, far away, far away, Dixie land." When the troops of the New York Sixty-ninth regiment opened camp on Arlington Heights on 30 May 1861 they celebrated the raising of their flag with a "new national song" set to the tune of "Dixie," with "some fourteen hundred voices thundering forth the refrain." In a remarkable example of how deeply Americans felt the connection between music and culture, song and politics, it has been claimed that shortly after the surrender of the Confederate army at Appomattox, Lincoln ordered a band in Washington to play "Dixie," observing that "as we had captured the rebel army, we had also captured the rebel tune."[19]

The Union's songs were also "captured" by the Confederates. "The Star-Spangled Banner," for example, was converted to "The Flag of Secession," with each verse ending: "And the flag of secession in triumph doth wave / O'er the land of the free and the home of the brave." Soldiers regularly seized weapons and supplies from the other side; songs were simply one more item to be captured and converted. Brander Matthews wrote of "The Songs of the War" in the *Century Magazine* in 1887 that "In the hour of battle a war-tune is subject to the right of capture, and, like the cannon taken from the enemy, it is turned against its maker." Even without such capturing, patriotic songs normally associated with one side sometimes crossed the lines in live performances. The encampments of opposing forces were often in close proximity, and although the next day might find them locked in mortal combat, soldiers of the two sides nonetheless bartered for tobacco, coffee, and other hard-to-find necessities, including song. Indeed, the singing and band music of each side were often clearly audible to the other, and, in a curious show of longed-for solidarity among warring parties, were sometimes performed not only with this audience in mind but with this audience as fellow singers and players. Thus patriotic songs associated with one side were sometimes embraced by soldiers of the other as sentimental evocations of life before the war. Under these circumstances, even "America" and "The Battle Hymn of the Republic," songs clearly affiliated with the Union cause, "were not objectionable to the Confederates."

In the spring of 1863, for example, when Union and Confederate troops were positioned on opposite sides of the Rappahannock River, the regimental bands played patriotic songs, such as "The Star-Spangled Banner" or "Dixie," as the troops for the designated side shouted their approval. At taps, however, one of the bands began playing "Home, Sweet Home," and was joined by that of the other side. "As the plaintive air died away across the Rappahannock," writes C. A. Browne, "cheer followed cheer until the hills, so lately resounding with hostile guns, echoed and re-echoed that responsive chord to which even the hearts of enemies could beat in unison."[20]

The question of songs enabling a musical form of impromptu cultural unison where more traditional politics had failed arises again and again in Civil War memoirs, thus indicating how aesthetics may serve as symbolic answers to historical crises that elude resolution. Usually, though, these musical moments of unison were short-lived and were seen as enigmatic and confusing. For example, in his memoir of the war, Confederate Lieutenant L. D. Young of Kentucky recalled hearing the Union bands play during his encampment near Sherman's forces after the battle of Chattanooga:

> Softly and sweetly the music from their bands as they played the national airs were wafted up and over the summit of the mountain. Somehow, some way, in some inexplicable and unseen manner, "Hail Columbia," "America," and the "Star-Spangled Banner" sounded sweeter than I had ever before heard them, and filled my soul with feelings that I could not describe or forget. It haunted me for days, but never shook my loyalty to the Stars and Bars or relaxed my efforts in behalf of our cause.[21]

Home Fronts: "Our Firm United Band"

By the time of the Civil War, the most widely employed venue for musical performance in America was the home. American manufacturers were producing twenty thousand pianos a year by 1860, many of them intended for home use. Family and friends gathered in parlors to sing and play music together, and during the war the typical family repertoire included many patriotic and military songs. The rapid and widespread dissemination of songs written during the war was facilitated by the prewar development of the American sheet music industry, particularly by steam-powered printing and typesetting machinery that permitted the quick release of songs in response to unfolding events. For example, sheet music for "The Palmetto State Song, music composed and respectfully dedicated to the signers of the ordinance of secession unanimously passed in convention at Charleston, S.C., Decr. 20th, 1860," was sold on the streets of Charleston within days of secession. George F. Root's song "The First Gun Is

Fired! May God Protect the Right!" was published on 15 April 1861, just three days after the attack on Fort Sumter. In addition to penning and publishing such topical songs quickly, Root also produced some of the most popular Union songs during the Civil War, including "Tramp, Tramp, Tramp" and "The Battle Cry of Freedom." He had once served as Lowell Mason's chief instructional assistant in the Boston school music program and, according to Michael Broyles, was more "Mason's musical heir" than any other composer. Like his famous mentor, Root was convinced of the extraordinary rhetorical power of song to deepen convictions and to mobilize individuals and groups. He was apparently not alone in this conviction; President Lincoln wrote to him regarding the persuasive power of his songs on behalf of the war effort: "You have done more than a hundred generals and a thousand orators." Root was later honored by veterans in 1889 as "The Maker of War Songs," "whose words can nerve the arm / Of freemen to their noblest trying, / And urge them on." Root's songs "inspired the living, cheered the dying, / Till war was gone."[22]

The combination of Mason's push to bring music into every home, school, and church and advancing means of inexpensive mass printing and distribution created the cultural and economic conditions necessary for "hit" songs such as Root's "Tramp, Tramp, Tramp." Indeed, like Mason, whose children's choirs and music collections had popularized "America," Root had a keen sense of marketing and publishing and was committed to the production of simple songs that even the musically challenged could perform. Prior to the war, new songs were popularized by professional singing groups and then published for home use. The market for songs, new and old, however, was dramatically expanded with the onset of war. In fact, more than ten thousand songs were published during the course of the war, over two thousand in its first year alone. Civilians supporting each side strove to develop new songs that would steel the troops, stir support on the home front, and celebrate the causes for which they were fighting. Abolitionist poet Julia Ward Howe composed the lyrics to "The Battle Hymn of the Republic" after watching McClellan's troops on parade in Washington. "My husband was beyond the age of military service, my eldest son but a stripling," she recalled; "I could not leave my nursery to follow the march of our armies." Her lyrics were published in the *Atlantic Monthly* in February 1862 and were quickly adopted by Union soldiers and their supporters. Patriotic poems that appeared during the war were quickly converted to song. John Sloan Gibbons published his poem "We Are Coming, Father Abraham" anonymously in the *New York Evening Post* of 16 July 1862 in response to General McClellan's call for three hundred thousand additional Union soldiers. Sixteen different composers had devised tunes for Gibbons's lyrics by the end of the year. Although limited by shortages of ink and paper, Confederate sheet music companies published over 650 pieces of music, many on war-related themes.[23]

What later historians and critics have come to call the "culture industry" may thus, in no small part, be traced back to the early phases of musical production and distribution during the Civil War.

Much like the early reform efforts of the public school music advocates, abolitionists, and temperance and women's suffrage activists discussed in chapters 2 and 3, these Civil War manifestations of America's entrance into a new world of mass culture often involved a tone of earnest, high moralizing. For example, George F. Root recalled in his autobiography, *The Story of a Musical Life*, that at the news of the war's beginning, the "bustling, cheery life" of Chicago "became suddenly grave and serious." "With what different eyes we saw everything around us," Root writes. "It was not the same sunshine that made the city so bright yesterday, and these were not the same faces of neighbors that then nodded so light-heartedly as they passed. The old flag had been fired upon, and that act had waked into stern determination the patriotism of every loyal heart." This awakened stern patriotism found expression in the thousands of topical songs written specifically for the war, yet newspapers on both sides also editorialized that the war was an opportunity to "purify national character" and to reestablish the patriotic spirit of the Revolutionary era. "Let no one feel that our present troubles are deplorable," wrote Horace Greeley, "in view of the majestic development of Nationality and Patriotism which they have occasioned." These hopes that the war would provide an opportunity for purifying the nation, for inculcating a new majesty amid what many reformers saw as a period of slackened morals, demonstrate that even war was viewed by high-minded reformers and commentators alike as an occasion for engaging in mass persuasion, mass moralizing, and mass reform. "The patriotic appeal" of Civil War "parlor music," writes Crawford, "lifted the matter, or at least it seemed to, to a higher, more public plane, so that the citizen who sang or heard patriotic music could tingle for a cause rather than merely for himself."24

Wars are sustained by civilians. Even when they are unacquainted with the deep political, economic, and institutional forces leading to war, civilians provide the personnel and financial support that make wars possible. During the Civil War, when what we call today the mass media was in its formative stages, widely distributed songs were used to encourage civilian enlistment, to build support for the sacrifices necessary for war, and to prompt less-than-enthusiastic civil warriors to "tingle for a cause." It comes as no surprise, then, to realize that antebellum patriotic songs such as "America" acquired new and more desperately urgent meanings in the context of the Civil War. Perhaps surprising, however, is the extent to which songs like "America" saturated parts of the culture that were less obviously tied to the machinery of war and propaganda. "America," for example, while serving the multiple Civil War functions already described, also remained a fixture of the public school classroom, only now with

explicit connections to the war effort. Mark Twain's report for the San Francisco *Morning Call* on the city's July Fourth celebration in 1864 noted the connections typically drawn in civic observances among schoolchildren, "America,"
and the war effort. Children from twelve schools marched in uniforms and military formation. The boys carried banners, including the motto "We are Coming, Father Abraham," coined earlier in the war to promote enlistment. Three
hundred girls rode in a procession of furniture cars, including one "gorgeously
costumed as the Goddess of Liberty." The program, held in the Metropolitan
Theater, included an overture of "National Airs" played by local bands and a
series of union war songs (including "The Battle Cry of Freedom," "The
Union," and "O Wrap the Flag around Me, Boys"). The program concluded—
in a gesture that would have warmed Mason's heart—with a children's choir
performing "America."[25] Thus, much as Mason used children as powerful tools
of persuasion for his evangelical, nationalist, class-specific socializing zeal, so the
Civil War found Americans again relying on the uncanny power of singing children to persuade themselves and their neighbors of the righteousness and sheer
historical necessity of their actions.

Two years before Twain's story, G. W. Rogers published "War," a song set to
the tune of "America" that chronicled the grim reality of war's presence in daily
life. In the nation's "dark hour," Rogers notes, "Men meet in deadly fray; /
Arms clash from day to day, / Mid cannons' roar." While these bleak lines emphasize the horror of war, most Civil War variations of "America" stressed the
need for heroism and dedication. For example, Frank Moore's anthology *Songs
of the Soldiers* included both Smith's original "America" and two alternate versions. Although promoted as a collection of songs used by Union soldiers,
Moore also marketed it to civilians, who were urged to sing in solidarity with
those in combat. "The Patriot's Hymn," by Reverend J. F. Mines, chaplain of
the Second Maine Regiment, is set to the tune of "America" and concludes
Moore's volume with a powerful call to rededicated effort, for "if the word must
be / Guardian of Liberty, / Unsheath its blade!" (see appendix A). In keeping
with the song's self-proclaimed status as a hymn, Mines's first verse closes with
repeated pleas to "Pray God that wars may cease, / Pray God to give us peace,
/ Pray God our hearts release / From discord's way." Appearing in 1864, when
northern support for the war had diminished and the peace candidacy of General McClellan threatened to unseat President Lincoln, "The Patriot's Hymn"
embraced the yearning for peace while simultaneously urging unity for the war
effort. In singing the song, civilians join with soldiers as a "firm united band"
sharing unabated antipathy toward a foe damned with the sung curse "Death
be the traitor's doom / Perish his name." Such denunciations were common
features in the songs of both sides, although, as noted previously, perhaps more
so on the home front than on the battlefield. Indeed, whereas soldiers were

forced into daily and therefore at least sometimes humanizing contact with the songs, stories, and sentiments of their foes, in "the Civil War parlor," Crawford observes, "*Ideology is absolute*; ambiguities and measured feelings are not expressed, and the motive of revenge is never far below the surface."[26]

"America" was also sung by Confederate civilians. In a combination of socializing and nationalizing evangelical fervor that would have made Mason and Woodbridge proud, Confederate children were taught to sing new lyrics set to the old melody in Sabbath schools. *The Sabbath School Wreath*, an 1864 songbook produced "for the benefit of the children in the Confederate states," includes an alternate version, as does *The Cymbal: A Collection of Hymns for Sabbath Schools* (1864). It is striking how many of the songs in these collections address the deaths that formed an indelible experience for millions of children during the war. In the last lines of "God Bless Our Sunday School," for example, the children sang for practical relief from the disruptions they faced in their education by the deaths of their teachers: "when death's arrows fly, / And useful teachers die, / Their places still supply— / God bless our school."[27]

"America" was further institutionalized in the Union during the Civil War through its use in public ceremonies and holiday programs, including the new national holiday of Thanksgiving. Sarah Josepha Hale, the influential editor of *Godey's Lady's Book*, had campaigned for decades for an official Thanksgiving holiday. By 1859 her efforts had produced celebrations of the holiday in thirty states and three territories. The onset of the Civil War gave new impetus to her efforts to establish Thanksgiving as a federal holiday, an occasion when patriotic songs, stories, and sermons might "awaken in American hearts the love of home and country." As the war quickly devolved into wholesale butchery and as support for the cause was understandably wavering, Lincoln was on the watch for symbols of and occasions for national spirit. Responding to Hale's activism and his own political imperatives, he signed a proclamation declaring the holiday on 3 October 1863. Thanksgiving had traditionally been a state holiday; Lincoln's proclamation thus completed what Gideon Welles describes as the "Nationalizing process," as the proclamation called on Americans to acknowledge the losses of the war and to pray for the restoration of the nation in "peace, harmony, tranquility and Union."[28] And so Thanksgiving was institutionalized as a nationally recognized wartime holiday linking home and hearth with the nation. Furthermore, "America" was typically the opening or closing song for public wartime Thanksgiving programs and the one number that audiences would generally join in singing.

The practice of having the audience join in singing "America" became a regular part of public ceremonies during the Civil War. For example, when the Washington Handel and Haydn Society played "America" at the third anniversary meeting of the Christian Commission, a civilian relief agency, on 29

January 1865 in the U.S. House of Representatives, the audience, including President Lincoln, joined in. After news of Lee's 9 April 1865 surrender, the crowd at the White House joined in singing "America" before Lincoln spoke. The fourth and final annual meeting of the Christian Commission was held on 11 February 1866, with the House chamber draped in memory of Lincoln, who had been assassinated on 14 April 1865, five days after Lee's surrender. Featured performer Philip Phillips, the "Singing Pilgrim," sang "America," and again the audience was asked to sing along.[29] Hence the Civil War ended much as it had begun, with Americans singing their politics, only now in tones somber and melancholy rather than heroic and militaristic.

The Mission of the War: "Cursed Be the Slaver's Might"

While each of the Civil War's combatants believed their cause was righteous, supporters of both the Union and the Confederacy disagreed about what had caused the war and about its desired outcomes. While these rhetorical struggles for interpretation have long outlived the physical conflict, they were also heated during the war, notably in the Union's slow and painfully contested embrace of emancipation. Given the arguments offered thus far regarding the relationships among song and politics, music and consciousness, it is no surprise to learn that music was an important medium for expressing the varied views of both soldiers and civilians regarding the mission of the war. Indeed, while Northerners sang of preserving the Union and fighting for freedom, Confederates sang of themselves as fighting for liberty, rebelling against an oppressive, machine-infested, money-grubbing, heartless Union. Emily Washington's "Confederate Song of Freedom," for example, urged soldiers to "Strike home for Liberty," while a song dedicated to "The Confederate Flag," performed in Portsmouth, Virginia, in 1861, pronounced the banner an "Emblem of liberty—symbol of truth."[30]

Nonetheless, despite such tributes to Liberty and truth, the southern version of these terms was ultimately rooted in the right to hold others in slavery. In fact, the Confederate constitution required that all states permit and protect slavery. Confederate vice-president Alexander Stephens made clear how fundamental slavery was to the construction of Southern national identity in his 21 March 1861 speech in Savannah's Athenaeum, where he observed that slavery was the "rock" on which Jefferson had correctly predicted that "the old Union would split." But whereas some of the drafters of the U.S. Constitution had believed that slavery was an evil that should pass away, "our new Government is founded upon exactly the opposite ideas; its foundations are laid, its cornerstone rests, upon the great truth that the negro is not equal to the white man; that slavery, subordination to the superior race, is his natural and moral condition." Stephens's emphatic explanation was applauded by his immediate audience and widely reprinted in Union and Confederate newspapers. Most northern abolitionists agreed with Stephens's assessment of the essential issue; African American abolitionists in particular had argued from the outset of the war that its stakes were inevitably slavery and freedom. "A blind man can see," John S. Rock told his audience at a meeting of the Massachusetts Anti-Slavery Society on 23 January 1862, "that the present war is an effort to nationalize, perpetuate, and extend slavery in this country."[31]

Despite such proclamations, most Union political and military leaders initially resisted the idea that the war had anything to do with slavery. Slavery, after all, existed in several states fighting for the Union, and in those where it was prohibited, abolition and abolitionists were unpopular. Boston mayor Joseph M. Wightman cautioned President Lincoln that in his city "and I believe in a large majority of the other cities and towns . . . the mingling of questions in relation to slavery with the crushing out of the present rebellion is viewed with the strongest feelings of disapprobation." This disapprobation was so strong nationally that early slave confiscation and emancipation orders issued by Union generals in Missouri and New Orleans were overturned by Lincoln. Indeed, at the outset of the war, Lincoln and powerful forces in every state opposed vigorously any arguments claiming that emancipation was an aim of the conflict. Within the Union army, debates over the meaning of the war were reflected in song. For example, the popular Hutchinson Family Singers from New Hampshire had included antislavery songs in their programs long before the Civil War and continued to do so during the conflict. The Hutchinsons helped popularize Root's new song "The Battle Cry of Freedom" and sang songs about the war in every public performance, but when the Hutchinsons performed for soldiers in the Army of the Potomac, singing that "In vain the bells of war shall ring" until the end "of slavery forever," the concert was disrupted by hissing from soldiers in the audience. Two days later, they were expelled from camp by General McClellan, the Union commander, who insisted that abolition was not the mission of the war. The Hutchinsons appealed to Lincoln, who pronounced their version of one of Whittier's antislavery verses "just the character of song that I desire the soldiers to hear" and ordered their readmission to the camps.[32] Nonetheless, the idea that the war was for the preservation of the union, not the abolition of slavery, persisted throughout the conflict and after.

In the first two years of the war, most popular Union war songs did not identify slavery as its cause, nor did they embrace abolition as the war's aim. James Walden's "God Save Our Native Land," published in the Sunday *New York Times* in 1861, is typical (see appendix A). It blends lyrical elements of "The Star-Spangled Banner" ("home of the free," "Long may our banner wave / Over the free and brave"), "God Save the King," and "America," which is designated as the melody for a song in support of a war to protect the nation "From the invader's hand." These "invaders" are "ruthless traitors" and "lawless bands" who "aim / To crush our nation's fame, / Yet still, in Freedom's name, / We cling to thee!" In fact, in a passage that typifies northern sentiments, Walden appeals to God to help the Union crush the insurrection: "O Lord! when, hand to hand, / Brothers as foes shall stand, / Shield thou the right!" These denunciations are leveled at "Brothers" marked as traitors not because of their defense of slavery but because in seceding from the Union they have "shatter[ed] freedom's shrine." Indeed, in Walden's (and many others') view, the war was primarily an effort to reestablish the previous Union, to restore its currently compromised white brotherhood.[33]

While ultimately committed to combating this version of white nationalism, abolitionists were placed in particularly difficult positions by the Civil War. Abolitionist meetings, fundraising activities, public events, and publications declined early in the war as many antislavery activists devoted their energies to what were perceived as the more urgent need of defending the Union. Those who remained active often turned to variations on national songs to help associate their understandings of the war's proper mission with the newly aroused patriotism of the times. "America," both in its original form and in numerous lyrical variations, was among the songs most frequently used to promote abolition as the war's primary objective. Among such revisionists, perhaps none were as successful as abolitionist Harriet Beecher Stowe, who wrote new lyrics to the tune of "America" for the flag-raising ceremony at Andover Theological Seminary on 5 June 1861, shortly after the outbreak of hostilities. Stowe's sensational 1852 novel *Uncle Tom's Cabin* had added renewed vigor to the abolitionist campaign and broadened its appeal. Published in book form after its serialization in the *National Era*, *Uncle Tom's Cabin* sold an astonishing half-million copies in five years, and (along with the despised Fugitive Slave Act) galvanized northern antislavery sentiment. Although probably apocryphal, Lincoln's famous greeting to Stowe on first meeting her in 1862, "So this is the little lady who started this big war," holds at least a grain of truth.[34]

By 1861, Harriet Beecher Stowe and her family had moved from Brunswick, Maine, where *Uncle Tom's Cabin* was written, to Andover, where Stowe's husband, Calvin, was a professor at the seminary. Ninety Andover seminary students organized themselves into a company (the "Havelock Grays") and drilled on the campus along with boys from Phillips Academy. The Stowes' son, Fred, had dropped out of medical school to enlist in the Seventy-third Ohio of the Army of the Potomac. Sixty-five Andover students and alumni served in the war, and many of those who remained behind assisted in the war effort on the home front. The Lockhart Society, a student choral group, sang "America" and other patriotic songs at public ceremonies and enlistment rallies. The performance of Stowe's alternative "America" at Andover must therefore have had particular resonance for those assembled both because of their deep personal investments in the war and also because it was in his student lodgings at the Andover Theological Seminary in the winter of 1831 that Samuel Smith had written the lyrics to "America." Indeed, the association of both Smith and his song with the school was a subject of local pride. Furthermore, Stowe was personally acquainted with Smith, as her father, Lyman Beecher, was among those Boston elites responsible for the first performance of "America" at her brother Edward's Park Street Church on 4 July 1831. Shortly after its premiere, Lyman Beecher left for Ohio to head the Lane Seminary. The eighteen-day "Lane Debates" on slavery staged in 1834 by Theodore Weld and other students eventually led to the transfer of those students to Oberlin and Lyman Beecher's dismissal and were a formative influence on Stowe's antislavery thinking.[35]

At Andover's 1861 recruitment ceremony, Stowe used Smith's "America" to revise the Union cause as abolitionist and to robe abolitionism in the traditional patriotic sentiments and civic ceremonials associated with Smith's song. When Smith was a student at Andover, the seminary was active in the Colonization Society, but in the mid-1840s Andover formed a small abolition society; by the onset of the Civil War, then, students and faculty joined in pronouncing abolition as the ultimate mission of the conflict. Since its premiere, "America" had been criticized by abolitionists as a false claim to liberty in a land of slavery. Stowe's "Hymn for a Flag-Raising" accordingly modifies and clarifies the claims of Smith's song, as it envisions freedom as something yet to be achieved, as a promise of the American Revolution that might be fulfilled in the Civil War. It comes as no surprise, then, to read in Henry Rowe's *History of Andover Theological Seminary* that the students "thrilled as they sang Mrs. Stowe's original hymn written for the occasion," for in singing Stowe's version of "America" they simultaneously celebrated Andover's progressive history, paid tribute to their illustrious alumnus, and pledged themselves to a righteous cause.[36]

In the opening line, Stowe links the Union cause with the American Revolution, situating her compatriots "Here, where our fathers came." Now, as then, Stowe suggests, the fate and direction of the nation are at stake. Along with this historical positioning, Stowe stresses the rhetorical and imagined nature of the nation, whose walls are "reared in air." More important, though, she articulates the sweeping yet vague promises of Smith's version as a challenge, as a historically specific task requiring citizens to "pledge your heart and hand." In addition, Stowe's lyrics and the performance site suggest divine support for the Union cause that the "God of our fathers" will "Judge and defend." Months before Lincoln would formally redefine the mission of the war, Stowe urges that the fight continue "Till there be not a slave." Indeed, the final verse of Stowe's

"Hymn for a Flag-Raising" is worded as an oath, sworn by seminarians who would be soldiers for abolition:

> God of our fathers! now
> To Thee we raise our vow,
>   Judge and defend;
> Let freedom's banner wave,
> Till there be not a slave,
> Show Thyself strong to save
>   Unto the end.[37]

Along with Harriet Beecher Stowe, Samuel Smith contributed to the association of his famous song with the Union cause and with abolition as the aim of the war. Smith joined the literary battle early in the war, not with a new version of "America" but with a poem that connected the famous song's sentiments and principles to the struggle at hand. His poem, "Thirty-Four," published in the *Essex (Massachusetts) County Register* of 18 September 1861, urges the nation to "marshal the legions for the fight." As in "America," Smith depicts liberty metaphorically as sound, in this case as the "bell of Freedom" whose

> Sound sweeps wildly o'er the land,
>   Sweeps o'er the bounding sea;
> It echoes, from each mountain-top,
>   The anthem of the free;
> It snaps the chain that sin has forged
>   It sings for liberty.[38]

In "Thirty-Four," as in "America," an "anthem of the free" rings "from each mountaintop." However, unlike the generalities of "America," in "Thirty-Four" the eradication of slavery is identified as the necessary precondition of national liberty, thus making explicit in 1861 what was ambiguous in 1831.

Abolitionists not only sought to persuade domestic audiences of the war's rightful mission, but also took their case abroad. In the first year of the war, Union abolitionists such as Stowe and Smith were appalled both by the lack of support they received from British antislavery organizations and by expressions of sympathy for the Confederate cause in the British press and Parliament. The British textile industry's supply of Southern slave-produced cotton was disrupted by the Union naval blockade; torn between its immediate business interests and its long-term commitment to human liberty (or at least the end of slavery), Britain wavered and left open the possibility of diplomatic recognition for the Confederacy. "The Confederate States the first political union built on negro slavery," Stowe wrote in June 1861, and "England the first state to raise the question of recognition." Although Britain generally honored the Union blockade of Southern ports and stayed out of the conflict, its neutrality remained in question through much of the war. Both sides mounted diplomatic campaigns to sway the British government and distributed speakers and printed materials in the hope of influencing the British public. Benjamin Quarles has studied the public speaking tours of Sarah Parker Remond and the other African American abolitionists who operated as "ministers without portfolio" in Britain during the war and has concluded that they had a substantial impact on British public opinion.[39]

In addition to such direct lobbying of the British, both Union and Confederate agitators employed the melody of the unofficial British anthem "God Save the Queen/King" as a vehicle for their appeals to British audiences. For example, "God Save the South," by "R. S. A.," appeared in the *Richmond Dispatch* in 1862 (see appendix A). Like so many Civil War versions of "My Country 'Tis of Thee," the song requests divine support for those "armed in such sacred cause," upon whom "No spot of wrong or shame / Rests on our banner's fame, / Flung forth in freedom's name." From this Confederate perspective, the Union is an "invader" so loathed that even the South's demure daughters sing "Death! death! to every foe, / Says each maiden low: / God save us all!" This "all," however, does not refer to Americans in general, for by the third verse (and for the rest of the song) the line asks instead "God save the South!" The belief that human events were directed by the hand of God was central to Confederate ideology; the early victories of the Confederate forces in turn confirmed for many Southerners the idea that God favored their cause and would assure their victory.[40] Like the British anthem and its early American variations (such as "God Save Great Washington"), "God Save the South" asks for God's protection of both the national leader, Jefferson Davis ("blessings upon him shower," "shield him from wrong"), and the population at large.

Supporters of the Union also made use of "God Save the Queen," sometimes in rebuke of the British. For example, the *New York Evening Post* offered a "New Version of an Old Song" on 29 May 1861, shortly after the *London Times* had editorialized in sympathy with the rebellion (see appendix A). One can imagine the venom with which these brilliantly sarcastic lines must have been sung:

> God save Cotton, our King!
> God save our noble King!
> God save the King!
> Send him the sway he craves,
> Britons his willing slaves,
> "Rule," Cotton! "Rule the waves!"
> God save the King!

This wickedly snide "New Version" was addressed to an implied British audience and "respectfully dedicated to the *London Times*," which had opposed

British emancipation and sided with manufacturers against Lord Shaftesbury's proposed factory reforms.[41] The "New Version" thus warns that if British textile industries, desperate for cotton, send the South "the sway he craves," they will be "his willing slaves," and cotton, not Britannia, will "rule the waves." The parody borrows the title line of the unofficial British anthem "God save the King" to deride the willingness of some Britons to permit cotton interests to dictate policy and monetary greed ("while we our pockets fill") to override antislavery principles long established in British law. In mockingly singing "'Rule,' Cotton! 'Rule the waves!,'" the penultimate line of the final verse also parodies James Thomson's 1740 ode "Rule, Britannia!", which had originally boasted "Rule, Britannia, rule the waves; / Britons never will be slaves." As Suvir Kaul has demonstrated, Thomson's poem "functioned virtually as the anthem of British nationalism and imperialism." The *Post*'s "New Version" of 1861 thus pointedly demonstrates that canonical British claims regarding the empire dovetailed nicely—so nicely as to be embarrassing—with the pretensions of American slaveholders. Along with Union military victories and the profits to be made from wartime trade with the Union, such abolitionist efforts played no small part in persuading the British to eschew formal recognition of or military support for the South.[42]

Along with these trans-Atlantic means of persuasion, American civilians also used the melody of "God Save the King" to explain the higher—and ultimately antislavery, if not abolitionist—purposes of the wartime sacrifices undertaken by soldiers, friends, and family. For example, George G. W. Morgan's 1861 "God Protect Us!" was "dedicated to England's gallant sons, THE NEW YORK BRITISH RIFLE REGIMENT, by their admiring fellow-countrymen":

> O Lord, we'd lead the van,
> E'er in behalf of man,
>   When held in thrall;
> Be with us in the fight,
> Now in the cause of right;
> Cursed be the Slaver's might,
>   God save us all![43]

Morgan's "God Protect Us!" declares abolition to be the purpose of the war, as the willingness of soldiers to fight and die is attributed to their dedication to liberate those "held in thrall" by "the Slaver's might." Abolitionists such as Smith, Stowe, and Morgan thus sought to turn the Civil War into a war for abolition.

These efforts were not unsuccessful. Indeed, despite their earlier reluctance, in a series of small but significant steps in 1862, Congress, Lincoln, and the armed forces moved toward emancipation and redefinition of the war's mission. On 6 March 1862 Lincoln proposed compensation to states agreeing to gradual emancipation; Congress then prohibited slavery in all U.S. territories and, in April, abolished slavery in the District of Columbia. By late 1862, Union forces throughout the occupied South welcomed African Americans who had escaped from slavery, although this was contrary to official policy. Union forces who witnessed slavery for the first time were shocked by what they saw. While some northern soldiers saw assistance to the fugitives as a way of punishing or transforming the South, others saw the former slaves as a valuable source of labor. "Whatever the motive," Stephen Ash observes, "one by one the soldiers of the Union army declared war on slavery." Thus, in songs such as the "Hymn of the Connecticut Twelfth," soldiers sang of a growing awareness of the injustice of slavery. The song's second verse is a bold call to redeem democracy from slavery:

> Break every yoke and chain,
> Let truth and justice reign
>   From deep to deep;
> Make all our statutes right
> In Thy most holy sight;
> Light us O Lord of Light,
>   Thy ways to keep.[45]

Although the lyrics are combative, as the first verse seeks God's assistance in "Crush[ing] Treason's serpent head," they also conceive of the rebels as wayward family members ("our sons misled") who may yet be redeemed and restored to the Union. The song thus identifies the twin missions of the war as the preservation of the Union and the abolition of slavery. In fact, borrowing a slogan from the abolitionist movement, the lyrics call on God to "Break every yoke and chain." In the final verse, the legal support of slavery through such actions as the Fugitive Slave Act is repudiated in the plea to "Make all our statutes right." The end of the war is thus conceived here not only as a military victory but as an opportunity for legislative and judicial reforms.

Government policy eventually ratified the practices of troops in the field, as the Confiscation and Militia Acts of 17 July 1862 authorized the seizure and employment of African Americans who had been enslaved by secessionists. On July 22, President Lincoln secretly submitted the first draft of the Emancipation Proclamation to his cabinet for review. At the same time, Lincoln made clear that his support for abolition was a result of military necessity—abolition was a product, rather than a mission, of the war. "My paramount object in this struggle is to save the Union, and is not either to save or to destroy slavery," he wrote to Horace Greeley in August 1862. "If I could save the Union without freeing any slave, I would do it; and if I could save it by freeing some and leaving others alone, I would also do that." Lincoln delayed announcement of the proclamation until September 22, following the battle of Antietam. The Emancipation Proclamation, effective on 1 January 1863, declared "forever free" all slaves in those Confederate states still in rebellion. The Union forces then quickly created "contraband camps" to accommodate those escaped or liberated from slavery, established a contract labor system for African American workers, and enlisted thousands of ex-slaves willing to risk their lives in what they had come to see as a mission to destroy slavery. Confederate president Jefferson Davis lent support to this view of the conflict when, in response to the Emancipation Proclamation, he ordered that all free African Americans living in or captured by the South would be forever enslaved.[45]

But even after the Emancipation Proclamation and Davis's incendiary response to it, abolition was not accepted by many Northerners as the proper mission of the war. The proclamation itself was, as historians have pointed out with some consternation, curiously conditional, as it permitted continued slavery in Union border states. Furthermore, the prospect of an "abolition war" outraged copperheads, the capitalist elites who favored a quick resolution of hostilities so they could resume their lucrative cotton trading. As described by Eric Foner in his magnum opus, *Reconstruction: America's Unfinished Business, 1863–1877*, the copperheads feared that "Black suffrage would disrupt the Southern labor force." Abolition, it was feared, would make for messy labor problems. In addition, Democratic Party leaders in August 1863 adopted a "peace" platform that would permit the continuation of slavery, thus appealing to white racists and seriously threatening Lincoln's reelection.[46]

Given the presence of such hostilities to abolition, the President's magnificent speech in July 1863, following the incomprehensible carnage of Gettysburg, may be read not only as a desperate attempt to salvage the war effort but also as part of a rhetorical effort to interpret the battle and, through it, the war, as a struggle for both emancipation and renewed national identity. Garry Wills thus observes in *Lincoln at Gettysburg* that "Words had to complete the work of the guns." But many besides Lincoln uttered such transformative words, and some of the most influential words were in songs, not speeches. Frederick Douglass toured incessantly during the winter of 1863–64, delivering his powerful lecture "The Mission of the War," in which he maintained that the abolition of slavery superceded and subsumed all other objectives, from the preservation of the Union to the hastened cessation of hostilities. The old Union and Constitution were dead, Douglass argued; they could not and should not be restored. "What we want now," Douglass proclaimed, "is a country—a free country—a country not saddened by the footprints of a single slave—and nowhere cursed by the presence of a slaveholder. We want a country which shall not brand the Declaration of Independence as a lie. . . . We now want a country in which the obligations of patriotism shall not conflict with fidelity to justice and liberty."[47]

As emancipation and Lincoln's reelection promised the creation of such a country, patriotic songs and oaths that had been anathema to most abolitionists in the decades before the war now became emblematic of what they saw as a new commitment to freedom. Previously dubious songs could now be sung without apparent "conflict with fidelity to justice and liberty." For many, then, Smith's original lyrics to "America" became a statement of the war's abolitionist cause and embodied the growing sense that the war had been an armed struggle to "let freedom ring" "from every mountainside" and to create a "sweet land of liberty" where none had previously existed. As millions of formerly enslaved African Americans finally gained their freedom, many freedpersons used the song to celebrate their liberation and loyalty to a nation reborn.

Emancipation: "The Choked Voice of a Race at Last Unloosed"

Antislavery variations on "America" had long imagined a time of jubilee, when emancipation would finally be accomplished. As the pace of emancipation accelerated during the latter stages of the war, eventually culminating in the Emancipation Proclamation (effective 1 January 1863) and the Thirteenth Amendment (passed by the Senate on 8 April 1864 and the House on 31 January 1865; ratified on 18 December 1865), Smith's original lyrics to "America" were used to celebrate newly won freedom, sometimes in so-called contraband camps. From the outset of the Civil War, African Americans escaped from slavery in large numbers and headed for Union encampments and territories. For example, "Aunt" Mary Dines escaped from slavery in Maryland and traveled in a hay wagon to a station of the Underground Railroad on Capitol Hill in Washington, D.C., where she eventually lived in one of the contraband camps (so called because, prior to the Emancipation Proclamation, African Americans who had escaped from slavery in Confederate territory were regarded as "contraband property") off Seventh Street, in wooden army barracks near the present site of Howard University. Mary Dines was literate and helped teach older freedpersons in the camp to read and wrote letters for those unable to write. She was also a renowned soprano singer with a powerful voice. In fact, black and white visitors flocked to the Seventh Street camp on weekends to hear Dines and others sing hymns, including various versions of "America." During these contraband camp concerts, many visitors, including members of Lincoln's cabinet and their families, offered financial support and helped instruct the freedpersons in reading, writing, sewing, and other skills designed to prepare them for independent living.

Lincoln knew Mary Dines from her occasional employment in the White

House and often visited the Seventh Street camp on his way to the Soldiers' Home. Dines later recounted the story of one of Lincoln's camp visits to John Washington, who included it in *They Knew Lincoln* (1942). One Saturday morning, it was announced that Lincoln was coming with an entourage to hear the freedpersons sing. Song-leader Dines "said that the thought of singing before the President nearly killed her." The freedpersons dressed in their best clothes, including reclaimed uniforms of both sides. Lincoln and his wife and guests arrived in fine carriages. While most of the visiting dignitaries sat on the platform, decorated with American flags, Lincoln stood with the older freedpersons and listened to the "spirit preacher," Uncle Ben. Then, after Ben finished his oratory, and in a remarkable example of the heady sense of freedom and solidarity that marked the close of the war, "all stood up and sang 'My Country, 'Tis of Thee' and President Lincoln took off his hat and sang too. Aunt Mary was standing near him and heard him: she said he had a good voice. . . . She said he was no President when he came to camp. He just stood and sang and prayed just like all the rest of the people." United with their president in singing the national hymn, the freedpersons celebrated their new liberties, pledged their loyalty to the union, and asserted their claim to citizenship. These sentiments gained new meaning when recounted by Washington in 1942, as he implicitly transferred these tales of Civil War loyalty and service to a new generation of Americans confronting the challenges of the Second World War.[48]

Lincoln remained linked with the song "America" for many African Americans for more than a century. Indeed, at civil rights demonstrations in front of the Lincoln Memorial, Marian Anderson sang "America" in 1939; Mahalia Jackson sang it there in 1957. Lincoln's statue was in the background of the national television images of Martin Luther King in 1963, when he used the lyrics of "America" to frame the last third of his address to the March on Washington. In *They Knew Lincoln*, Washington recalls his own visit to Oak Ridge Cemetery in Springfield, Illinois, where he saw "a large number of colored people, both young and old, standing about the tomb of Lincoln singing, 'My country, 'tis of thee'," a song "that Lincoln had first made a reality for them." There is considerable debate regarding Lincoln's positions on slavery and emancipation, yet celebrations of the Emancipation Proclamation were held throughout the North and occupied territories. Many of these gatherings featured impassioned singing of "America." "It is a day for poetry and song," Frederick Douglass declared on 28 December 1862 (after Lincoln had made his Proclamation and only a few days before it took effect) — this sensibility was broadly shared. The largest and most exuberant celebrations were in the occupied South, where those who had recently escaped from slavery gathered in huge crowds. For example, the Port Royal region, a group of occupied islands around South Carolina's Beaufort River, was home to thousands of African Americans who had escaped from slavery. Union Brigadier General Rufus Saxton issued a "Happy New-Year's Greeting to the Colored People in the South" in late 1862 encouraging celebrations of January 1 by Port Royal freedpersons "whose hopes it comes to brighten and bless." Saxton encouraged them to combine their voices in a "grand chorus of liberty" that would be heard in surrounding communities. Thousands of freedpersons and many white soldiers and civilians responded to the call, arriving in Port Royal in steamers provided by Saxton. By ten o'clock in the morning, an enormous and excited crowd had gathered in a live oak grove on the former Smith plantation. A dozen whole oxen were roasted overnight for the communal feast that would follow the day's lengthy program and dress parade.[49]

Colonel Thomas Wentworth Higginson, in command of the First Regiment Colored South Carolina Volunteers, the first Civil War regiment consisting of newly liberated slaves, presided over the ceremony. Most African American soldiers, once they were finally admitted to the Union army, were commanded by white officers, such as Higginson or Robert Gould Shaw of the Massachusetts Fifty-fourth. Higginson was a Massachusetts minister, president of the Massachusetts Anti-Slavery Society, and one of the "Secret Six" who funded John Brown's raid on Harper's Ferry. He is probably best remembered today as the *Atlantic Monthly* editor who rejected the poems of Emily Dickinson. In his memoir *Army Life in a Black Regiment* (1870), Higginson recalled that the high point of the 1863 New Year's Day emancipation ceremony was a spontaneous rendition of "America" by the freedpersons. "The President's proclamation was read" by South Carolinian and former slaveholder Dr. W. H. Brisbane, Higginson remembered, and

> then followed an incident so simple, so touching, so utterly unexpected and startling, that I can scarcely believe it on recalling, though it gave the key-note to the whole day. The very moment the speaker had ceased, and just as I took and raised the flag, which now for the first time meant anything to these poor people, there suddenly arose, close behind the platform, a strong male voice (but rather cracked and elderly), into which two women's voices instantly blended, singing, as if by an impulse that could no more be repressed than the morning note of the song-sparrow.

> > "My Country, 'tis of thee,
> > Sweet land of liberty,
> > Of thee I sing!"

> People looked at each other, and then at us on the platform, to see whence came this interruption, not set down in the bills. Firmly and irrepressibly the quavering voices sang on, verse after verse; others of the colored people joined in; some whites on the platform began, but I motioned them to silence. I never

Figure 4.2. Drawing of the New Year's Day celebration of emancipation on Port Royal Island, 1863, from *Leslie's Illustrated Weekly Newspaper* (24 January 1863). Courtesy of The University of Illinois Rare Book and Special Collections Library.

saw anything so electric; it made all other words cheap; it seemed the choked voice of a race at last unloosed. . . . Just think of it! The first day they had ever had a country, the first flag they had ever seen which promised anything to their people, and here, while mere spectators stood in silence, waiting for my stupid words, these simple souls burst out in their lay, as if they were by their own hearths at home! When they stopped, there was nothing to do for it but to speak, and I went on; but the life of the whole day was in those unknown people's song.[50]

For newly free men and women, the act of singing "America" marked their first symbolic step toward citizenship after generations in bondage. For the first time, the assembled freedpersons at Port Royal sang of the nation and its liberties as their own (see figure 4.2).

Along with singing traditional versions of "America" at such festivities, the song was also adapted in new lyrics written specifically for use in emancipation celebrations. For example, a "Song of Freedom," dedicated to Frederick Douglass, appeared in the April 1863 issue of *Douglass' Monthly*, inviting participants to

Come sing a cheerful lay,
And celebrate this day
     Throughout the land;
Oh! Let us joyful be,
For freedom's sons are we,
In this land now the free
     At Thy command.[51]

Such joyous eruptions of a now-reconceived nationalism were encouraged by northern elites anxious to move the nation beyond sectional and racial violence. Indeed, freedpersons were encouraged to sing Smith's "America" by northern teachers who came south during the war. In January 1862, Treasury Secretary Salmon P. Chase sent his friend Edward Pierce to investigate the situation of freedpersons in the Port Royal area. Pierce submitted a report calling for educational and cultural assistance for the thousands of newly free African Americans who had been forcibly denied literacy while enslaved. Within a week of receiving the report, Thomas W. Sherman, commanding officer of the Department of the South, issued a general appeal for northern philanthropy and volunteers. Freedmen's aid societies were formed throughout the North to provide clothing, supplies, and teachers. Edward Pierce, appointed as government agent for the freedpersons in the Port Royal area, accompanied the first group of fifty-three teachers to their new post and instructed them in their mission: "You go to elevate, to purify, and fit them for the duties of American citizens" (see figure 4.3). Eight schools for freedpersons were established in the Port Royal region by May 1862; in each of them students were taught patriotic songs, including "America." These songs were invariably included in public performances and inspections by visiting officials as demonstrations of the progress the freedpersons were making toward citizenship.[52]

Both the 1 January emancipation celebration of 1863 in Port Royal and the subsequent freedpersons' school performances, then—like other such occasions both during and after the war—were the culmination of concerted efforts orchestrated by elites, who, following the lessons learned from Mason and Smith and Woodbridge in the 1830s, saw music as a crucial tool for socializing and nationalizing previously excluded or marginalized citizens. The 1989 film *Glory*, which tells the story of the Massachusetts Fifty-fourth Colored Infantry, includes a scene of one such performance. In occupied Beaufort, South Carolina, in June 1863, Robert Gould Shaw (played stoically by Matthew Broderick) and other white Union officers and their families are entertained by a group of African American schoolchildren, recently freed from slavery. They sing the first stanza of "America," having practiced for weeks in anticipation of the Fifty-fourth's arrival, Shaw is told. In his memoir *After the War: A Tour of the Southern States, 1865–1866*, Whitelaw Reid recalls a similar ceremony, this one on Saint

NOON AT THE PRIMARY SCHOOL FOR FREEDMEN, VICKSBURG, MISSISSIPPI.—[See Page 396.]

PRIMARY SCHOOL FOR FREEDMEN, IN CHARGE OF Mrs. GREEN, AT VICKSBURG, MISSISSIPPI.—[See Page 396.]

Figure 4.3. Drawings of freedpersons' schools in Mississippi, from *Harper's Weekly* (23 June 1866). Courtesy of HarpWeek.

Helena's Island, South Carolina, at which a white teacher led her newly freed African American students in the performance of "America." These stories demonstrate that teaching citizenship was as important a mission for many of the freedpersons' schools as instruction in reading and writing. In fact, the Port Royal programs were considered so successful that they were adopted by the federal government as a model for the training of freedpersons elsewhere.[53] Thus, thirty years after its initial performance in a Boston church segregated by color, "America" was used in a South still smoldering from war as a musical vehicle for celebrating democracy, socializing new citizens, and uniting individual voices within collective communities.

Indeed, for many African Americans, whether enslaved or nominally free before the war, the Union victory and the passage of constitutional amendments abolishing slavery and granting citizenship and the franchise (to males) produced a new national affiliation that was often voiced in song. Freedpersons celebrating the Fourth of July in Hampton, Virginia, in 1865 sang "America" to begin the ceremony, then formed a procession "more than a thousand strong, of Volunteers, once all slaves, but now all free to be slaves no more." They marched through the streets of Hampton, carrying a large American flag. The festivities in Hampton were no exception; African American communities throughout the South celebrated the Fourth of July in 1865, and while many resentful Southern whites refrained from participating in such celebrations, freed blacks sang "America" at many of these gatherings.[54]

"America" was also an important part of celebrations for the passage of the Thirteenth Amendment. Secretary of State William H. Seward issued an official proclamation on 18 December 1865 announcing the ratification of the Thirteenth Amendment to the Constitution, which abolished slavery in all states. The headline of Seward's broadside, quoting Leviticus, proclaimed "Liberty throughout all the land, unto all the inhabitants thereof." At last "America" in song seemed to resemble America in fact, as the end of slavery meant that a "sweet land of liberty" where freedom promised to ring "from every mountainside" was at least possible, perhaps even forthcoming. Americans of all political persuasions accordingly sang "America" to express their jubilation. In the House of Representatives on 31 January 1865, for example, when the Thirteenth Amendment was passed, the *New York Times* reported:

> Thereupon rose a general shout of applause. The members on the floor huzzaed in chorus with deafening and equally emphatic cheers of the throng in the galleries. The ladies in the dense assemblage waved their handkerchiefs, and again and again the applause was repeated, intermingled with clapping of hands and exclamations of "Hurrah for freedom!" "Glory enough for one day," &c. The audience were wildly excited, and the friends of the measure jubilant.

Never was a scene of such joyous character before witnessed in the House of Representatives, certainly not within the last quarter of a century.[55]

Amid this "scene of such joyous character," following huzzahs and exclamations, the crowd rolled in to a spontaneous rendition of "America." Bishop Benjamin Arnett, who was among the many African Americans in the House galleries that day, later recalled joining with the congressional representatives in singing "My country, 'Tis of Thee" as the cannons and bells of the city "carried the glad tidings in the air."[56]

It is perhaps difficult for Americans today to fathom how revolutionary this moment felt and how completely it seemed to alter the possibility of America itself. Contemporaries understood, however, that a brilliant new day had arrived. For example, addressing an anniversary celebration of the Thirteenth Amendment in 1874, John Mercer Langston explained that "in our emancipation it is fixed by law that the place where we are born is *ipso facto* our country." While slavery existed, even nominally "free" African Americans were excluded, but the Thirteenth, Fourteenth, and Fifteenth amendments created a "new nation," Langston argued, to which African Americans owed "the duty of allegiance" in exchange for governmental protection of their liberties. Indeed, the war, the abolition of slavery, and the promise of civil rights deepened national affiliation for many African Americans and encouraged them to seek justice in a land where change, finally, seemed possible. As Vincent Harding writes in *There Is a River*, "The confluence of the river of struggle and the terrible chariots of war had broken open the way," and

The children of bondage were crossing over, bearing visions of a new land, challenging white America to a new life.

> My country. My country.
> 'Tis of thee I sing.
> Country still unborn.
> Sweet land yet to be.[57]

The Compromised Spectacle of Reconstruction: "A Nation of Performers"

The jubilee nation promised by the Union victory and reconstruction was not realized. Efforts to reassimilate the former Confederates and to secure the rights stipulated in the Thirteenth, Fourteenth, and Fifteenth amendments met with great resistance. For years before the war, many white Southerners had regarded themselves as unaffiliated with the national political culture. The Confederacy was premised on a distinct national idea, a "slaveholders' republic," as

George Rable has termed it, with its own ideas of liberty and the role of government. Fealty to the North's version of democracy was therefore compromised, not the least because during the war Union occupying forces imposed martial law and suppressed expression of pro-Confederacy or anti-Union sentiments, fulfilling the prophecies of repression trumpeted by Southerners. Indeed, the Washington, North Carolina, provost warned in 1862 that "Whosoever shall utter one word against the Government of the United States will be at once arrested and closely confined."[58] Allegiance to the Union, then, which even before war and the imposition of martial law was hard to come by, was not easily compelled, even after the collapse of the Confederacy. Many white Southerners refused to take loyalty oaths administered by Union authorities, while others swore but did not heed them. "Union Leagues" and "Loyal Leagues" were established throughout the South but were reviled by most white Southerners, who used violence, shunning, and other forms of intimidation against those who joined them. Reconstruction was therefore a period marked by paralyzing contrasts between the utopian sense of a cleansed nation finally opening it arms to new citizens, the lingering, festering, rotting bitterness of secessionists and racists who refused to recognize either the Union or emancipation, and the vast, overwhelming majority of citizens who simply longed for peace and prosperity after years of devastating sacrifice.

Throughout the war Lincoln spoke of the Confederates as wayward members of the Union family whose return to the fold was welcomed. Never one to avoid a Biblical metaphor, he had come to view and speak of the war as God's punishment of both North and South for the sin of slavery. But southern resistance and northern desires for retribution and reformation greatly complicated postwar efforts at reunification. On what basis should the former Confederate states and sympathizers be readmitted to the Union? What should be required of them? When President Andrew Johnson opposed the Radical Reconstructionists' program of southern reforms and advocated minimal requirements for readmission he was impeached and escaped a guilty verdict in 1868 by a single vote. Yet by the end of 1868, Democrats and moderate Republicans were joined by some Radicals in the desire to minimize conflicts over reconstruction and to relegate arguments over slavery and secession to the past. Indeed, much as debate regarding slavery was shunted into the future by the Founders, who thought the subject too divisive to address at the close of the eighteenth century, so Reconstruction saw debate regarding black freedom and citizenship shunted into the past, where it would not disturb what were seen as more pressing issues. Thus, over the next eight years, federal troops were withdrawn, the Confederate states were readmitted to the Union, and African American suffrage, civil liberties, and economic opportunities were quashed throughout the South.

Despite significant residual differences, white politicians of the reunited North and South constructed a shared rhetoric that Paul Buck once dubbed "the new patriotism." This was a nationalism that acknowledged differences in regional culture, permitting Southerners to think of the South as a distinct unit within the larger nation and Northerners to regard their region as "more characteristically American than any other part of the Union." National unity of these disparate cultures was grounded in the shared experience of the war, in which all regions, classes, and races had suffered. Curiously, particularly considering the pivotal role of slavery in the war, both sides tried to talk past or through the issue of race. Indeed, shared sacrifice in the past, rather than projected freedoms in the future, provided a powerful sense of white common national experience.[59] Veterans of each side undertook speaking tours of the other's region, where they recounted battle stories and praised the bravery of their former opponents, whom they met and embraced at battle reunions. The "new patriotism" was thus based on a rhetoric of white reconciliation in which the substantial issues of the war were buried beneath heroic tales memorializing shared experiences of battle and struggle.

Postwar reconciliation was most spectacularly ceremonialized in Patrick Gilmore's National Peace Jubilee. Held in Boston in 1869, the Jubilee featured a huge chorus and orchestra, internationally renowned musical celebrities, and national songs and symbols, all in a celebratory enactment of the reconstituted union. The emotional highlight of the festivities was a thunderous fifty-thousand-voice rendition of "America." Patrick Sarsfield Gilmore, the Jubilee's producer, was born in Ireland and came to the United States in 1849, at the age of twenty, whereupon he led a series of popular bands in Boston during the decade before the Civil War. When the war began, the Gilmore Band enlisted en masse to accompany the Twenty-fourth Massachusetts Volunteer Regiment. While stationed in North Carolina, Gilmore organized regimental minstrel troupes to entertain the soldiers. In 1864, he went to New Orleans as chief bandmaster for General Banks and the Union occupation forces. On 4 March, Gilmore staged what he termed a "monster concert" for the inauguration of Governor Michael Hahn and to celebrate a "Free and Restored Louisiana." He assembled many local bands into a single unit of five hundred instrumentalists and gathered an immense chorus of five thousand schoolchildren, who waved American flags during "The Star-Spangled Banner." Their renditions of national songs, *Watson's Art Journal* reported, "fell upon the ear as though the very heavens had opened, and all the angels therein were participating in the great event of the day."[60]

The idea of the "monster concert" had been developed twenty years earlier by French composer and conductor Hector Berlioz. For the 1844 World Exposition of Industrial Products in Paris, Berlioz produced a music festival featuring five hundred singers and an orchestra of 480 musicians. Berlioz's exaggerated

scale made live performance a mass medium befitting the pretensions of industrial progress and nationalist grandeur. His program included not only classical numbers but popular and patriotic songs, closing with his own *Hymne à la
France*. The following year, Berlioz staged another monster concert, in part as
a showcase for his *Marche triomphale*. Berlioz's model of the monster concert was
adopted by other conductors and promoters in other countries, including the
American composer and pianist Louis Moreau Gottschalk, who in 1861 staged
a music festival in Havana featuring a 450-piece orchestra and forty pianists.
Gottschalk later staged monster concerts throughout South America. Monster
concerts were often nationalistic in character, as patriotic songs were featured
prominently in the programs. In Yorkshire in 1856, for example, the Halifax
Sunday School Jubilee assembled a choir of 24,787 teachers and students and
a five-hundred-piece orchestra. The program concluded with a passionate rendition of "God Save the Queen," in which the choir was joined by the eight
thousand audience members. Thus, in a significant merging of new technologies—transportational, organizational, and musical—the monster concert
marked a new moment in mass politics that blended musical performance,
mass popular culture, and patriotic pep rally into a spectacle of nationalism.[61]

After the Civil War, Patrick Gilmore brought the monster concert to an even
grander scale. Indeed, the 1869 National Peace Jubilee was larger in attendance, number of performers, and ideological pretensions than any previously
attempted monster concert. In 1867 and 1868 Gilmore envisioned the Jubilee as
a musical spectacle that could unite the fractured nation. Unfortunately, with
President Johnson facing impeachment and constant news reports of continued
violence in the former Confederacy, such a celebration seemed premature to
the potential backers whom Gilmore approached in New York City. Nonetheless, in 1868, Gilmore convinced Boston business and civic leaders to support
the Jubilee by emphasizing both the leading role of Massachusetts as an agent
of national reconciliation and, perhaps more persuasively, its prospective financial windfall from tourism related to the event.

Gilmore was a skilled promoter with a keen sense of what would attract and
please a crowd. He adopted Grant's presidential campaign slogan "Let us have
Peace" for the Jubilee and publicized the popular general's likely attendance.
Gilmore solicited endorsements for the Jubilee from prominent politicians, musicians, and newspaper editors. He distributed circulars and advertised in newspapers, announcing that the Jubilee would be the *"most important event in American
History* to be celebrated by the grandest outpouring of National, Patriotic, and
Sublime Music ever heard upon the American continent." Gilmore spent ten
thousand dollars in advertising and gained substantial free publicity from the
over 330 newspapers covering the planned events. Gilmore's media blitz emphasized that the National Peace Jubilee was designed to celebrate "the restora-

tion of peace and union." No such "demonstration of national character," he believed, had yet taken place since the war. The "Official Programme" for the event boasted that Gilmore had invited "THE PRESIDENT OF THE UNITED STATES, members of his cabinet, Heads of Departments, Governors of all the States, And many distinguished persons from all parts of the country" (see figure 4.4). The interior decoration of the coliseum and the musical program would reflect the theme of national reconciliation: "What nobler form could this commemoration take than that of a grand outburst of song—the universal harmonizer?" he asked. The Jubilee, Gilmore declared, would "manifest to the world the joy of a nation for its deliverance from a fratricidal war." This idea was expressed in the Jubilee's opening (and virtually inaudible) oration, where Alexander Rice assured the participants that they would find "the loudest din of battle hushed in the melody of song."[62]

Every element of the 1869 National Peace Jubilee was spectacular. To house the concert, Gilmore proposed construction of "the largest public structure ever built in the United States," a temporary wooden building that would accommodate over fifty thousand people. Gilmore initially suggested that the structure be built on Boston Common, but after fierce local opposition he settled on St. James Park. Because of the siting controversy and other delays, construction had yet to begin as late as March, with the Jubilee but three months away. Again demonstrating his keen skill at manipulating early forms of mass media and nationalism, Gilmore issued a call to "every city, town, and village in Massachusetts" to provide a corps of volunteer construction workers, and many did so. The coliseum, *Dwight's Journal of Music* reported, "went up as by magic." Engravings of its construction and finished form were published in illustrated periodicals across the country (see figure 4.5). Like the giant building constructed for the occasion, the scale of the performances was gargantuan and included a ten-foot-wide drum built especially for the event, a powerful organ, and a massive chorus assembled from choirs and singing clubs invited from around the nation. Indeed, 103 musical societies eventually assembled to form a choir of ten thousand voices, accompanied by a one-thousand-piece orchestra. It was to be, Gilmore claimed in the promotional circulars, "the greatest concert ever staged anywhere in the world."[63]

As in the monster concert he had produced in New Orleans, Gilmore organized an enormous children's chorus drawn from the Boston school music programs that had been initiated by Lowell Mason three decades earlier. Gilmore understood that child performers would attract the paid attendance of their families and help publicize the show; hence on 18 January 1869 he wrote to Dr. J. B. Upham, superintendent of music in the Boston public schools, announcing that all grammar school children and all children over eight years old in the primary schools would be automatically admitted to the chorus. Gilmore pre-

"Let us have Peace."

OFFICIAL PROGRAMME.

Great National Peace Jubilee!

(PROJECTED BY MR. P. S. GILMORE,)

TO BE HELD

IN THE CITY OF BOSTON,

June 15, 16, 17, 18, and 19, 1869,

TO

COMMEMORATE THE RESTORATION OF PEACE

THROUGHOUT THE LAND.

THIS GLORIOUS EVENT IN OUR NATIONAL HISTORY WILL BE CELEBRATED
BY THE

Grandest Musical Festival

EVER KNOWN IN THE HISTORY OF THE WORLD.

THE PRESIDENT OF THE UNITED STATES,

**Members of his Cabinet, Heads of Departments,
Governors of all the States,**

And many other distinguished persons from all parts of the country, together with the
Representatives of Foreign Governments at Washington, have been invited
by the Mayor and City Council of Boston to become the

GUESTS OF THE CITY DURING THE FESTIVAL.

AN IMMENSE COLISEUM,

The largest structure in America, capable of accommodating FIFTY THOUSAND
PERSONS, has been erected especially for this occasion, the
interior of the building being

MAGNIFICENTLY DECORATED

WITH EMBLEMS OF NATIONAL PEACE AND HARMONY.

The extraordinary expense incurred in preparing for this great Festival has been met,
with remarkable generosity, by the public-spirited, art-loving citizens of Boston, and
the Executive Committee take great pleasure in announcing the following

Figure 4.4. The "Official Programme" for Patrick Gilmore's 1869 National Peace Jubilee. Courtesy of The Special Collections of the University of Illinois Music Library.

Figure 4.5. This exterior view of the "Festival Hall" built for the National Peace Jubilee, from P. S. Gilmore, *History of the National Peace Jubilee*. Courtesy of The Special Collections of the University of Illinois Music Library.

scribed uniform clothing for the student participants: white dresses for the girls, each adorned with a red, white, and blue sash, worn "Highland style"; dark jackets for the boys, with a red, white, and blue rosette on the left breast. Gilmore proposed to assemble "the largest and most charming chorus of children that have ever been seen or heard in any part of the world." "Such a legion of well-trained young voices, supported by the harmony of a thousand musical instruments," he promised, "will inspire and enchant the assemblage beyond the power of language to describe."[64] The Boston School Committee, however, refused to permit the participation of schoolchildren, based largely on safety concerns prompted by the recent deadly collapse of a local skating rink. At last, in May, Gilmore hit upon the idea of moving the children's performance from the first day, when the safety of the building was untested, to the final day. If the building were to collapse under the weight of the huge crowd, he argued, it would already have done so before the children performed. This satisfied the school authorities, and the children's chorus was assembled.

The interior of the coliseum was decorated with banners and symbols "historically emblematic of state and national progress since the formation of the Union." Behind the arches was a painted background of clouds, with two colossal angels, each holding a scroll with the inscription "Peace." The inner columns supporting the balcony were each adorned with a medallion bearing the portrait of a famous composer and the flag of the composer's native land, reflecting the promotion of the Jubilee as (at least in part) a must-see musical event, an unprecedented opportunity for a massive audience of listeners of all classes to hear songs written by internationally renowned composers. Several musical superstars were engaged for the performances, including Ole Bull and Carl Rosa, who led the violin section, the renowned cornetist Matthew Arbuckle, Johann Strauss and his orchestra, and Carl Zerrahn (former director of the Boston Handel and Haydn Society) as conductor. The soprano Euphrosyne Parepa-Rosa, billed as the only human whose voice was large enough to fill the coliseum, was hired to perform several numbers, including Gounod's "Ave Maria" accompanied by two hundred violinists. The Jubilee also drew on regional orchestras, choruses, and singing clubs, in the hope of linking regional styles and vernaculars with European traditions and cultures. While a forest of flags "including one or more of every nation on the globe" lined the columns of the coliseum, the interior decoration was also strongly nationalistic. Red, white, and blue streamers covered the balconies, crowning the hall with the colors of the national flag. Medallions bearing the seals of the thirty-six states, each flanked by U.S. national flags, adorned the outer columns. The eighteen seals on each side of the hall mixed former Confederate and Union states together in random order, to make clear that "no partiality is shown" (see figure 4.6; note at the end of the hall the giant drum and organ built for the occasion).[65]

The Jubilee lasted five days, beginning on the morning of 15 June 1869 and ending on the evening of the 19th. The first day was devoted to inaugural proceedings and was designated a "Day of Prayer." Ticket sales for the first day were disappointingly slow until Gilmore announced that a performance of the "Anvil Chorus" would be added to the program. Slated already for the third day's "Popular" program, the "Anvil Chorus," from Verdi's opera, *Il Trovatore,* had been the focus of intense publicity and public interest as well as great derision from music critics. Gilmore's announcement set off a flurry of ticket sales, but still only an estimated eleven thousand attended on the first day, fewer than the twelve thousand performers. Lacking any kind of public address technology, the unamplified prayers and addresses were completely inaudible to most of the audience. The musical performances, on the other hand, were both deafening and visually spectacular. For the "Anvil Chorus" Gilmore recruited one hundred members of the Boston fire department to strike one hundred anvils, lined in two columns. The firefighters marched into the hall wearing matching red flannel shirts, white belts, and helmets and carrying long-handled smith's hammers on their shoulders like a military drill formation. They struck their anvils in dramatic accompaniment to the chorus and orchestra.

Twice as many concert-goers attended the second day, devoted to "Symphony and Oratorio." President Grant and Admiral Farragut were among the

Figure 4.6. Interior view of the "Festival Hall" built for the National Peace Jubilee, from Gilmore, *History of the National Peace Jubilee*. Courtesy of The Special Collections of the University of Illinois Music Library.

many celebrity guests. The Jubilee suffered its only fatality when Parepa-Rosa sang "Let the Bright Seraphim" from Handel's *Samson*, during which a woman in the audience "was overcome with emotion and quietly expired." Boston was crowded with visitors; to the dismay of music critics, nine of every ten tickets sold in advance were for the third day of the Jubilee, dedicated to "Popular Music." Forty to fifty thousand people attended the day's performances, and many more were attracted by the excitement of the event. The program for the fourth day was classical and the audience somewhat smaller. Still, all the seats and half the standing room were filled. The fifth and final day was designated "Children's Day," and a choir of seven thousand school children performed hymns and national songs, including "America." Even the skeptical *Dwight's Journal of Music* concluded—in a tone that no doubt made Lowell Mason smile—that the Jubilee's mass performances had kindled "a new belief in Music, a new conviction of its social worth; above all, of its importance as a pervading, educational, and fusing element in our whole democratic life."[66]

The emotional high point of the Jubilee, according to many accounts, was a spectacular performance of "America" that closed the first day's program. Gilmore himself conducted the patriotic numbers and had a special fondness for "America," which he pronounced "the grandest and most majestic of all national airs." At the National Peace Jubilee it was performed (like the "Anvil Chorus" that immediately preceded it) with full chorus, organ, orchestra, military band, drum corps, "all the bells of the city in chime," and cannon accompaniment from the Second Massachusetts battery, which fired in time to the music. For "America" only, the program states that "the audience is requested to join in singing the last stanza." Concert-goers more than complied. In fact, the *New York Times* reported that during the performance of "America" "the audience stood on the benches and shouted and made extraordinary demonstrations." According to the *Boston Post*, at the conclusion of the song the crowd erupted in "a demonstrativeness of enthusiasm that had scarcely been reached during the afternoon." The audience clamored for and received a repeat performance of the song, in which they joined in, followed by an even louder and more sustained ovation.[67]

Gilmore's advance circulars advertised the Jubilee as a symbol of the reconstituted union, as an event that "will bring together in fraternal greeting the leading men of the Nation, and people from all parts of the land" in the "FIRST GRAND NATIONAL REUNION since the close of the War." Press accounts made much of those who had traveled from Nebraska and California to attend and of Gilmore's invitations to national figures and former Confederates. The recruitment of singers and instrumentalists from throughout the United States, according to the *Boston Post*, produced "a nation of performers." Although the audience was overwhelmingly white and from New England, many observers saw in the vast numbers of people attending and performing in the Jubilee a simulation of the national population. Perhaps more than anything else, however, the "NATIONAL REUNION" was an occasion to forget past hurts. Indeed, the causes and issues of the Civil War were not mentioned in the National Peace Jubilee. In a telling article, the *Boston Post* stressed the event's success in soothing "into coveted oblivion those animosities and hatreds which once distracted and divided a nation." Those who attended the Jubilee, the *Post* continued, had "gathered to forgive and forget the past" and to "join in the bands of a glorious harmony a separated people." Efforts to forgive and forget constructed the war as a terrible mistake, a regrettable conflict between white brothers. And so the tone was set for Reconstruction.[68]

DURING the Civil War, "America" and its many variations were used to redefine the mission of the conflict and to mark the redeemed promise of freedom for African Americans. In the National Peace Jubilee, however, "America" was part of a larger effort to bury the contentious issues of the Civil War beneath a spectacularly banal carnival of musical nationalism. The National Peace Jubilee illustrates, then, how the complexities of reunification were finessed by downplaying slavery's role in the conflict and by embracing instead the glories of

Figure 4.7. Thomas Nast, "Worse than Slavery," from *Harper's Weekly* (24 October 1874). Courtesy of HarpWeek.

white fraternal nationalism. "The road to reunion," however, as John Hope Franklin reminds us, "was paved with new laws of social segregation and new practices of racial discrimination." Indeed, within the thundering bombast of the anvil chorus, or the treacly sweetness of seven thousand singing children adorned in matching uniforms, it was easy to forget that white supremacist views were as intimately linked as ever in the minds of many Americans with national identity.[69] In fact, it would not be long before many Americans, both white and black, were bitterly observing that the trying conditions fostered by postwar racism were in some ways "worse than slavery" (see figure 4.7).

FIVE

Reforming the "Sweet Land of Knavery"

"America" and Political Protest, 1870–1932

THE religious revivals that swept the United States prior to the Civil War invigorated movements for social and political reform, as preachers of a variety of denominations stressed the necessity of both individual and national salvation. As demonstrated in chapters 2 and 3, the faithful were fired with perfectionist ideas of a destined nation that could be redeemed through collective political and evangelical action. Feeding off of this cultural energy, political activists worked to construct an ideal society and to promote legal reforms through quasi-religious organizations that bridged the secular and the sacred, the nationalist and the evangelist, while invoking patriotic texts and symbols. Furthermore, the various revivals of the Second Great Awakening often overlapped with antebellum reform movements for abolition, temperance, suffrage, and peace, among other causes, both in their universal appropriation of "My Country 'Tis of Thee" and in their shared memberships and core assumptions about what it meant to be an American. Indeed, despite their political differences, antebellum reform movements all believed that mass persuasion and reform were necessary and possible, that the fate of the nation hung in the balance of their efforts, that effective campaigns required the use of a variety of persuasive media, and that among these music was singularly effective. As detailed in chapter 4, however, the cataclysmic eruption of the Civil War forced activists to make difficult choices regarding their political commitments; one result of these difficult choices was the slackening of grassroots activism, especially for temperance and women's suffrage. Hence, while mass spectacles such as the 1869 National Peace Jubilee in Boston sought to reunify the shattered nation in the comforting amnesia of forgiving white nationalism, the rejuvenation of post–

Civil War democracy in America is more accurately indicated by the rebirth of the temperance, women's suffrage, labor, and school reform movements.

As we explain hereafter, each of these post–Civil War movements relied heavily on appropriated versions of "America" to persuade fellow citizens of the efficacy of their proposed reforms. Much like their antebellum predecessors, these post-Civil War movements understood that politics were powerful when sung. In his 1888 history of the temperance movement, for example, Senator Henry Blair described music as "the vehicle of moral transitions" that is "both an accompaniment and a weapon of revolution." "Lately," he observed, "the Union has turned attention more and more to its neglected power as an agent for the regeneration of human nature." Blair's characterization of music as both "the vehicle of moral transitions" and "a weapon of revolution" would not have struck his contemporaries as hyperbolic, as post–Civil War movement songs were heard in churches, schools, homes, and civic ceremonies, while popular song collections and the programs of popular entertainers frequently included reform songs. The Hutchinson Family Singers of New Hampshire, for example, who were among the most popular singing troupes in the United States for nearly fifty years, built their antebellum and Reconstruction-era performances around songs from the temperance, abolition, and women's suffrage movements and occasionally dedicated entire programs to the support of organizations such as the Sons of Temperance or the Equal Suffrage Society. In their popular song "If I Were a Voice" they imagined their influence as "a persuasive voice, / That could travel the whole world through." While such global ambitions are seen through postmodern eyes as part of the discourse of colonization and imperialism, they were recognized at the time as a sign of deep, righteous commitment to the democratic premises of persuasion and activism that were then fueling both reform-based and evangelical versions of nationalism.[1]

Like "If I Were a Voice," thousands of post–Civil War movement songs were published as broadsides and in newspapers and song collections. Most reformers turned to familiar melodies for their songs, which enabled them to quickly turn out songs adapted to specific occasions and purposes. More important, such topical songs based on familiar melodies enabled large groups to sing them on first reading. For example, the title page of Walter K. Fobes's 1889 *Temperance Songs and Hymns* explained: "these songs are written to familiar tunes so that all may join together in singing for the grand temperance cause." Similarly, J. N. Stearns wrote in the preface to the 1880 *National Temperance Hymn and Song Book* that he had chosen to "present new and stirring words" set to "such old tunes and airs as are familiar to the public" because they "can be taken up by almost any congregation and 'all unite in singing.'"[2] "America" was among the old tunes familiar to the public most often adapted for use by the social and political movements of the latter nineteenth century. In fact, post–Civil War reform movements produced more than one hundred alternate versions of the song. Some of the variations were employed in organizational rituals, drawing on the solemnity and majesty associated with "the national hymn" to dignify their own ceremonies. Most postwar variations, however—like those produced by the abolitionists and other reform movements of the antebellum period—used Smith's song to present their own visions of the nation.

Indeed, as we demonstrate hereafter, temperance activists used appropriated versions of "America" to equate liberty with sobriety; the women's suffrage movement relied on the song to argue that the liberties described in Smith's song had not yet been extended to all Americans; labor activists sang versions claiming that there is no freedom without bread; and school reform proponents hoped to use the song to rejuvenate lagging nationalist pride by more aggressively socializing working-class and immigrant children. This final movement demonstrates how powerfully class- and race-based fears drove the political energies of some Reconstruction, Gilded Age, and early-twentieth-century Americans. But for the most part, the post–Civil War reformers' variations on "America" addressed hereafter imagined a nation still in the process of becoming truly free, as a righteous yet compromised web of unfulfilled promises that needed to be secured through mass political action directed at transforming public opinion and laws.

"The Temperance Flag Unfurled / Shall Wave Throughout the World"

The Civil War left America shattered. While Reconstruction is often thought of as the postwar period in which radical Republicans sought (ultimately unsuccessfully) to rebuild the nation along premises closer to genuine democracy than apartheid, it may also be understood as a period when the entire nation struggled to rebuild civic institutions, community bonds, and a sense of national belonging. One of the first signs of this postwar national resurgence in political activism was the launching of the National Temperance Society, which was formed in 1865 by a convention of delegates from twenty-five states. With the founding of the Women's Christian Temperance Union (WCTU) in 1874, the movement gained enormous grassroots support and national political power. Its slogan, "For God and Home and Native Land," reflected the activists' understanding of their efforts as protecting the home and preserving the nation, with both tasks fired by heavenly imperative. By 1887 the WCTU claimed to have ten thousand local unions and two hundred thousand members, amounting to a separate temperance government composed entirely of women administering the affairs of a temperance nation. Such organizing was so successful that by

1913 nearly half of the American population lived in states that restricted the use of alcohol. Temperance activism culminated in the Eighteenth Amendment (ratified in 1919 and then repealed in 1933), which legislated that "the manufacture, sale, or transportation of intoxicating liquors . . . is prohibited."[3]

While Prohibition is now generally understood as an ill-conceived attempt to legislate personal behavior, the grassroots movement that prompted it nonetheless stands as a remarkable example of citizens engaging in the democratic process. Indeed, while Americans might cringe at its heavy-handed moralizing, the temperance movement is nonetheless a fascinating case study in political persuasion, particularly as regards its specific appropriations of "My Country 'Tis of Thee" and its more general commitment to singing politics. For example, Mrs. E. J. Thompson, a leader of the women's movement that became the WCTU, and an activist so important that Senator Henry Blair later called her the "Mother of the Crusade," believed that song was essential to secure broad changes in American society. Thompson's musical ideas inspired the Baptist Social Union of Boston to stage a "sacred concert" in 1886 for eight hundred "American workmen." "The concert was so arranged that often all could take part," Henry Blair reports, "singing 'America' and like tunes." One such temperance version of "America," entitled "Temperance, Thy Noble Name," an 1889 song by Walter Fobes, demonstrates the depth of commitment many activists brought to the movement. After opening with a bold promise that "Temperance, thy noble name, / We will to all proclaim / With trumpet blast," the song pledges commitment to the cause "While life shall last."[4]

Like Fobes, other temperance activists composed dozens of sets of alternate lyrics to Smith's "America." The popular 1880 *Good Templar Songster for Temperance Meetings and the Home Circle*, for example, includes Smith's "America," identified as the "National Hymn," and seven alternate versions, with six grouped together on facing pages. Founded in central New York in 1851, the Independent Order of Good Templars, the group that produced the *Good Templar Songster*, trumpeted their "sole purpose" as delivering "the land and the world from the curse of intemperance." By 1886 the Good Templars had chapters in every state and in more than twenty other nations; these chapters held over ten thousand meetings each week and sang songs at most of them. Thirty-nine songs were prescribed by the Good Templars for use in their rituals. The *Good Templar Songster* collected and disseminated these songs, including multiple versions of "America," for meetings and rituals, so that "in all parts of the world the same ritual is in use, the same songs are sung."[5] Despite this pursuit of a homogeneous movement relying on the same rituals and songs, the versions of "America" in the *Good Templar Songster* have markedly different purposes and audiences. One, "God of the Temp'rance Cause," is a prayerful invocation for opening temperance meetings; another, "Children's Temperance Hymn," was written two decades earlier by John Pierpont for use in Sabbath schools and juvenile temperance societies. Yet another version praises "Our State" while another sings of "Our Cause." Three are millennial portrayals of the nation redeemed from alcohol. In Reverend C. S. H. Dunn's "My Country, 'Tis To Thee," the title and opening line of Smith's song are changed by one word, from "of" to "to," thus expressing the rhetorical ambitions of the Templar singers: "My country! 'tis to thee, / From ocean unto sea, / I'd raise my song." Dunn reinterprets Smith's "Let freedom ring" as a command to save the nation from "Rum" and in the last verse combines the language of nationalism, temperance, and religion as he calls on God to "Protect this Nation, bright, / From Rum's long reign of night, / Give freedom's holy light / In this dark hour."[6]

Like their antebellum predecessors, and as demonstrated so clearly in *The Good Templar Songster*, the post–Civil War temperance movement mastered the means of mass-produced print persuasion, thus blanketing the nation with affordable songbooks, hymnals, teaching manuals, and organizing manifestoes. It comes as no surprise, then, to learn that over one hundred thousand copies of the WCTU's *Popular Campaign Songs* had been sold by the time the Eighteenth Amendment was ratified in 1919. Temperance songs were not only popular in such movement-generated materials, however, but were often included in general collections of popular songs, where they were sometimes printed alongside such popular drinking songs as "Little Brown Jug." Nonetheless, temperance versions of "America" were popularized mostly via their inclusion in temperance songbooks, which provided large collections of songs for meetings and home use and stressed that temperance songs could be sung by one and all, not just by talented vocalists. An advertisement for *Temperance Battle Songs* (1884) thus promised "the most stirring" pieces that could "be made very effective with ordinary voices." The songs, the editor and publisher S. W. Straub assured, were "perfectly adapted to all temperance occasions."[7] Many songbooks, like *The Temperance Chimes* (1867) and *The Temperance Songster* (1845), were published as pocket-sized books that, like traditional hymnals, were easily portable and could be printed relatively cheaply (see figures 5.1 and 2.6). Furthermore, most temperance songbooks and guides included extensive lists of other available materials, creating a self-referential cycle in which each temperance book pointed to others that then pointed to others. *The Temperance Orator* (1874), for example, a "choice collection of prose and poetical articles and selections," includes seven pages of ads for temperance materials, including songbooks such as *The Temperance Chimes* and *Bugle Notes for the Temperance Army* (see figure 5.2).[8] The success of the post–Civil War temperance movement, then, like that of the antebellum abolitionists and temperance activists before it, was based in no small part on its mastery of the political economy of publishing.

Following the successful strategy pioneered by Mason, Woodbridge, and the

Figure 5.1. The front cover of *Temperance Chimes* (1867). Courtesy of The University of Illinois Rare Book and Special Collections Library.

children's music education movement of the 1830s and 1840s, most major post–Civil War temperance organizations sponsored children's auxiliaries and devoted substantial attention to temperance instruction of the young. Indeed, by 1887 the Independent Order of Good Templars had approximately half a million adult members and 139,951 Juvenile Templars. "Compared with the child," Senator Blair argued, "it is of little consequence what becomes of the sot or even of the moderate drinker." Temperance leaders accordingly urged the mass education of children through public schools, Sabbath schools, and choirs. Temperance activists were so successful in this aspect of their work that by the 1880s half the states required alcohol education in public schools and the other half were considering such legislation. Along with this emphasis on public schools, Blair and others placed high priority on the development and distribution of suitable materials for children's temperance instruction.[9] The National Temperance Society's 1880 *National Temperance Hymn and Song Book*, for example, includes a full-page advertisement of children's temperance materials published by J. N. Stearns. A prominent New York publishing agent, Stearns offered pamphlets, membership certificates, and songbooks for use by juvenile temperance organizations and Sabbath schools. Ten sets of concert exercises for Sunday

The National Temperance Society's Books.

Esther Maxwell's Mistake. 18mo, 236 pages. By Mrs. E. N. JANVIER, author of "Andrew Douglass," **$1 00**

This book is full of Gospel truth, and written in a simple but earnest style, showing the utter absurdity of endeavoring to forget trouble by the use of strong drink, which Esther, like many others, found soon formed habits not easily broken. Her sudden awakening to this fact, and turning to her Saviour for pardon and help to renounce the temptation to drink, make one of the most touching narratives ever written.

Wealth and Wine. 12mo, 320 pp. By Miss MARY DWINELL CHELLIS, author of "Temperance Doctor," "At Lion's Mouth," **$1 25**

This book is written in her best style, showing the deception of the wine-cup and the power of woman's influence, together with the evil influence of social and moderate drinking. Its moral and Christian tone is excellent, and none can fail to be profited by its teachings.

The Life Cruise of Captain Bess Adams. 12mo, 413 pages. By Mrs. J. MCNAIR WRIGHT, author of Nothing to Drink, etc., **$1 50**

A sea-story, filled with thrilling adventures on the deep, and intensely interesting scenes on land in the midst of a quaint old sea-coast town, proving effectually that alcoholic drinks are not needed on shipboard or on land, and should be absolutely banished. The brave Christian character of Captain Adams and the heroism of his daughter, Bess, together with the pure religious tone pervading every page, make this one of the most interesting books ever written.

The Model Landlord. 18mo. By Mrs. M. A. HOLT, author of "John Bentley's Mistake," "Work and Reward," . . **$0 60**

It shows how a "model landlord" who keeps a gilded saloon for fashionable wine-drinkers, though he may attend church, give money to the poor, and circulate in the "first society," may be the greatest instrument in leading the young down to destruction.

Miscellaneous Publications.

The Bases of the Temperance Reform. 12mo, 224 pages. By Rev. DAWSON BURNS, ... **$1 00**

This is an English prize essay, which took the second prize under the liberal offer of James Teare for the best essay on the entire temperance question.

Bacchus Dethroned. 12mo, 248 pages. By FREDERICK POWELL, **$1 00**

This is an English prize essay, written in response to a prize offered by James Teare, of England, for the best temperance essay. The question is presented in all its phases, physiological, social, political, moral, and religious. It is very comprehensive.

The National Temperance Orator. 12mo, 288 pp. By Miss L. PENNEY, **$1 00**

This is issued in response to the many urgent calls for a book similar to the "New Temperance Speaker," used widely throughout the country. Is contains articles by the best temperance writers of the day, poems, recitations, readings, dialogues, and choice extracts from speeches from some of the ablest temperance speakers in the country, for the use of all temperance workers, Lodges, Divisions, Bands of Hope, etc., etc.

Bugle Notes for the Temperance Army. Price, paper covers, **30** cents; boards, ... **$0 35**

A new collection of Songs, Quartets, and Glees, for the use of all Temperance gatherings, glee clubs, etc., together with the Odes of the Sons of Temperance and Good Templars.

Temperance Chimes. Price, in paper covers, **30** cents, single copies; **$25** per hundred. Price, in board covers, **35** cents; per hundred, ... **$30 00**

A Temperance Hymn and Tune-Book of 128 pages, comprising a great variety of Glees, Songs, and Hymns designed for the use of Temperance Meetings and Organizations, Bands of Hope, Glee Clubs, and the Home Circle. Many of the Hymns have been written expressly for this book by some of the best writers in the country.

Bound Volumes of Sermons, $1 50

Seventeen sermons delivered upon the invitation of The National Temperance Society, and published in the National Series, have all been bound in one volume, making 400 pages of the best temperance matter of the kind ever published. The sermons are by Revs. Henry Ward Beecher, T. L. Cuyler, T. De Witt Talmage, J. B. Dunn, John Hall, J. P. Newman, J. W. Mears, C. D. Foss, J. Romeyn Berry, Herrick Johnson, Peter Stryker, C. H. Fowler, H. C. Fish, H. W. Warren, S. H. Tyng, and W. M. Taylor.

Text-Book of Temperance. By Dr. F. R. LEES, ... **$1 50**

We can also furnish the above book, which is divided into the following parts: 1. Temperance as a Virtue. 2. The Chemical History of Alcohol. 3 The Dietetics of Temperance. 4. The Pathology of Intemperance. 5. The Medical Question. 6. Temperance in Relation to the Bible. 7. Historical. 8. The National Question and the Remedy. 9. The Philosophy of Temperance.

Figure 5.2. Advertisements from "Publications of the National Temperance Society," appended to Miss L. Penney, ed., *The National Temperance Orator* (1874). Courtesy of The University of Illinois Rare Book and Special Collections Library.

schools are advertised here, including "The Cup of Death" and "The Alcohol Fiend." Julia Colman's song "The Temperance School" promises "full directions for organizing and conducting a Temperance School."

Juvenile temperance organizations and materials, as reflected in Stearns's advertisement, were designed both to persuade children of the evils of alcohol (through materials such as "Pictorial Tracts for Children") and to train them as agents to persuade others. The Stearns advertisement thus includes scripts for declamations and dramatic dialogues (such as "Curing a Drunkard, for four girls") through which children could appeal to adult listeners. Stearns also offered L. Penney's *National Temperance Orator* and his own *Temperance Speaker*, a collection of speeches for presentation by young people to adult audiences. In fact, teaching righteous children to persuade wayward adults to join the temperance movement became one of the key components of late-nineteenth and early-twentieth-century temperance activism. For example, in *The Curse of Drink: Stories of Hell's Commerce* (1910), Elton Shaw recounts an incident in which sixteen tavern customers and the owner supposedly swore off drinking after a little girl, brought to the bar by her widowed mother, sang "Mother's a Drunkard, and Father Is Dead." A popular twist on this story was the song "Mother Is Dead," in which a little girl sings pathetically: "Life is so hard since mother is dead; / It is so hard to beg for my bread; / No one for months on me has smiled; / Pity and pray for the poor drunkard child."[10] The 1880 *National Temperance Hymn and Song Book*, which includes both Smith's "America" and two alternative temperance versions, took the different route of addressing children directly. "Come with Us to the Spring," for example, a song directed to youthful drinkers, asks: "Why to the wine-cup's brim / Where mirth and folly swim / Press thy young lip?" Instead, the young listener is encouraged in the second verse to "Come join us at the spring! / Come join us while we sing / Cold water's praise."[11] Much as in antebellum reform movements, then, late-nineteenth- and early-twentieth-century temperance activists approached children both as *targets of* and *agents for* musical persuasion.

Along with this complicated relationship to children, Reconstruction and Gilded Age temperance activists relied on hefty doses of hyperbole to persuade the unconvinced. One popular form of hyperbole was the threat that even moderate drinking would lead to both physical death and eternal damnation. For example, along with a prose argument regarding "Moderation vs. Total Abstinence," the *Temperance Almanac* of 1880 printed a wonderfully provocative image of moderation leading inevitably to death (see figure 5.3). Note that the "Teetotal Bridge" bears a cross on its awning, while distressed witnesses on the shore pray for victims hurtling over the edge of the waterfall of drinking. Some hapless victims falling off the "Moderation Bridge" into the deadly waters below are even drawn to look transparent, as if their moderate drinking has not only lead

Figure 5.3. Drawing of "Moderation vs. Total Abstinence," from *The National Temperance Almanac and Teetotaler's Year Book* (1880). Courtesy of The University of Illinois Rare Book and Special Collections Library.

to their death but also, prior to their death, to their literally losing themselves — they are hollow, fuzzy, lost souls. Hence the politics of temperance veer into heavy-handed religious moralizing, complete with hyperbolic threats of death and damnation.[12]

Post–Civil War, Gilded Age, and early-twentieth-century temperance activists also relied on appropriated versions of "America" to invoke the still resonant symbolism of the War of Independence. For example, in "America's New Tyrant" (1905) Harriet Castle compares the scourge of alcohol to both British and Satanic tyranny: "Once more a tyrant reigns; / Rum is the tyrant's name; / At Satan's call he came / Our land to spoil."[13] Such simultaneously religious, political, and historical imagery portrayed temperance, like the Revolution, as a cause of national liberation. Indeed, the nation was at stake, and those who sought to save it from Rum—represented here as Satan's chosen weapon— accordingly described themselves as righteous patriots, as evangelical nationalists. The metaphor of the Revolution served two additional persuasive purposes. First, it offered hope for victory against great odds, just as the ragged Continental Army had overcome the powerful British. Second, it produced a sense of moral and historical obligation, linking support for the temperance movement to respect for the Revolution. For example, "The saloon is a most dangerous enemy of the republic," William Windom intoned on 4 July 1886, and must be destroyed "if the hopes of our fathers and our own ambition for this great republic are to be realized."[14] The temperance movement thus sought to honor the revolutionary "hopes of our fathers" by redeeming a nation awash in a mind-clouding and body-bloating sea of alcohol.

As a corollary to this method of looking back through time to honor the dead, temperance songwriters and speakers also peered into a glorious future where they imagined a nation redeemed from sin. These visions encouraged movement workers to imagine the prize for which they labored, to cherish the imminent glory of the country to follow upon its salvation from alcohol. The best of these forward-looking persuasive attempts simultaneously drew on long-standing national symbolism, collapsing past and future into the obligations of a revolutionary present. For example, "Our Land Redeemed" (1886), set to the tune of "America," opens with a powerful interlacing of present dangers and past struggles:

> My country! broad and fine,
> Cursed both by beer and wine,
>   Of thee I sing.
> Land where my fathers died,
> Land where King George defied
> And slavery set aside,
>   Thy deeds shall ring.

The song then shifts into a speculative voice that imagines the nation "Redeemed from rum and wine," hence enabling a utopian return to glory: "Oh, may our country shine, / And we may be wholly Thine, / Great God, our King."[15] "Our Land Redeemed" thus appropriates Smith's "America" while merging revolutionary past, temperance present, and utopian future in a righteous prayer of national salvation.

Indeed, long before national prohibition was enacted in law, temperance activists imagined a future hypothetical nation in which their cause had triumphed. Walter Fobes's 1889 "Temperance, Thy Noble Name," for example, predicts in lyrics set to the tune of "America" that

> When thy victory's won,
> And all our duty's done,
>   We'll sing thy praise;
> Honor and peace be there,
> Freedom for all to share,
> And joy beyond compare,
>   To endless days.[16]

Those singing "Temperance, Thy Noble Name" describe how they will feel and act "when thy victory's won," demonstrating how the prospect of victory sustains the sacrifices of the present. One finds such temporal displacements throughout temperance songs, as antialcohol forces frequently depicted in song a future sober republic where freedom from "the Demon Rum" would ring "from every mountainside." One of the curiosities of such visions is that they assumed—both before and after the Civil War—that a dry republic would serve as a moral beacon for other nations, until "the Temperance flag unfurled / Shall wave throughout the world / In every land."[17] Thus, much as Lyman Beecher had previously spoken of temperance and "empire" in the same breath (see chapter 2), so Fobes revels in the colonizing energy that projects white middle-class reformers "throughout the world / In every land."

It may seem odd today to hear temperance writers such as Fobes describe legal restrictions on drinking as "freedom for all to share," particularly when couched in verse that clearly invokes such empire-building zest, yet it was believed at the time that those who were "enslaved by the cup" could never be considered truly free. In short, because dependence on alcohol diminishes the capacity for free choice, "freedom to drink" is an oxymoron. Such arguments in turn enabled temperance activists to think of themselves as abolitionists, as activists fighting against a new form of slavery. In fact, temperance activists found this provocative image so powerful that long after the passage of the Thirteenth Amendment abolishing slavery they continued to use the slavery metaphor to describe intemperance. "Alcohol, the foe of freemen," Mrs. J. Hitchcock wrote after the war, "Binds us fast in slavish chains." In *The Temperance Movement*, Senator Blair devoted a chapter to the necessity for a "New Emancipation" (total abstinence), based on the constitutionally established truth that slavery is incompatible with democratic liberties. Such claims were riven with contradictions, for despite the strong presence in the antebellum temperance movement of abolitionists and free blacks, most postwar national temperance organizations were segregated and sought to gain support in the South by using racist appeals that associated problem drinking with African Americans and foreigners. Indeed, the WCTU and other temperance groups organized whites by appealing to racist stereotypes and fears. White prohibitionists in Birmingham, Alabama, for example, sought to gather support in 1907 by warning of "PICTURES OF NUDE WOMEN ON BOTTLES OF WHISKEY SOLD TO NEGROES."[18] Thus, much like the muddled drug warriors of today, temperance speakers of the late nineteenth and early twentieth centuries drew lurid portrayals of drink-crazed African Americans and foreigners, whom they blamed for violent crime and society's moral decline.[19]

The Eighteenth Amendment was submitted to the states for ratification in December 1917, at the height of World War I (and only six months after the free speech–destroying Espionage Act of 15 June 1917), in large part as a "patriotic" reaction against the millions of recent immigrants, especially poor Germans and Irish, who were identified both with the enemy Central Powers and with the sale and use of alcohol.[20] Prohibition was advanced then—and ratified in 1919—in large part as a "patriotic" wartime measure to rescue the nation from the corrupting influences of mass immigration. Thus, despite the reliance of nineteenth-century temperance activists on the enabling rhetoric of revolution, democracy, and the abolition of slavery, the movement's culminating achievement in the twentieth century may be linked directly to longstanding white middle-class fears about racial and national outsiders.

Suffrage: "Our Birth-Rights Claim We Now"

Despite their remarkable contributions to antebellum abolitionism, temperance, suffrage, and school reform movements, and despite their heroic roles in serving the nation during the Civil War, American women of the Reconstruction and Gilded Age were still second-class citizens. The passage of the Fourteenth Amendment in 1868 and the Fifteenth Amendment in 1870, which together granted full citizenship to all black men, including the vote, was thought by many women's suffrage activists to be a precursor to their own imminent enfranchisement. However, while the complicated geopolitical imperatives of Reconstruction induced radical Republicans to support black male voting rights, which it was thought would guarantee Republican control in the South, women were still thought to be too politically unpredictable to be of much use to either party. In fact, arguing for women's suffrage was considered a political handicap that could derail what were considered more pressing Reconstruction goals. As Ellen Carol DuBois has noted, "abolitionists' increased political power made them more reluctant to support feminist demands than they had been before the War." Reconstruction-era suffrage activists accordingly felt betrayed by both abolitionists and Republicans yet were also heartened by the belief that dramatic Constitutional changes were within their grasp. This dual sense of bitterness and cautious hope is evident in "Foremother's Hymn," an 1885 version of "America" that laments: "Land where we stand and wait; / Like supplicants at the gate, / Debarred by laws of State / Thy praise to sing." Hence Reconstruction found women's suffrage activists fighting for entrance to full citizenship, hoping to be able to sing "Thy praise" to a land where liberty and freedom were no longer restricted by gender.[21]

The women's rights movement produced far fewer songbooks than the antislavery or temperance movements. Several of those that were published, however, including May Wheeler's *Booklet of Song* (1884), were distributed in large quantities. Wheeler, a Minnesota suffragist and temperance activist, published two alternate versions of "America" in her collection. Her own version, "My

Native Country," adopts the first-person voice of Smith's original to make a personal plea for political recognition:

> My native country, now
> Before whom nations bow,
>   O hear my song!
> May this fair land be free,
> From golden gate to sea,
> That laws may equal be,
>   As years prolong.[22]

Wheeler also reprinted Elizabeth Boynton Harbert's "The New America," which was composed and performed for the annual convention of the National Woman Suffrage Association (NWSA) in Washington, D. C., in January 1883. The NWSA was founded in 1869 by Elizabeth Cady Stanton and Susan B. Anthony; its national conventions featured delegates from many states. "The New America" became a staple of the NWSA and other suffrage groups and has been rediscovered by modern women's rights groups. In fact, Elizabeth Knight recorded "The New America" for her 1958 Folkways album *Songs of the Suffragettes*. Like "Rights of Woman" in 1795 (see chapter 2 and appendix A), "The New America" in 1883 (see appendix A) urged an activist reclamation of liberty, freedom, and justice, three of the touchstone democratic promises so long denied to women. The song opens with this bold claim: "Our country now from thee, / Claim we our liberty, / In freedom's name." The second verse argues that women have waited too long for their natural rights and that such rights will now be seized: "Our birth-right claim we now— / Longer refuse to bow." Thus, whereas Smith's 1831 lyric begins with an acknowledgement of the freedoms enjoyed by the singer, as an implied *he* sings of the country as a "sweet land of liberty," in "The New America" women singers announce their intention to wrest their liberty *from* a reluctant country. Harbert's lyric draws on the principles and precedents of the American Revolution ("their zeal our own inspires") to support the cause of women's rights, and depicts the suffrage movement as a continuation of "the work so well begun" in the Revolution. The middle stanza, however, in an astute play on the emotions of the assumed guilty parties—and in a move that clearly parallels the way temperance activists appealed to guilty parents—appeals to men, who are asked to act on behalf of their "mothers on bended knee" to "Rise, now in manhood's might" to unite with women in the suffrage cause.[23]

After its premiere in 1883, "The New America" became a regular part of NWSA meetings. The song's popularity may be traced in large part to Harriet May Mills and Isabel Howland's *Manual for Political Equality Clubs*, an 1896 pamphlet that compiled set programs for NWSA meetings. Designed primarily for new chapters, the *Manual* outlined each meeting, providing canned prayers, speeches, and songs. The *Manual* thus provides a detailed look at the proceedings of many local meetings and at the efforts of the NWSA to unify the beliefs and efforts of its individual chapters. One obvious aspect of these meetings is that songs were included in each program, with the *Manual* instructing chapters that "all present should join in the singing." "The New America" was featured in the model program for the second meeting, which is devoted to the question of "How the People Govern." Group singing of "The New America" follows the opening prayer, which implores God to "incarnate Thy perfect will in the laws and customs of the world" by effecting equality between the sexes. The song is followed by the chapter president's address (with choral responses from the membership) on the exclusion of women from governance.[24] Hence, much as Smith's original 1831 version of "America" benefited from its institutionalization in the form of hymn books, school readers, and both abolitionist and temperance anthologies, so "The New America" benefited from its institutionalized place within NWSA meetings and its wide distribution in the *Manual for Political Equality Clubs*.

Another aspect making "The New America" so popular was its obviously parodic play on both Smith's original and Smith himself. Indeed, in another example of intertextual reference, of one writer borrowing themes and melodies from another to help make a claim more familiar, Harbert's "New America" describes women suffragists as the "daughters of patriot sires," clearly playing off of the title of Smith's second most popular song, "Patriot Sons of Patriot Sires." Perhaps even more important, however, "The New America" turned Smith's song toward political goals that he adamantly opposed, hence making the parody that much more pointed. Temperance and antislavery adaptations of Smith's "America" were to some extent in accord with Smith's own political beliefs, as he was a supporter of both causes and published songs and poetry devoted to them. But women's suffrage was another matter. In fact, Smith was unalterably opposed to the women's rights movement and made his opposition public in an unfortunate piece entitled "Women's Rights":

> 'Tis my creed,—perhaps I'm wrong,
> But I'll say it for a song,—
>   Their right is to promote us
> From bachelors to men,
> To excel us with the pen,
>   But never to outvote us.

Smith's "Women's Rights" is addressed to a male readership, whom Smith feels confident will share his view of men as "the lords of this creation" and of women's suffrage as a threat to their power. The only "right" to be yielded to women, Smith advises, is "the right / To be witty, brave, and bright." For Smith, women's proper station is that of "mothers to our boys" and "sunlight of the home"; they should have no part in public affairs. Women's suffrage, he warns, will "run the nation, / From zenith down to nadir." Smith thus argues in "Women's Rights" that while motherhood is a patriotic duty yet political power is an exclusively male dominion. Hence the author of what was known lovingly at the time as "the national hymn" voices the traditional patriarchal version of American democracy: politics are for men, domestic space is for women. Feminists of course contested this idea of the nation. The African American suffragist Mary Ann Shadd Cary, for example, speaking for the NWSA before a committee of the U.S. House of Representatives in 1872, insisted that "the strength and glory of a free nation, is *not so much* in the size and equipment of its armies, as in the *loyal hearts* and willing hands of its *men* and *women*," who have an equal right to be governed by their own consent.[25]

Despite Smith's intransigent loyalty to patriarchy, suffragists used "America" as a vehicle both to criticize the nation as then constituted and to project a future nation, one true to its principles and more inclusive in its liberties. Thus the final stanza of "The New America" imagines a country in which "Women are free." As in the hypothetical temperance nation, however, there were limits to the inclusiveness of the nation imagined by many white suffragists. Despite the efforts of Cary, Sojourner Truth, and other African Americans active in the NWSA, the suffragist nation as expressed by Stanton, Anthony, and other white leaders, as Philip Cohen has observed, was "based on exclusive citizenship that was conditioned on whiteness." In fact, postwar suffrage organizations largely abandoned the rhetoric of natural and equal rights that had once formed the basis for a coalition with abolitionists. The NWSA and other suffrage groups adopted instead an essentialist rhetoric that often stressed white women's innate moral qualities and that sought support for white women's suffrage as a means of offsetting African American men's votes.[26] Much like the moralizing and racially driven fears of the temperance movement, white suffragists' nationalist discourses portrayed white women's suffrage as a necessary element of nation-building, as a call for the "Daughters of Patriot sires" to redeem the nation from its vices and from the corrupting influences of its diverse population. Indeed, even while arguing for their own empowerment the women's suffrage movement continued the national tradition of pursuing democratic rights segregated by both class and color. Nonetheless, while gender equality — even on this limited model — was to prove far more elusive than the vote, the passage of the Nineteenth Amendment (submitted in 1919; ratified in 1920) was celebrated as the culmination of more than a century of struggle for women's rights.

Labor and Economic Reform: "Dark Land of Tyranny . . . [Where] Capital Is King"

One of the most persistent challenges of American democracy is balancing the foundational claims to life, liberty, and the pursuit of happiness, particularly when one understands that the latter two of these terms, following the long philosophical tradition of seventeenth- and eighteenth-century liberalism, were rooted ultimately in notions of private property. Indeed, whereas Greek notions of democracy hinged on the desire of citizens to participate in public debate regarding the good of society, liberal versions of democracy increasingly came during the late eighteenth and early nineteenth centuries to view governments not as public forums for pursuing virtue but as institutional apparatuses that could facilitate the accumulation of individual wealth.[27] Hence, from the earliest days of America, those who wanted to see democracy as a means of publicly debating questions of virtue and justice found themselves battling those who wanted to see democracy as a means of privately organizing property. From the first questions raised about slavery and indentured servitude in the early 1700s through the federalist debates of 1787 and 1788, up through Reconstruction and the Gilded Age and on toward our contemporary debates regarding computer monopolies and the regulation of cyberspace, Americans have struggled to balance justice and capital, democracy and property, equality and wealth. While this broad subject has received ample attention elsewhere, our hope here is to convey the urgency with which Americans of the Gilded Age addressed the apparent contradictions between democracy and capitalism and to demonstrate the remarkable role of "America" in enabling them to explore possible alternatives.

Many labor activists attributed unique rhetorical qualities to song, particularly in its ability to reach those whom other forms of persuasion could not. Thus A. W. Wright, editor of the *Journal of the Knights of Labor*, wrote that songs "will reach thousands to whom arguments would at first be addressed in vain." Labor songs appealed to workers not only because of their entertaining and participatory performance but as a form of literature that treated issues from the viewpoints of workers themselves and that reflected long traditions of work songs among miners, weavers, and other laborers. Indeed, from as early as the late 1820s and early 1830s the rise of trade unions and workers' political parties produced a substantial labor press—totaling upwards of fifty labor weeklies—that distributed pamphlets, broadsides, songbooks, poems, and manuals to workers. By the 1880s, there were hundreds of labor publications, representing dozens of different occupations and all major (as well as most minor) union and labor organizations; their editors solicited songs from readers and published many of these grassroots submissions. These worker-produced songs were typically set to the melodies of popular and national songs, a practice that some scholars have attributed to workers' lack of leisure time for composition. As discussed in each of our previous chapters, however, the use of familiar melodies was more likely motivated by other considerations, including the less expensive printing costs of publishing verse without musical scores and the comparative ease with which such revised songs could be learned and performed. For example, Karl Reuber advertised his 1871 *Hymns of Labor* as "Remodeled From Old Songs," presumably in the belief that this would be a feature attractive to consumers and activists alike.[28]

As a universally popular cultural icon, a widely used protest song, and an established component of ceremonial and performative traditions that lent nationalist dignity to meetings and rituals, Samuel Smith's "America" was an obvious target for appropriation by labor songwriters. For example, when Ira Steward and the National Labor Union (NLU) stepped up the campaign for the eight-hour day after the Civil War, the labor movement actively solicited songs that could be used in eight-hour league meetings and other union functions. Jonathan Fincher, the editor of *Fincher's Trades' Review*, announced a contest for eight-hour day songs in the summer of 1865. In the September 23 issue he published an anonymous reader's submission, set to the melody of "America":

> Ye noble sons of toil,
> Who ne'er from work recoil,
> Take up the lay.
> Loud let the anthems roar
> Resume from shore to shore,
> Till time shall be no more.
> Eight Hours a Day.[29]

Steward and the NLU believed that the eight-hour day campaign would unify workers across trades and that, when won, the shorter work-day would give workers sufficient leisure time both to educate themselves and to change the social order. Fincher clearly supported this vision, as did his anonymous contributor, who, like so many reformers before her, recognized the efficacy of appropriating "America" to achieve these ends.[30]

Largely as a result of the tireless efforts of labor activists, by late 1868 six states had adopted eight-hour day legislation and Congress had done so for federal employees. But these gains were lost with the onset of the six-year depression that began in September 1873 and left over three million people unemployed, thus forcing workers to accept large pay cuts while enabling employers to blacklist labor organizers. Unions were devastated. Farmers were hit particularly hard by the depression of the 1870s, as railroad rates increased (driving up shipping costs) and overproduction drove prices down. As the price of wheat plunged from a high of one dollar and five cents per bushel in 1866 to sixty-seven cents per bushel in 1895 and the yield per acre doubled during the same period, farmers were left in a precarious position. One result of such economic changes was that farmers began losing their land. As Sean Dennis Cashman observes, farm tenancy "increased as the century drew to a close, from 25 percent in 1880 to 28 percent in 1890 and 36 percent in 1900."[31] Thinking in broad terms, the downturn in prices and the loss of their land, coupled with the rise of industrial production, meant that after the Civil war, farmers slowly lost political power, especially at the federal level, to the rising classes of (among others) manufacturers, bankers, and railroad men.

Farmers organized in response to these pressures by forming cooperatives, which pooled equipment and resources, and fraternal societies, which served as hubs of political and cultural activism. Hundreds of songs, including several set to the melody of "America," were written for use at these gatherings. In fact, from as early as the Revolution farm workers had used the melody of "God Save the King" and then "America" in their households and social gatherings as a hymn to the value of their labors. By the Civil War, at least three farmers' versions were in wide use, including I. F. Shepard's "Thanksgiving Hymn" (1842), James Montgomery's "Praise to the God of Harvest" (c. 1854), and "God Bless the Farmer's Toil" (1861), which was "sung at Harvest Home celebrations, Agricultural Fairs and Festivals, &c." These songs extol the virtues of the farmer, who "nobly tills the ground / From sun to sun." Set to the melody of the national hymn, the farmers' "America"'s portray the harvest of the "fruitful field" as the nation's bounty, their role in that process as a kind of stewardship, and the farming life as a dignified calling blending virtuous toil and God's blessing.[32] Such musical claims are supported by an image from 1875 that positions a noble farmer surrounded by a series of other occupations. Whereas the banker says "I fleece you all" (there are nine other roles, none as bleak as banking), the farmer says "I feed you all" (see figure 5.4).

Thus "America" was used to celebrate the Jeffersonian values of land and labor. Much as Jefferson feared, however, the rise of modernity was slowly transforming America from an agricultural into a manufacturing society, forcing farmers to fight for political power as their long-term economic situation eroded. Among the political organizations used by farmers in these struggles, perhaps none were as successful as the "Grange." Founded in 1867 by six government clerks in Washington, D.C., by 1875 The Order of the Patrons of Husbandry (the Grange) had thirty thousand chapters nationwide and over two million members. At the peak of Grange activity, in February 1874, an average of eighty new lodges were established each day. Modeled on the Masonic Order, the Grange employed secret rituals and signs. Symbolically laden degrees of membership were established for men (including Laborer, Cultivator,

Figure 5.4. Granger lithograph (1875). Courtesy of The Library of Congress.

Harvester, and Husbandman) and women (such as Maid, Shepherdess, Gleaner, and Matron). Much as at abolitionist, temperance, and suffrage gatherings, songs were performed at Grange meetings, and activist farmers, like their fellow reformers, used alternative versions of "America" to voice their concerns. For example, the 1872 songbook *Songs of the Grange* includes A. B. Curry's version of "America." Written as a prayer, it asks: "Thou who hast taught the worth / Of *labor*, bring us forth / From East, West, South, and North, / In proud array." In singing the song Grangers depicted themselves as part of a national organization of workers whose efforts were blessed by God. Although officially nonpolitical, the Grangers were active in a variety of causes and campaigns, particularly railroad regulation and civil service reform.[33]

Labor also reorganized in the 1870s, largely in secret, while fueled by the conviction, as Clark Halker writes, that "the nation's ruling elite had set the nation on a course of ruin and that only workers and their unions could save the Republic." This urgent sense that nothing less than the fate of the nation was at stake was reflected in labor appropriations of national songs that both laid claim to national principles and offered visions of a nation yet to be realized in which laborers would enjoy power, prosperity, and security. At a practical level, labor's appropriations of national songs borrowed from the performative traditions of their much-loved melodies. At a deeper historical level, however, using "America" and other popular national songs was a way of participating in a long-standing dialogue with American culture itself. We have established in the preceding chapters that national songs were often performed as public loyalty oaths, that they have served historically as statements of identity and belonging, and that they have traditionally been sung at public events, ceremonies, and protests. National songs are therefore remarkably flexible vehicles for challenging political realities while still claiming citizenship, so that one may attack the nation while still being of it and in it. Labor organizations clearly recognized the dual functions of such national songs—serving both as criticism of a policy *and* celebration of citizenship—and thus often used their versions of national songs to open and close meetings, hence singing protest material while ritualizing codes of membership and behavior. Indeed, some songs were institutionalized in prescribed rituals in which all were expected to join in singing. As explained by Terence Powderly, Grand Master Workman of the Knights of Labor, "no one member was selected to sing alone."[34]

The Knights of Labor were formed in 1869 and remained a secret organization until 1881. They had a penchant for oaths, rituals, secret handshakes, and elaborate officer titles; songs were an essential element of their meetings and public communications. The Knights of Labor encouraged their members to write songs promoting the cause of labor, and their national offices accordingly received numerous submissions. For example, in 1886 John Cotter, a printer in Saginaw, Michigan, and Master Workman of Local Assembly 2897 of the Knights of Labor, composed an "Initiation Ode," set to the melody of "America," that was adopted by the national organization and used in most locals. Such songs and rituals contributed to the sense of the Knights, as Philip Foner has written, as "a mass fraternal lodge, a working-class Masonic order." Although half a century earlier farmers and skilled craftspersons had formed the nucleus of the American anti-Masonic movement, they now created their own equivalents of the Masonic Order. And much as earlier Masons had used songs based on the melody of "America" and "God Save the King" to lend ceremonial dignity to their meetings and rituals, so the Knights and Grangers followed suit.[35]

The strength and influence of the Knights of Labor increased dramatically during the 1880s. At its height in 1886 the organization had seven hundred thousand members, including African American and white, male and female, native-born and immigrant workers from all regions of the country. "An injury to one," the order's slogan announced, "is the concern of all." The Knights opposed the use of strikes and organized workers in mixed assemblies rather than trade unions. They supported a broad platform of social legislation, including government ownership of railroads and communications and the elimination of the private banking system. As described by Philip Foner, they sought to promote the "financial and industrial emancipation of the World's Workers from

Corporate Tyranny and Wage Slavery." The Knights of Labor declared the education of workers their primary mission and accordingly established schools, lecture programs, and reading rooms. They placed particular emphasis on songs and poems as media for educating workers about important issues; "America" was among the melodies most frequently used for such topical productions.[36] For example, Ralph E. Hoyt published an alternate version of "America" in the *Journal of the Knights of Labor* on 3 July 1890 (see appendix A). The song opens with a wry lament: "Our Country, 'tis of thee, / Sweet land of knavery, / Of thee we sing!" This knavery is mass produced and well financed, however, as the nation is now a "Land where fond hopes have died, / Where demagogues reside, / Monopolies preside, / And misery bring." In the second verse the implied singers, like those of Smith's lyrics, proclaim their love of America's "rocks and rills," but in Hoyt's "America" they qualify their affection: they love "not thy bitter ills" and view the nation's postwar proclamations of "freedom" and "equal rights" as "somewhat hollow." In the last verse, Hoyt yearns for a nation that is a "true land of liberty," which Smith's song presumes already exists. Lamenting America's shortcomings, Hoyt imagines how it would be to sing in earnestness a "cheerful song" in "loud praise" of the nation that might someday be.[37] Hoyt's "America," like those produced by the suffrage, temperance, and antislavery movements, thus ends with a visionary glance toward a future America cleansed of its Gilded Age hypocrisies and compromises.

In comparison to such forward-looking, utopian versions of "America," many labor activists and economic reformers portrayed Smith's "America" as a paradise lost, a land of liberty that once existed but had been corrupted and betrayed. Indeed, the recurring economic downturns of the post–Civil War decades and growing cynicism about governmental corruption and the monopolistic power of big business lent a hollow ring to proclamations of national progress. In "A New National Anthem" (1891), for example, Thomas Nicol writes "My country 'tis of thee, / *Once* land of liberty." In Nicol's despondent view, Americans "*were* so pure and free / *Long, long ago*." H. W. Finson's 1891 version of the song also describes an America in which "Our liberties are gone, / Justice no more is done."[38] Two years earlier H. C. Dodge published in *Baker's Journal* a similarly bleak version of "America" entitled "The Future America." Despite its title, Dodge's song is less about the future than the lost past and a botched present. Smith's "America" here becomes a bitter benchmark of an age of corruption and greed:

> My country 'tis of thee
> Land of lost Liberty,
> Of thee we sing.
> Land which the millionaires,
> Who govern our affairs,
> Own for themselves and heirs—
> Hail to thy king.

Dodge uses Smith's "America" to decry the failure of the American Revolution, ending with a statement of regret that Americans have not "Put down the cursed wrong / That makes a king." In this tragic version of history gone wrong, Americans threw off the yoke of one monarch only to raise up another in the form of "the millionaires, / Who govern our affairs." For Dodge, the United States is no longer a "sweet land of liberty." Instead, it is a "land of lost liberty," a country "betrayed by bribery," a greed-infested swamp where sweet Freedom has died, leaving workers as merely "wretched slaves." Dodge's song is thus a fatalistic lament for a democracy ruined by capitalism: "Alas!" he writes, it is "too late" to realize America's once revolutionary promise.[39]

Urban workers were joined by farmers in their dim assessment of the state of the union. In 1886, the Farmers' Alliance spread throughout the South, as thousands of local organizations were established and loosely affiliated in an effort to gain political power. In 1890 the Alliance swept through the Midwest, where it gained control of several state legislatures; in the South it elected forty-five representatives and three senators to Congress. By 1891 the Northern and Southern Alliances, along with the Colored Farmers' National Alliance and Cooperative Union, had more than three million members and formed a coalition with the Knights of Labor, thus forming the nucleus of the Populist Party. The Alliance held mass regional meetings where thousands of farmers gathered to socialize, hear speeches, and sing songs. The Alliance solicited movement songs from its members and sponsored competitions for farmer glee clubs. Many farmers and laborers responded to the call, and their songs were published in newspapers, broadsides, and collections. The most popular Alliance songbook was Leopold Vincent's *Alliance and Labor Songster* (1891). Along with his father and brother, Vincent edited the *Winfield (Kansas) American Nonconformist*, which supported the Alliance and alcohol prohibition. Vincent's *Alliance and Labor Songster*, a compilation of songs by various writers, sold over forty thousand copies in the first ten months and was reprinted in several editions. *The Alliance and Labor Songster* includes Smith's "America" and five alternate versions, including Dodge's "The Future America" (see figures 5.5 and 5.6). One version, "Once More We Meet to Clasp," is suggested as an "opening ode" for labor meetings. Three others link labor's struggle with the patriot cause in the American Revolution, whose soldiers fought "Through foul and fair, and shine" to victory. In all five alternate versions, farmers and other workers sing for freedom from the oppression of monopolists, tyrannical employers, and economic insecurity, hence illustrating how they saw capitalism (like monarchy before it) destroying the promises and possibilities of democracy.

Much as in the 1870s, the political power produced by the alliance of the farmers' movement with labor was shattered in the 1890s by a crippling economic crisis. In fact, from 1893 to 1897 the United States experienced the worst depression to that point in its history. By the end of 1893 over sixteen thousand businesses had failed and between two and four million workers were unemployed.[40] Down-and-out workers traveled long distances seeking jobs, only to be turned away. Half the "tramps" studied in fourteen cities were found to be skilled workers who had been driven to the streets by their inability to find work. Without effective social welfare programs, homelessness and starvation became commonplace. Membership in the Knights of Labor and most unions dwindled, so that by 1895 the ranks of organized labor were no greater than they had been at the end of the Civil War. One response to this economic catastrophe was that the South was swept with racial violence as depressed white farmers and workers unloaded their anxieties and frustrations by attacking their black neighbors.[41] Even when not resulting in violence, the severe economic hardships, combined with the loss of organized economic and political power, produced an overwhelming sense of despair. For example, in "America—1895," O. J. Graham updated Smith's song to depict the nation in the midst of depression. "We once had liberty," Graham proclaims, "Peace and prosperity," but "Now, want and misery / All through our land." In lines that clearly foreshadow the biting style of Woody Guthrie, Graham describes a shattered land where "Tramps line our public way, / Men starving every day, / How just, how grand." This ironic nod to botched justice and tarnished national grandeur is followed by lines that detail the sources of the nation's difficulties: "Laws made by plutocrats, / And mugwump democrats, / All owned by autocrats / From a foreign land."[42]

In April 1895, one month before Graham's remarkable version appeared in print, thousands gathered in Boston to pay tribute to Smith as the author of the "national hymn." His death a few weeks later prompted eulogies and ceremonial performances of "America" in many states. But by 1895 Smith's 1831 portrayal of the country stood in striking contrast to the daily struggle for survival faced by millions of Americans who had lost their jobs, homes, and sustenance. Indeed, after two years of deep depression, Smith's "America" seemed irretrievably lost, a "Land where *once* all were free" and where "We *once had* liberty." Graham's song thus fulfills a doubly melancholic function as it honors the passing of a leading activist and songwriter of the reform movement while detailing the drowning of Smith's vision of liberty in the cesspool of trusts, monopolies, and corruption.

The labor variations on "America" produced at the end of the nineteenth century were bleak and fatalistic, far from the hopeful perfectionism that had once been expressed in antebellum reform versions of the song. And for good reason, as more than thirty-eight thousand strikes and lockouts, involving over seven and a half million workers, occurred in the "labor wars" from 1881 to 1905. During these bitter times employers increasingly relied on violence and

THE

+ALLIANCE·*and*·LABOR·SONGSTER+

A COLLECTION OF

LABOR AND COMIC SONGS,

FOR THE USE OF

Alliances, Grange Debating Clubs and Political Gatherings.

COMPILED BY

LEOPOLD VINCENT,

Winfield, Kas.

WINFIELD, KANSAS
H. & L. VINCENT, PRINTERS.
1891.

Copyright, 1891.

Figures 5.5, 5.6. The front cover of Leopold Vincent, comp., *The Alliance and Labor Songster* (1891), and the sheet music for H. C. Dodge, "The Future 'America'" (from the same source). Courtesy of The John Hay Library, Brown University.

scab labor to break strikes and unions and used the labor surplus created by the economic depression to force increases in working hours and cuts in wages. Local, state, and federal governments collaborated with employers by criminalizing union activities and lending military assistance. By 1900, when Rose Alice Cleveland's "Hymn of the Toilers," set to the tune of "America," was published in Charles Kerr's *Socialist Songs*, many union gains had been reversed,

Figure 5.6.

leaving working Americans depressed, ragged, and singing "When life and justice, asked, / Still further down were cast, / Even sobs were hush'd at last, / And hope seem'd dead."[43]

This hopelessness was nowhere more evident than in Colorado, where the powerful Western Federation of Miners (WFM) was destroyed in 1903–4 by the concerted efforts of mine owners, their governmental allies, and armed thugs. In fact, mine owners used militia to take over fifteen hundred striking miners prisoner and to banish two hundred from the state. The mining company–

backed Citizens' Alliance, operating as a vigilante government, destroyed union halls and printing presses and sponsored mob violence that killed dozens of mine workers. The collusion between government and mine owners to crush the unions and trample the civil liberties of mine workers produced deep disillusionment among union supporters about the state of American liberties and the possibility of social justice within the capitalist system. As Harry A. Floaten, a socialist supporter of the WFM, expressed in a bitter version of Smith's "America":

> Colorado, it is of thee,
> Dark land of Tyranny,
>   Of thee I sing.
> Land wherein labor's bled
> Land from which law has fled
> Bow down thy mournful head,
>   Capital is king.[44]

The alternate versions of "America" produced by farmers' and laborers' movements in the nineteenth and early twentieth centuries speak from the experiences of groups and individuals who believed, like Floaten, that their access to the liberties heralded in Smith's song had been denied or limited or simply crushed by the unflinching greed of a capitalist "tyranny" in which "Capital is king." At the same time, most of the alternate versions cited earlier embraced the ideals of Smith's original while simultaneously contrasting them with contemporary national realities. If in Smith's "America" the national character seems fixed as an already accomplished state to be celebrated, then labor's alternate versions speak of "America" as a land still becoming, as a troubled nation where sweet Freedom is elusive, lost, or yet to be achieved.

As the economic crises of the late nineteenth century deepened and as the American public came increasingly to attribute these difficulties to an unholy alliance between a lecherous government and vulturelike bankers, big businesses, and trusts, so the songs of activists came to reflect a profound disillusionment with the possibility of democracy surviving in the face of capitalism. What use is political participation, they asked, when the masses are starving, when workers are gunned down like dogs, when the press is bought and sold at the whim of robber barons, when political parties are indistinguishable, and when the police are but hired thugs of the trusts? "America" was a popular vehicle for expressing these doubts and angers. Ambrose Bierce's version, "A Rational Anthem," stands as perhaps the most bitter example of such appropriations. Bierce (1842–1913) served as a volunteer in the Union army during the Civil War and afterward moved to San Francisco, where he worked as a reporter and editor. In January 1881, after a series of financial mishaps and health problems, Bierce accepted a position as editor of the San Francisco *Wasp*, a Democratic anti-railroad weekly renowned for its nasty edge and color lithographs. In his columns—entitled "The Town Crier," "Prattle," and "The Devil's Dictionary"—"Bitter Bierce" railed against robber barons and political corruption. He waged a courageous campaign against the Central Pacific Railroad and its leaders, Leland Stanford (whom he parodied as $tealand Landford!), Collis Huntington, and Charles Crocker. Bierce was relentless in his criticism of the railroad barons, whose Central Pacific dominated the California economy and whose lobbyists had corrupted the legislature and press. He believed the nation was doomed by the forces of economic and political inequality represented by the railroad barons' power. Bierce described the United States as "a great, broad blackness with two or three small points of light struggling and flickering in the universal blank of ignorance, bigotry, crudity, conceit, tobacco-chewing, ill-dressing, unmannerly manners and general barbarity."[45]

This disenchantment is expressed in "A Rational Anthem" (1882; appendix A). Set to the tune of "America" and published in the *Wasp*, the song stands as a remarkable tribute to the sense that the Gilded Age marked the final dissolution of our "sweet land of liberty" into a swamp of corruption, greed, and decadence. Bierce's indictment extends beyond the Gilded Age, however; the first verse describes America as the "Land where my fathers fried / Young witches and applied / Whips to the Quaker's hide / And made him spring." By 1882 such vicious practices have become bureaucratized, as "Federal employees / And rings rob all they please" and "office-holders make / Their piles and judges rake / Our coin. For Jesus' sake, / Let's *all* go wrong!" This ironic appeal to Jesus is then turned around in the closing verse, which ends with Bierce picturing America as hell-on-earth festering "'Neath Satan's wing."[46] This final verse was apparently so provocative that some of Bierce's early biographers and anthologizers pretended it wasn't there, printing the song with only three verses.

Bierce later returned to Smith's "America" in another parody, "Land of the Pilgrims' Pride," in which he wrote: "The land is foul with crime, and none declares / Our shame and downfall." But Bierce himself was more than willing to do so. When asked if he does not, despite its faults, still love his country, Bierce responded: "Faith I would, / But 'tis infested by my countrymen."[47] These harsh words indicate how deeply some Americans had become disillusioned with the unchecked power of railroads and trusts and banks. Indeed, the century came to a close with activists and observers like Bierce using "America" as a vehicle for voicing their disgust with the fact that the promises and possibilities of democracy were crushed beneath "thieving bills," corrupt "mobs" and "rings," and crooked "Federal employees" and "judges." These sentiments are captured nicely in an 1882 illustration from the back page of Bierce's *Wasp* (see figure 5.7). Entitled "Patriotism, Past and Present," this lithograph by Freder-

Figure 5.7. G. Frederick Keller, color lithograph of "Patriotism, Past and Present," from the San Francisco *Wasp* (26 May 1882), back page. Courtesy of The University of Illinois Rare Book and Special Collections Library.

ick Keller depicts a heroic past in which "Uncle Sam" rides "Patriotism" amid shouts of allegiance from a farmer, sailor, soldier, and iron-smith. The botched present finds "Bribery," "Monopolies," "Grabbing," and "Official Corruption" devouring the rotting and bloodied carcass of the once proud "Patriotism."[48] Despite the image's nostalgia and its depiction of America as consisting of only white males, one would be hard pressed to find a more telling depiction of the despair gnawing away at many Americans at the close of the nineteenth century.

"To Arouse Enthusiasm for the Higher Values": Schooling and Mandatory Patriotism

While rowdy social critics like Bierce could sarcastically sneer "Let's *all* go wrong!" in the face of the Gilded Age's rampant political corruption and economic depression, elite leaders were clearly worried about what seemed to be a culture rapidly spinning out of control. Hence, as so often has been the case throughout American history, elite leaders of the late nineteenth and early twentieth centuries responded to the crises of faith, patriotism, and sociability among the disaffected working classes by turning to education as an apparatus of socialization. Patriotism slowly evolved, then, from a grassroots-based, evangelically driven, reform-minded love of the nation into a state-imposed fealty to order. As in the eighteenth and nineteenth centuries, "America" played an important role in this shift toward mandatory patriotism. Indeed, by the late nineteenth century, "America" was routinely performed (particularly in the Northeast and Midwest) at public events, and audiences were *expected* to join in singing it. By order of the governor of Massachusetts, all schoolchildren in the state simultaneously sang "America" in their classrooms on 21 October 1892, which was both Columbus Day and Samuel Smith's eighty-fourth birthday.[49] Hence, some sixty-one years after the song first premiered at a Fourth of July gathering organized by temperance activists, it had become a required aspect of an increasingly bureaucratic state.

The subtle link between patriotism, independent cultural activists, and state-organized institutions is illustrated nicely by Henry B. Carrington's popular 1894 *Beacon Lights of Patriotism*, a collection that offered sample programs of appropriate readings and music for "Memorial Observances" of Columbus Day, Arbor Day, Labor Day, and Washington's Birthday. The last, Carrington observed, was the holiday most likely to fall when school was in session; he accordingly offered a detailed program for school exercises honoring the occasion. A picture of Washington was to be placed on an easel at the front of the auditorium. Thirteen girls, each with a banner bearing the name of one of the original colonies, were to accompany their teacher, "who carries a wand or flag, and the insignia 'Columbia' upon brow, breast, or belt," to the stage. A program of songs and readings (such as "Washington as a Guide for Youth" or Jared Sparks's song "The Lesson of the Revolution") was offered, concluding with "America," which was to be "sung by all, standing." Such guidebooks instructed community groups in how to stage a proper ceremonial observance. Silver, Burdett, the publishers of Carrington's collection, appended eight "suggested programs for various public occasions" to their edition of the sheet music for Samuel Smith's "Patriot Sons of Patriot Sires: A Song for Young America" in 1895. Each program, like Carrington's for Washington's Birthday, consisted of a series of readings and songs (all selections from *Beacon Lights of Patriotism*) to be performed in a designated order. "America" was suggested as the appropriate opening song for Forefathers' Day and as the closing number for Independence Day, Washington's Birthday, Patriots' Day, Discovery (Columbus) Day, Arbor Day, and Labor Day. Schoolchildren and public audiences were expected to know "America'"s four verses and to join in singing them. Hence we see that by the turn of the century the song had become institutionalized as a crucial component in a series of culture-solidifying and nationalism-cementing holidays and ceremonies—in short, that it had become part of a carefully orchestrated system of mandatory patriotism.[50]

One particularly evocative example of the complicated uses made of "America" is Anna D. Cooper's 1907 illustrated pantomime of "America," "staged and posed for public exhibition" at public gatherings. The stage directions call for a stage decorated with flags. The performer is to wear Greek costume with "a large American Flag draped on the back, fastened on the shoulders, with the Stars uppermost." As "America" is played and sung, the performer strikes a series of poses, with the music "carefully modulated to conform with the illustrations and text, in their patriotic and devotional changes of sentiment and expression":

> "My Country, 'tis of thee, Sweet land of liberty, Of thee I sing." Take weight on right foot, the left free at side.
>
> On "My country," clasp flag with right hand, high toward left shoulder; left hand holds folds of flag at left side. Head bends tenderly over flag and face turns upwards to right. Picture No. I.
>
> On first word of "Sweet land of liberty," transfer weight to left foot; on second word, put out right foot and take weight upon it.
>
> Raise trunk to full height on "land," taking a deep inspiration; and on "liberty," carry out arms at side, drop flag, open palms and turn them about a quarter upwards. When finishing wave of arms, the hands will always fall slightly backwards on wrists if the unfolding sequence is properly made.
>
> "Of thee I sing." Keep same foot-position, carry arms higher, three-fourths to front. Palms lifted in praise. Trunk full height. Head tipped slightly back, face uplifted in song of praise.
>
> "Land where my fathers died." On first words, take weight back on left foot. Arms down left, clasped hands. Look down calmly, reflectively, as though the patriots' death had made hallowed memories.[51]

Cooper's pantomime instructions continue through all four verses. On the one hand, the pantomime artist, earnest and devout, wrapped in the flag, personifies the nation moving in response to "America." On the other hand, the sheer bathos of the text, its utter overdetermination of affect, demonstrates how such nationalist sentiments were thoroughly *orchestrated* (see figure 5.8).

The slow transformation of "America" from its grassroots, activist, and reform-based origins into a tool of school-administered mandatory patriotism was supported by Samuel Smith. Indeed, as he gained national fame after the Civil War for his authorship of "America," Smith often spoke and wrote about the value of patriotic songs in public schools. He even composed additional lyrics to the song that spoke about both the importance of education in the life of the nation and the role of songs in school. In 1898, four of the five original verses of "America" were published together with four new verses under Smith's name in

Figure 5.8. Picture X from Anna Cooper, *My Country 'Tis of Thee: An Illustrated Pantomime* (1907). Courtesy of The John Hay Library, Brown University.

R. L. Paget's *Poems of American Patriotism*.[52] The four new verses were largely forgotten until revived in 1932—amid the Great Depression—for the celebration of the bicentennial of Washington's birth and the mistaken "centennial" of Smith's lyrics. The *National Education Association Journal* urged that "children should be taught the complete version of 'America,' especially some of the verses which have usually been omitted and which are particularly significant to children because they emphasize education and the school." In fact, the U.S. Office of Education's *School Life* published the "education" verses in its October 1933 issue and recommended them for use by schools in connection with American Education Week programs, which were observed by over three million students and teachers in 1932.[53] In Massachusetts and other states, boards of education encouraged classroom teachers to teach these rediscovered verses (see appendix A) to their pupils, beginning with the celebratory opening lines "Our glorious Land to-day, / 'Neath Education's sway, / Soars upward still." The grand assumptions behind such claims are extended in the second verse, where Smith promises that "No tyrant hand shall smite, / While with encircling might / All here are taught the Right / With Truth allied." Revived at the height of the Great Depression, nearly four decades after Smith's death, the added lyrics promise renewed prosperity and morality through education, "whose bounties all may share." Considering the devastating hardships faced by millions of Americans at the time, this paean to collectively shared bounties must have struck unemployed workers, hungry farmers, and out-of-school youths alike as little more than balderdash, the worst kind of nationalist cheerleading in the face of hard times.

The pedagogical question of how students were to be "taught the right" was addressed in another of Smith's essays, where he described the educational process as a "seal, laid on pliant wax," that could be "cancelled never."[54] Given the massive social unrest of the 1930s, it is not surprising to find the Office of Education aggressively marketing lyrics that sing cheerfully of a nation "soaring upward still," guided by "progress" toward "unity sublime." Yet the convergence of this bureaucratic myth-making and Smith's notion of school-age children as "pliant wax" awaiting proper imprinting by the state cannot help but suggest a troubling stage in the slow transformation of patriotism into mass-produced propaganda. But even by the turn of the century, a generation before the Office of Education began promoting Smith's "lost" educational lyrics, patriotic songs were sung at least weekly in most American classrooms and in school ceremonies and assemblies that emphasized order, authority and patriotism. For example, in 1908 Frank Damrosch (1859–1937), supervisor of music for New York City's public schools, described the role of music in the ideal school assembly:

> The orderly, symmetric marching into place, the soft and pure singing of the opening hymn, the short reading from the Scriptures, the musical response. Then the salute to the flag, spoken or sung, the patriotic song, not shouted, but sung with spirit and enthusiasm, a chorus or part-song for two or three part chorus, a brief address by the principal or distinguished visitor, a closing song and the march back to the class rooms. This is an opening of the day which cannot but react favorably on the pupil and teacher.[55]

The alarming regimentation of Damrosch's ideal assembly, with its "orderly, symmetric marching into place," was intended to unify students and classes in a militaristic hierarchy where they pledged obedience to school and nation. Damrosch, who, fittingly, later cofounded a school for army band leaders, insisted that mere compliance with the school's requirement to sing was insufficient and that patriotic songs were to be performed not perfunctorily but "with spirit or enthusiasm" that reflected sincere belief.[56] Thus continuing a trajectory consistent with at least one branch of its long and complicated history, we see "America" serving the dubious function of coerced obedience, sliding from folk lore into organizational regime, from the people's song of allegiance into the elite's tool of socialization.

This move toward a homogenizing and socializing school system serving the political needs of the state had been advanced dramatically in the years leading up to America entering the First World War, as all states adopted compulsory education requirements designed in part to insure the loyalty of millions of recent immigrants. Public schools were to be the "chief instrument of Americanization," and music was regarded as among the most important vehicles for training in citizenship. Even after the close of the war, Frank V. Thompson, assistant superintendent of Boston schools in 1920, argued that patriotic songs should be included in the weekly curriculum of every class so as "to arouse enthusiasm for the higher values of human devotion, aspiration and sacrifice, particularly for those things which the American spirit holds dear." "America" figured prominently in such school-based Americanization programs. State eighth-grade diploma examinations in Michigan, for example, required pupils to "recite from memory" the first stanza of "The Star-Spangled Banner" and all of "America." In South Dakota schools one hour of class time per week was set aside for singing "America" and other patriotic songs. By 1921 the National Conference of Music Supervisors unanimously adopted a Standard Course in Music requiring all students to spend at least twenty-five minutes each class day in music instruction. They recommended by the end of the sixth year that "Every child shall have acquired a repertory of songs which may be carried into the home and social life, including 'America' and 'The Star-Spangled Banner.'"[57]

Much as in its earliest phases of institutionalization in the late eighteenth and early nineteenth centuries, then, during the early decades of the twentieth century "America" became a ubiquitous focal point for those who sought to unify the masses behind a desired political identity. The song was so effective in this function that in addition to its use in schools "America" was adopted as part of the citizenship training exercises of many extracurricular youth organizations, including the Girl Scouts and Children of the American Revolution, a youth auxiliary of the Daughters of the American Revolution, whose members pledged "to promote the celebration of all patriotic anniversaries; to hold our American flag sacred above every other flag on earth; and to love, uphold, and extend the institutions of American liberty and patriotism and the principles that made and saved our country."[58] Thus, by the early twentieth century, most

American children were expected not only to know "America" and to sing it regularly in schools, at public ceremonies, and with their civic organizations but also to know that in singing the song they were fulfilling expectations of performing mandatory patriotism.

DESPITE its widespread use in civic ceremonies and public events and its unparalleled use as a familiar text for voicing political protest, "America" has always had its detractors. In his 1909 report on national songs Oscar Sonneck of the Library of Congress concluded that "'America' is perhaps too hymn-like and devotional in character for a national anthem, and possibly is pervaded too much by a peculiar New England flavor." In 1921, amid increasing efforts to select an official national anthem, Edward Ninde also expressed concern over the song's geographical specificity. "'Rocks and rills' and 'templed hills' suit New England," Ninde observed, "but nothing is said of the rolling prairies of the great West. . . . 'Land of the pilgrim's pride' is objected to as introducing a sectarian bias, while 'My native country, thee' unfits the hymn to be sung by the multitudes from other lands." "It must also be admitted," he added, "that some of the lines are not above criticism from a literary point of view."[59] Such objections to the song had long been expressed, along with concerns (discussed in chapter 1) regarding the incompatibility of the melody's foreign origins—as "God Save the King"—and the nation's rising status as a self-made and thoroughly exceptional world power.

Despite these longstanding concerns about the song's ancient British origins, we have demonstrated in this chapter that during Reconstruction, the Gilded Age, and the early twentieth century, temperance activists, women's suffrage proponents, and a vast array of workers' and farmers' organizations relied on alternative versions of "America" to voice their anger, their hope, and their vision of what it means to be an American. The fact that these angers, hopes, and visions are so contradictory demonstrates the remarkable flexibility of our concepts of self, community, and nation. While the versions of "America" discussed here sing of a nation roiling in racial-, gender-, moral-, and class-based battles over power and citizenship, they point simultaneously to a series of shared assumptions about the fundamental premises of the nation. And while those premises were manipulated by men like Damrosch and Smith to stand as justifications for incorporating children and immigrants into tightly regimented educational regimes that demanded patriotism as a sign of sociability, activists from a remarkable number of perspectives in turn used such imposed patriotism as wonderfully productive vehicles for renegotiating the bonds of nationhood. And so, much as our ancestors had been doing since the days of the Revolution, Americans of the first third of the twentieth century argued about democracy in America by singing "My Country 'Tis of Thee."

Epilogue

"America," "God Save the Queen," and Postmodernity

THE 1831 premiere of Samuel Smith's "America" in Boston's Park Street Church featured a well-drilled children' choir and the moral pretensions of temperance activists gathered to celebrate a properly righteous July Fourth unsullied by the drunken revelry of their social inferiors. For much of the rest of the nineteenth century the song was employed in a variety of similarly ceremonial but also frequently oppositional occasions. Whether using Smith's original lyrics in dignified celebrations of the nation or any number of the hundreds of parodied variations used to protest the nation's failures, most of the grassroots activists using "America" held the song to be an iconic symbol of American identity. One might argue about whether the promises and ideals of "sweet freedom's song" had been fulfilled and were cause for celebration or whether in fact they had been buried beneath generations' worth of hypocrisy and fear and were cause for protest, but it was generally agreed that democracy was an evolving experiment and that singing one's politics, both individually and collectively, was a healthy and productive means of making sure that the nation continued to learn (albeit slowly, painfully slowly) how to be more true to its foundational principles. Thus, while "America" was a universally popular *and* contested song, one senses that the myriad groups appropriating it shared the assumptions that democracy was serious business and that participating in political struggle—particularly via song—was part of what it meant to be an American.

The gradual development of mass media has led, however, to the production of a culture awash in an almost infinite number of images, sounds, and commodities, hence to the creation of a world in which very little is agreed on, let alone shared as an icon worth fighting for. Not surprisingly, "My Country 'Tis of Thee" played a central role in the evolution of this situation, for it was among the first songs recorded and sold on a mass scale, contributing to the production of what scholars now refer to as "the culture industry." The first commercial recordings were developed in 1889 for use in phonograph parlors, where patrons paid a nickel, spoke the name of a song into a tube, and listened to their selection through a separate tube connected to a phonograph in the room below. In 1890, North American Records developed the first cylinder duplication machinery. Jules Levy, who billed himself as "the world's greatest cornet player" and who was the first major musician to be extensively recorded, scored a number one hit with his 1893 version of "America," as did the Columbia Mixed Double Quartet in 1916. Two different versions, including one by "March King" John Philip Sousa's band, charted in 1905. Sousa then included the song in his collection *National, Patriotic and Typical Airs of All Countries*, which became the standard text for American service bands for the next fifty years.[1] Thus, much as "America" was a crucial component of the Civil War–era developments in production and distribution that historians have come to call the print-capitalism revolution (see chapters 3 and 4), later versions of the song were among the first "hits" of the fledgling culture industry.

But the culture industry is not monolithic, as both its products and its means of mass-marketing have always been open to appropriation by groups of all political and religious persuasions. For example, in 1910, the Mormon Tabernacle Choir achieved national celebrity through the release of their recording of twelve hymns and patriotic songs, including "America."[2] Just twenty-three years earlier, the Mormons had been considered un-American by Congress, which had forced legal and social reforms through the Edmunds-Tucker Act. In response to such persecution, the Choir's recordings blended church songs and patriotic anthems to assert their patriotism. Perhaps as a nod to the complicated costs and benefits of this quintessential example of assimilation, "America" has been regularly featured in the Choir's concerts ever since. The sense that "America" was the nation's unofficial hymn—a claim that we have shown was pushed forcefully by the song's author, Samuel Smith—thus merged nicely with the new means of production and distribution enabled by the recording industry. It is wonderfully appropriate, then, that the twenty-five-thousand-voice choir of the evangelist Billy Sunday recorded "America" in 1918. The song was then included in *Songs for Service*, the popular evangelistic hymn collection compiled by Sunday's musical director, Homer Rodeheaver.[3] Thus, by the early twentieth century, "America" had crossed many contexts—secular and sacred, performed and recorded, popular and official, civilian and military, home and stage—to become a staple element of American public life and a touchstone for the discussion of what it means to be an American. One is forced to wonder, however, if the ever-accelerating capability for mass-producing recorded songs and corresponding songbooks—all fetching fancy profits as commodities—has come to the point where there are simply too many objects of consideration for any one of them to fire the collective imagination the way "God Save the King" and then "America" did from roughly 1750 through 1932.

There has been much debate on the subject of postmodernity. Rather than engaging in an extended review of the relevant literature here, we will simply say that most observers of postmodernity agree that it includes a blurring of genres of art and culture, a blurring of national boundaries and identities, and a blurring of the differences between what were once understood to be the separate realms of private and public—in short, postmodernity has opened up what many observers see as both a dizzying new world of possibility *and* a daunting new world of media saturation, political confusion, and cultural vertigo. Hence, other than the flag, the "Star-Spangled Banner," and the Pledge of Allegiance, which are all protected through a series of intricate legal and institutional codes that have isolated them from the fray of cultural appropriation and parody, one would be hard pressed to imagine any song stirring the kind of heated passions and debates that made "America" a touchstone for activists in the late eighteenth, nineteenth, and early twentieth centuries.[4] One obvious result of this logic of oversaturation and inundation is the rise of a new kind of irony that is devoid of the political convictions that made appropriation and parody so radical in the eighteenth and nineteenth centuries. "In this situation," Fredric Jameson observes, "parody finds itself without a vocation . . . and that strange new thing pastiche slowly comes to take its place. Pastiche is, like parody, the imitation of a peculiar or unique, idiosyncratic style. . . . But it is a neutral practice of mimicry, without any of parody's ulterior motives, amputated of the satiric impulse. . . . *Pastiche is thus blank parody.*[5] This sense that what was once parody has become vacuous and facile may explain in part the slow decline of "America" as an object of serious and passionate consideration.

On the other hand, one might just as persuasively argue that "America" has fallen out of the public's favor because it has been superseded by other, more contemporary songs. Kate Smith's 1938 version of Irving Berlin's "God Bless America" and Woody Guthrie's 1945 "This Land Is Your Land," for example, have both enjoyed remarkable popularity through the years. Guthrie's song in particular clearly fulfills the role "America" previously played for generations before it, as singing the song is simultaneously an act of protest and celebration: you sing the song to protest democracy's compromised status while hoping to someday celebrate the nation for living up to is utopian promises. Nonetheless, it is telling to observe that in Jody Rosen's recent essay on Smith and Guthrie and national anthems, "My Country 'Tis of Thee" is not mentioned once.[6]

The fact that one can discuss national songs and not immediately think of

"America" is evidence of the foreshortening of our national sense of history and tradition, which in turn closes off options for cultural production and protest. Indeed, as we have demonstrated, "America" has been sung for the past two hundred and sixty years *mostly* as a vehicle of protest. One wonderful example of how our forebears used "America" to lampoon a nation rocketing along on what many thought was a fast track to destruction is George S. Kaufman and Morrie Ryskind's 1931 Broadway musical *Of Thee I Sing.*[7] With its title drawn from Smith's "America," *Of Thee I Sing* lampooned campaign politics in the midst of the depression. Candidate John P. Wintergreen is elected to the presidency by ignoring the social catastrophes all around him, instead playing up his romance with Mary Turner, who has promised to marry him if he wins. His campaign song (written by George and Ira Gershwin) turns Smith's "America" into a wickedly ironic pop hit:

> Of thee I sing, baby,
> You have got that certain thing, baby.
> Shining star and inspiration
> Worthy of a mighty nation,
> Of thee I sing!

Wintergreen serenades Mary with the song; mesmerized voters sing it to him. The satire reaches epic proportions when Wintergreen's inauguration is also his wedding ceremony. Once in office, however, he is bedeviled by charges that he has jilted a woman who, by winning his campaign-sponsored national beauty contest, was supposed to have married him. The Senate, unconcerned about the catastrophic effects of the depression ("The Committee on Unemployment is gratified to report that due to its unremitting efforts there is now more unemployment in the United States than ever before"), nonetheless tries to impeach Wintergreen. Mary's pregnancy announcement forestalls the impeachment proceedings, convincing the president that, in a goofy paraphrase of Hoover, "posterity is just around the corner." He finally resigns from office, and the curtain closes with Wintergreen's aides and the justices of the Supreme Court reprising the title song.[8] At a time when political leaders seemed incapable of dealing with the country's social problems, *Of Thee I Sing* used "America" to parody vacuous political sloganeering and to caricature the decline of democratic politics into a deadening distraction of romantic and patriotic spectacle.

Four years after *Of Thee I Sing* opened on Broadway, sixteen-year-old Ella Fitzgerald recorded a similar parody of Smith's "America" with the Chick Webb Orchestra. Her "Vote For Mr. Rhythm," released at the height of the depression, describes an imaginary feel-good candidate:

Everyone's a friend of his.
His campaign slogan is:
"Change your woes
into a-wo-de-ho."
Vote for Mr. Rhythm,
Let freedom ring,
And soon we'll all be singing,
Of thee I swing.[9]

With its platform of promised good times, Fitzgerald's "Vote for Mr. Rhythm" is played over the closing credits of D. A. Pennebaker's revealing documentary of the 1992 Clinton presidential campaign, *The War Room*. A song performed as an ironic critique of feel-good politics during the depression is thus revised as an equally ironic critique of feel-good politics in the age of the Teflon presidency.

Whereas Smith's 1831 "America" sang of proud citizens whom we know first gathered to sing the song in choral form in a temperance gathering in a church, this 1935 parody (and its 1992 appropriation) speaks of cynical citizens who come to recognize democracy as a lark, a romp, "a-wo-de-ho" that leaves the masses swinging. Following Fitzgerald's 1935 "Vote for Mister Rhythm" and the Gershwins' 1931 title song from *Of Thee I Sing*, "America" was used in the second half of the twentieth century mostly as a humorous prop symbolizing political naïveté and the surreal politics of conventioneers' straw hats and slogan-adorned banners. Indeed, it would appear that the song has become either a token of lost innocence, immediately identifiable as nostalgic musical quotation, or an object of merciless pastiche in which the song's promises are not only no longer taken seriously but lampooned as the deluded rhetoric of hopelessly idealistic dreamers.

Despite these preliminary observations on the cultural saturation of postmodernity and despite the obvious fact that "America" is no longer as ubiquitous as it once was, one may still find the song playing creative roles in the few remaining liminal spaces where culture and politics meet. For example, Charles Gross's musical soundtrack to Everett Aison's 1968 film *Post No Bills* uses eleven comical variations on "America" (including bluegrass, Dixieland, and cocktail lounge versions). The ten-minute film opens with a shot of a beautiful lake surrounded by trees; the camera pans to a billboard with the exhortation "Drink Beer!" In the next image, a lone man (Bob Brady) tears down the billboard and burns it, then moves on to destroy another. A police officer catches him in the act and arrests him. As he exits the courthouse after sentencing, he is met by a crowd of cheering supporters who are holding signs protesting billboards. They lift him on their shoulders and carry him to a bar to celebrate by drinking beer, the very activity urged by the billboard he had destroyed. He becomes a celebrity and appears on a television talk show; as he is applauded by the mindless studio audience, he smiles and lights a cigarette. The film ends with this bitter image dissolving to a shot of the protagonist's image displayed on a billboard with the slogan "Smoke the rebel's cigarette." Gross's multiple variations on "America" are dispersed throughout the film. Thus, in the year of the assassinations of Kennedy and King, the Tet Offensive, and the riotous Democratic National Convention in Chicago, Smith's song is used to illustrate the voracious banality of a nation in which protest and patriotism have been absorbed as little more than the raw material for corny sloganeering and commercial kitsch. Gross's point would appear to be clear: democracy has become little more than a joke, a façade for consumerism—believing in the promises and possibilities of democracy amounts then to a kind of naïve sentimentalism as outdated as "America."

A similarly critical use of the song may be found in Chip Lord's 1981 video short *Get Ready to March!* Newly inaugurated president Ronald Reagan is shown waving to the crowd at a parade while text scrolls by explaining that the president's proposed budget for the National Endowment for the Arts will be less than the allocation for military bands. The brilliant soundtrack accompaniment is a trumpeter stumbling through "America," thus symbolizing the perilous predicament of the arts in an age of unprecedented military expenditures. Addressed to an implied audience whose opposition to Reagan has been outvoted, Lord's video concludes with the admonition: "Get Ready to March!" America the nation and "America" the song are here mutually botched by Reagan's headlong rush into barbarism. While Aison's *Post No Bills* and Lord's *Get Ready to March!* offer wickedly biting commentaries, they also illustrate the paradoxical role of "My Country 'Tis of Thee" in postmodernity. Indeed, whereas prior generations of activists used the song both to criticize the nation and to celebrate its utopian promises, in these two films the song stands as little more than an outdated symbol, a throwback, a decayed reminder of just how completely democracy has slid into meaninglessness. In this sense, then, Aison's and Lord's appropriations of "My Country 'Tis of Thee" recall "Bitter" Ambrose Bierce's despair. But whereas Bierce and his Gilded Age contemporaries bemoaned a nation sinking beneath the weight of gross political corruption and deadly capitalist exploitation, our postmodern predicament is generally understood, for better or worse, as more properly cultural, as a result of the incredible multiplication of images and sounds and tastes and other commodities.

This sense that the sheer abundance of culture made possible by postmodernity has evacuated the political bite of parody, leaving in its wake what Jameson calls pastiche, "bland parody," is illustrated nicely by a story from 30 July 1979. Robert Fripp, guitar god and technological wizard, collaborator with Brian Eno, and key member of the once-great King Crimson, was playing a show in U.C. Berkeley's "Bear's Lair" (the student center pub, where students and faculty still gather on Friday afternoons). As Fripp tells the story,

A gentleman from the audience called out for me to play the "Star Spangled Banner" in commemoration of the tenth anniversary of Woodstock [where Jimmie Hendrix played his ripping, gut-wrenching version of the song]. I replied that as another guitarist had played that tune, perhaps it was more appropriate for me as an English guitarist to play "God Save the Queen," and developed a Frippertronic improvisation on the opening notes of that well-known anthem.[10]

"Frippertronics" was a (then revolutionary) technique of tape-looping sound while on stage. Fripp could play a line, record it, and have it loop back in real time while recording another melody over the original part; these now merged sounds would again loop back as Fripp played another line, and so on, with the entire "song" running through banks of processors, creating cascading walls of sound. One musician, then, with just one guitar, some tape, and some gadgetry could spontaneously produce waves of sculpted "ambient" sound. The idea struck many listeners as brilliant.

What makes this particular story of Frippertronics so telling for our purposes, however, is that the promised version of "God Save the Queen," clearly framed by Fripp as the proper Englishman's response to the American's request for the "Star-Spangled Banner," is empty of all intelligible musical reference to any original. The "song" is beautiful in precisely the way one has come to expect from Fripp, yet *there is no recognizable melody* — he could be parodying "Hey Jude" or "Night in Tunisia" or "Hello Dolly" or any other song that comes to mind, but there is nothing resembling a melodic quotation, not a hint of what even the most adventurous listener might associate with either "My Country 'Tis of Thee" or "God Save the Queen." Nationalism, then, is something that the American audience and the British performer recognize as having substance: they recognize that one song speaks to and of America while a different set of lyrics to the same melody speaks to and of Britain — yet the traditional musical content of this song, as played by Fripp, is irrelevant. What matters here is not the song as musical material but the invocation of nationalism as a preface for the performance of technological mastery and guitar virtuosity. What matters here is thus the gesture, the nod to nationalism: the song is irrelevant, for of course the traditional melody and lyrics of the song are but nostalgic gestures that speak of a world long gone. This is what Jameson means by pastiche.

One final observation is in order regarding the incomprehensible, almost comically obscene use of "America" for commercial purposes. The list here could be extended at will, but one example will suffice; in this case, the guilty party is AT&T. In a full-page ad in the *New York Times*, complete with a full-size picture of a cordless phone painted in the Stars and Stripes, large letters announce "200 more reasons to let freedom ring." Smith's original version of the song, as we have demonstrated, was complicated by a variety of tricky intentions and subtle exclusions, yet there is no doubt that he envisioned his song speaking of *political* freedoms. In 1831 "Let freedom ring" was a call for the realization of the nation's then-and-still radical promises of justice and equality for all. But in 2000 the phrase "let freedom ring" is a call for a "$50 cash back" deal that, when you sign on to the AT&T juggernaut, includes "NO ROAMING. NO LONG DISTANCE CHARGES."[11] One cannot imagine a more representative example of the conflation of politics with commerce, of the confusion of the individual's consumption privileges with the community's political obligations.

In contrast to the wonderful and confusing instrumental version created by Fripp and the vulgar advertising version of AT&T, our sense is that one of the most significant factors in the long popularity of "My Country 'Tis of Thee" is the simple beauty and inescapable presence of the human voice. At the April 1997 Central States Communication Association conference in St. Louis, for example, Bob presented some of the materials in this book to a packed room of fellow historians, rhetorical critics, and music lovers. While Bob told the story of the song, complete with slides and video, friends read some versions of the song while I and others sang some of the variations of the song. The presentation was greeted with something I have never seen before at an academic conference: a standing ovation, complete with some members of the audience crying. It would seem that even the most ironic of postmoderns still want to love their country, still thrill at the sheer depth and wonder of a historical story when well told, and still cherish the simple pleasure of hearing their friends and colleagues and neighbors bust out a good song—"My country 'tis of thee, / Sweet land of Liberty, / Of thee I sing," indeed.

Appendix A

*Sixteen Versions of "God Save the King" and
"My Country 'Tis of Thee," Organized Chronologically,
1744–1891*

1. This is the first known version of "God Save the King," printed in 1744 in *Thesaurus Musicus* during a period of both foreign and domestic peril in Britain. The third verse was published in 1745. All three verses are reprinted in William Cummings, *God Save the King: The Origin and History of the Music and Words of The National Anthem* (London: Novello, 1902), 84–85.

> God save great George our King.
> Long live our noble King,
> > God save the King.
> Send him victorious,
> Happy and glorious,
> Long to reign over us,
> > God save the King.
>
> O Lord our God arise,
> Scatter his enemies,
> > And make them fall;
> Confound their Politicks,
> Frustrate their knavish Tricks,
> On Thee our hopes we fix.
> > God save us all.
>
> Thy choicest gifts in store,
> On George be pleas'd to pour,
> > Long may he reign.
> May he defend our laws,
> And ever give us cause,

> With heart and Voice to sing,
>   God save the King.

2. One of the many examples of colonial Americans adapting "God Save the King" to fit their revolutionary goals, "A New Song, to the Tune of— GOD SAVE THE KING" was published in the *Boston Independent Chronicle* on 4 December 1777 (reprinted in Gillian B. Anderson, *Freedom's Voice in Poetry and Song* [Wilmington, Del.: Scholarly Resources, 1977], 375).

> FAME, let thy Trumpet sound,
> Rouse all the World around,
>   With loud alarms!
> Fly hence to Britain's land,
> Tell George in vain his Hand
> Is raised 'gainst FREEDOM's Band,
>   When call'd to arms.
>
> Each Island of the Main
> Free'd from the Tyrant's Chain,
>   Shall own our Sway!
> Loud Songs of Thankfulness,
> Each Bosom shall possess;
> Fondly fair FREEDOM's Bliss,
>   They shall display!
>
> LEXINGTON's Plains proclaim,
> From brazen Trump of Fame,
>   Our Strength in Fight;
> DEATH shew'd his Arrows round,
> And purpl'd all the Ground
> Nor one had Safety found,
>   But in swift Flight.
>
> Again they bend their Course,
> With full united Force,
>   To BUNKER-HILL;
> Asham'd of their Late Flight,
> With an envenom'd Spite,
> They fiercely rush to Fight,
>   Our blood to spill!
>
> But FREEDOM's Sons once more,
> Did Vengeance on them show'r,
>   And check their Pride;
> Of wounded and of slain,
> Full fifteen Hundred Men,

With Blood the Field did stain,
　　On BRITAIN's Side! . . .

Behold! Those Sons of Shame,
Who falsely boast of Fame,
　　In War acquir'd!
Hark!—How our Cannon roar!—
They fly fair BOSTON's Shore!
Nor can resist our Power,
　　By FREEDOM fir'd.

Come MUSE! Fly hence apace,
NEW JERSEY claims a Place,
　　In War's rude Song
Our March, through Hail and Snow,
To meet the murd'rous Foe!
And sing their overthrow,
　　To me belong.

O' gen'rous Sons of Worth!
Nobly have ye stept forth,
　　Your rights to Guard;
On FAME's swift Pinions driv'n,
Th' approving Nod from Heav'n,
To crown You, shall be giv'n
　　Your just Reward.

3. In 1789 George Washington was inaugurated as the first president of the United States. Samuel Lowe's "Ode, To Be Sung on the Arrival of the PRESI-DENT of the UNITED STATES" (see figure 1.7) welcomed Washington to New York Harbor for the ceremony. Lowe's "Ode" was published both as a broadside (held by the New-York Historical Society) and in *The Gazette of the United States* (25 April 1789), 3.

Hail thou auspicious day!
Far let America
　　Thy praise resound;
Joy to our native land!
Let ev'ry heart expand,
For WASHINGTON's at hand,
　　With Glory crown'd!

Thrice blest Columbians hail!
Behold, before the gale,
　　Your CHIEF Advance;
The matchless Hero's nigh!

Applaud HIM to the sky,
Who gave [us?] Liberty
    gen'rous France.

Illustrious Warrior hail!
Oft' did thy Sword prevail
    O'er hosts of foes;
Come and fresh laurels claim,
Still dearer make thy name,
Long as Immortal Fame
    Her trumpet blows!

Thrice welcome to this shore,
Our leader now no more,
    But Ruler thou;
Oh, truly good and great!
Long live to glad our State,
Where countless Honors wait
    To deck thy Brow.

Far be the din of Arms,
Henceforth the Olive's charms
    Shall War preclude;
These shores a HEAD shall own,
Unsully'd by a throne,
Our much lov'd WASHINGTON,
    The Great, the Good!

4. One of the first American feminist songs known to exist, "A Lady"'s version of "God Save the King," entitled "Rights of Woman," appeared in the *Philadelphia Minerva* on 17 October 1795.

God save each Female's right,
Show to her ravish'd sight
    Woman is Free.
Let Freedom's voice prevail,
And draw aside the veil,
Supreme Effulgence hail,
    Sweet Liberty.

Man boasts the noble cause,
Nor yields supine to laws
    Tyrants ordain.
Let woman have a share,
Nor yield to slavish fear.
Her equal rights declare,
    And well maintain.

Come forth with sense array'd
Nor ever be dismay'd
  To meet the foe,—
Who with assuming hands
Undid the iron bands,
To obey his rash commands,
  And vainly bow.

O Let the sacred fire
Of Freedom's voice inspire
  A Female too,—
Man makes his cause his own,
And Fame his acts renown,—
Woman thy fears disown,
  Assert thy due.

Think of the cruel chain,
Endure no more the pain
  Of slavery;—
Why should a tyrant bind
A cultivated mind
By reason well refin'd
  Ordained Free.

Why should a Woman lie
In base obscurity,
  Her talents hid,
Has providence assign'd
Her soul to be confin'd;
Is not her gentle mind
  By virtue led?

With this engaging charm,
Where is so much the harm
  For her to stand,
To join the grand applause
Of truth and equal laws,
Or lend the noble cause,
  Her feeble hand.

Let snarling critics Frown,
Their maxims I disown,
  Their ways detest:—
By man, your tyrant lord,
Females no more be aw'd,
Let Freedom's sacred word,
  Inspire your breast.

Woman aloud rejoice,
Exalt thy feeble voice
    In cheerful strain;
See Wolstonecraft, a friend,
Your injur'd rights defend,
Wisdom her steps attend,
    The cause maintain.

A voice re-echoing round,
With joyful accents sound,
    "Woman be Free."
Assert the noble claim,
All selfish arts disdain;
Hark now the note proclaim,
    "Woman is Free!"

5A. In the winter of 1831 music educator and booster William Woodbridge commissioned Samuel Smith to translate German schoolbook songs into English. Smith came upon a melody that inspired him and wrote "America." The song was first performed as part of the "Celebration of American Independence, by the Boston Sabbath School Union, at Park Street Church, July 4, 1831" (program held by the Chapin Library Special Collections, Williams College).

My country! 'tis of thee,
Sweet land of liberty,
    Of thee I sing:
Land, where my fathers died;
Land of the pilgrim's pride;
From every mountain-side,
    Let freedom ring.

My native country! Thee,
Land of the noble free;
    Thy name I love:
I love thy rocks and rills,
Thy woods and templed hills;
My heart with rapture thrills,
    Like that above.

No more shall tyrants here
With haughty steps appear
    And soldier-bands;
No more shall tyrants tread
Above the patriot dead;
No more our blood be shed
    By alien hands.

Let music swell the breeze,
And ring from all the trees
    Sweet freedom's song:
Let mortal tongues awake,
Let all that breathes partake,
Let rocks their silence break,
    The sound prolong.

Our fathers' God! To thee,
Author of liberty!
    To thee we sing:
Long may our land be bright
With freedom's holy light;
Protect us by thy might,
    Great God, our King!

5B. Sixty-seven years later, amid a period of great national turmoil—including massive immigration and working-class agitation—Smith wrote an additional four verses to be added to the original text of "America." Known as the "education verses," they celebrate the socializing powers of schools. The verses first appeared in R. L. Paget, ed., *Poems of American Patriotism, 1776–1898* (Boston: L. C. Page, 1898) 1–3, but were forgotten until 1933, when the U.S. Office of Education's magazine *School Life* [XIX: 2 (October 1933): 28] recommended them as a helpful part of depression-era school curricula.

Our glorious Land to-day,
'Neath Education's sway,
    Soars upward still.
Its halls of learning fair,
Whose bounties all may share,
Behold them everywhere
    On vale and hill!

Thy safeguard, Liberty,
The school shall ever be,
    Our Nation's pride!
No tyrant hand shall smite,
While with encircling might
All here are taught the Right
    With Truth allied.

Beneath Heaven's gracious will
The star of progress still
    Our course doth sway;
In unity sublime
To broader heights we climb,
Triumphant over Time,
    God speeds our way!

Grand birthright of our sires,
Our altars and our fires
　　Keep we still pure!
Our starry flag unfurled,
The hope of all the world,
In Peace and Light impearled,
　　God hold secure!

6. Published in the *Liberator* (3 May 1839), Theta's "America—A Parody" stands as one of the most powerful examples of an activist appropriating "My Country 'Tis of Thee" for abolitionist purposes.

My country! 'tis of thee,
Stronghold of Slavery—
　　Of thee I sing:
Land, where my fathers died;
Where men *man's* rights *deride*;
From every mountain side,
　　Thy deeds shall ring.

My native country! thee —
Where all men are born free,
　　If *white* their skin:
I love thy hills and dales,
Thy mounts and pleasant vales;
But hate thy *negro* sales,
　　As foulest sin.

Let *wailing* swell the breeze,
And ring from all the trees
　　The *black* man's wrong;
Let every tongue awake,
Let *bond* and free partake,
Let rocks their silence break,
　　The sound prolong.

Our father's God! To thee—
Author of *Liberty*!
　　To thee we sing;
Soon may our land be bright, —
With *holy Freedom's* light —
Protect us by thy might,
　　Great God, our King.

7. John Pierpont's 1842 "Fourth of July Ode" interlaces nationalist symbols with the temperance cause. Here are three of the six verses that appeared first

in Charles Young's *Temperance Song Book of the Mass. Temperance Union*, 2nd ed.
(Boston: Kidder and Wright, 1842), 37.

> With patriotic glee,
> Columbia's jubilee
>   Once more we hail;
> Let nothing damp our joys,
> The *Temp'rance pledge* destroys
> The last foe that annoys.
>   Quail, monster, quail!
>
> Our fathers, when they broke
> Proud Britain's galling yoke,
>   Fought *one* good fight!
> A *better* one fight they
> Who "cast the bowl away,"
> And toast this glorious day
>   In water bright.
>
> Reformers! Go ahead!
> No more let it be said
>   By freedom's foe,
> That this, our fair domain,
> Wears worse than British chain!
> Upholds the tyrant reign
>   Of "Death & Co."

8. Published in 1854, Joshua McCarter Simpson's "Fourth of July in Alabama"
was one of the abolitionist versions of "My Country 'Tis of Thee" printed in his
collection *The Emancipation Car, Being an Original Composition of Anti-Slavery Ballads*
(Zanesville, Ohio: E. C. Church, 1854; Sullivan and Brown, 1874), 41–42. This
was one of the first books of verse written entirely by an African American.

> O, thou unwelcome day,
> Why hast thou come this way?
>   Why lingered not?
> I watch with restless eye,
> Thy moments slowly fly—
> Each seems to stop and die—
>   And leave a "blot."
>
> Though cannons loudly roar,
> And banners highly soar—
>   To me 'tis gloom.
> Though "lads" and "lasses" white,
> With face and spirits bright—

Hail thee with such delight,
    With sword and plumes.

I hear the loud huzzas,
Mingled with high applause,
    To Washington.
The youth in every street,
Their notes of joy repeat;
While Patriots' names they greet,
    For victory won.

Brass bands of music play
Their sweet and thrilling lay,
    Which rend the skies;
Old fathers seem to feel
New animating zeal,
While tones of thunder peal
    On every side.

Yet we have got no song.
Where is the happy throng
    Of Africa's sons?
Are we among the great
And noble of the State,
This day to celebrate?
    Are we the ones?

No! We must sing our songs
Among the Negro Gongs
    That pass our doors.
How can we strike the strains,
While o'er those dismal plains,
We're bleeding, bound in chains,
    Dying by scores?

While e'er four million slaves
Remain in living graves,
    Can I rejoice,
And join the jubilee
Which set the white man free,
And fetters brought to me?
    'Tis not my choice.

O, no! While a slave remains
Bound in infernal chains
    Subject to man,
My heart shall solemn be—
There is no song for me,

> 'Till all mankind are free
> From lash and brand.

9. James Walden's "God Save Our Native Land" was first published in the *New York Times* in 1861 and then in the "Poetry and Incidents" section of Frank Moore, ed., *The Rebellion Record: A Diary of American Events, etc.* (New York: Putnam, 1862), 1:17. Conspicuous in its silence regarding slavery, the song conveys the popular belief—at least at the start of the Civil War—that the conflict was about shattered white brotherhood.

> God save our native land
> From the invader's hand,
>   Home of the free!
> Though ruthless traitors aim
> To crush our nation's fame,
> Yet still, in Freedom's name,
>   We cling to thee!
>
> O Lord! we humbly pray,
> Far distant be the day
>   Ere that shall be;
> Though lawless bands combine
> To shatter freedom's shrine,
> With faith and hope divine
>   We cling to thee!
>
> O Lord! when, hand to hand,
> Brothers as foes shall stand,
>   Shield thou the right!
> Stay these unhappy wars,
> Join us in one great cause—
> To guard our nation's laws
>   With freemen's might!
>
> Lord! may this strife soon cease;
> Grant us a lasting peace,
>   Parted we fall!
> Long may our banner wave
> Over the free and brave,
> O Lord! our country save,
>   God save us all!

10. Also printed at the opening of the American Civil War, this version relies on wicked satire to attack Britain's feared alliance with the Confederacy. "Anonymous'" "A New Version of an Old Song" appeared in the *New York Evening Post* (29 May 1861) and then in Moore, *The Rebellion Record*, 1:120.

> God save Cotton, our King!
> God save our noble King!
>   God save the King!
> Send him the sway he craves,
> Britons his willing slaves,
> "Rule," Cotton! "Rule the waves!"
>   God save the King!
>
> God save Cotton, our King!
> God save our noble King!
>   God save the King!
> Outweighing truth and fame,
> Cotton shall cloak our shame,
> Freedom an empty name.
>   God save the King!
>
> God save Cotton, our King!
> God save our noble King!
>   God save the King!
> Careless of good or ill,
> Cotton is sovereign still,
> While we our pockets fill
>   God save the King!

11. One of the many Civil War versions of "America" to defend the Confederacy, "God Save the South," by "R. S. A.," appeared in the *Richmond Dispatch* in 1862 and then in Moore, *The Rebellion Record,* 4:36–37.

> No spot of wrong or shame
> Rests on our banner's fame,
> Flung forth in freedom's name
>   O'er mound and sea.
>
> Then let the invader come;
> Soon will the beat of drum
>   Rally us all.
> Forth from our homes we go—
> Death! death! to every foe,
> Says each maiden low:
>   God save us all!
>
> Then, 'mid the cannon's roar,
> Let us sing evermore:
>   God save the South!
> Ours is the soul to dare;
> See, our good swords are bare—
> We will be free, we swear!
>   God save the South!

12. "The Patriot's Hymn," published in early 1864 when the Civil War was going badly for the North, offers a rousing call for rededicated effort and enthusiasm. Written by Reverend J. F. Mines, the chaplain of the Second Maine Regiment, the song was included in the "Poetry and Incidents" section of Moore, *The Rebellion Record*, 2:48–49.

> While the loud drum and fife
> Angrily call to strife,
>   Still let us pray,
> Pray God that wars may cease,
> Pray God to give us peace,
> Pray God our hearts release
>   From discord's way.
>
> Yet if the word must be
> Guardian of Liberty,
>   Unsheathe its blade!
> Grasping the trusty brand,
> Heart joined to heart, we'll stand,
> Our firm united band,
>   God giving aid.
>
> Shame to the coward come,
> Death be the traitor's doom
>   Perish his name!
> True be their hearts who rear
> Our starry flag in air,
> Ever their praise we'll bear,
>   Deathless their fame!
>
> Run up the Stripes and Stars,
> Borne in our fathers' wars,
>   Victor through all;
> For it, on battle-field,
> Their sons the sword will wield,
> Never the flag will yield,
>   Though we may fall!

13. Elizabeth Boynton Harbert's "The New America," composed and performed for the annual convention of the National Woman Suffrage Association in Washington, D.C., in January 1883, stands as one of the period's most powerful feminist statements. Published in L. May Wheeler, comp., *Booklet of Song: A Collection of Suffrage and Temperance Melodies* (Minneapolis: Co-operative Printing, 1884), 15–17.

> Our country now from thee,
> Claim we our liberty,

In freedom's name.
Guarding home's altar fires,
Daughters of patriot sires,
Their zeal our own inspires
Justice to claim.

Women in every age
For this great heritage,
Tribute have paid—
Our birth-right claim we now—
Longer refuse to bow;
On freedom's altar now,
Our hand is laid.

Sons will you longer see,
Mothers on bended knee,
For justice pray?
Rise, now in manhood's might,
With earth's great souls unite
Of freedom's day.

Our garnered sheaves we yield,
Gleaned from each glorious field
Women have wrought.
Truth's standard raising high,
Ready to do or die,
Enriching life for aye,
With deed and thought.

Grateful for freedom won—
The work so well begun,
Patriots by thee!
Ended shall never be,
Until from sea to sea,
Chorused the song shall be,
Women are free.

14. Ralph E. Hoyt published this version of "America" in the *Journal of the Knights of Labor* on 3 July 1890. During this period of economic depression, the *Journal* solicited worker-authored songs for singing at organizational meetings, strikes, and socials.

Our Country, 'tis of thee,
Sweet land of knavery,
Of thee we sing!
Land where fond hopes have died,
Where demagogues reside,

Monopolies preside,
  And misery bring.

We love thy rocks and rills,
But not thy bitter ills—
  And griefs that follow.
Thy boasts of "equal rights,"
Made through thy leading lights,
In rhetoric proud flights—
  Are sometimes hollow.

Land of true liberty,
We'll sound loud praise to thee,
  In cheerful song.
Then will the oppressed arise,
The dawn salute all eyes,
Souls swell with glad surprise—
  God speed the day!

15. Published in the San Francisco *Wasp* (16 September 1882), 581, Ambrose Bierce's "A Rational Anthem" stands as a bitter indictment of the rampant corruption driving the Gilded Age.

My country, 'tis of thee,
Sweet land of felony,
  Of thee I sing—
Land where my fathers fried
Young witches and applied
Whips to the Quaker's hide
  And made him spring.

My knavish country, thee,
Land where the thief is free,
  Thy laws I love;
I love thy thieving bills
That tap the people's tills;
I love thy mob whose will's
  All laws above.

Let Federal employees
And rings rob all they please,
  The whole year long.
Let office-holders make
Their piles and judges rake
Our coin. For Jesus' sake,
  Let's *all* go wrong!

Our Father's God (whom we
Call Satan) unto thee
   Our Song we sing.
Long may each blatherskite
Grab all he sees, and Might
Protect be from Right,
   'Neath Satan's wing.

16. Thomas Nicol's 1891 "A New National Anthem" is one of many Gilded Age versions of "America" that attack greed, corruption, and the spoiling of democracy at the hands of modern capitalism. Printed originally in Leopold Vincent, ed., *The Alliance and Labor Songster* (Kansas, 1891).

My country 'tis of thee,
Once land of liberty,
   Of thee I sing.
Land of the Millionaire;
Farmers with pockets bare;
Caused by the cursed snare—
   The Money Ring.

My native country thee,
Thou were so pure and free;
   Long, long ago.
Yet still I love thy rills,
But hate thy usury mills,
That fill the bankers' tills
   Till they overflow.

So when my country thee,
Which should be noble, free,
   I'll love thee still;
I'll love thy Greenback men,
Who strive with tongue and pen,
For liberty again,
   With right good will.

And then my country thee,
Thou wilt again be free;
   And freedom's tower.
Stand by your fireside then,
And show that you are men,
Whom they can't fool again,
   And crush their power.

Appendix B

*Selective List of Alternative American Versions of
"God Save the King" and "America," 1759–1900*

1759   Enoch Freeman, "A New Song on the Success of 1759," in James Leamon, *Revolution Downeast* (Amherst: University of Massachusetts Press,
1993), 31.

1764   "O Lord our God Arise! . . . George and Franklin," in *The Election, a
Medley* (broadside, Library Company of Philadelphia), in Vera Brodsky
Lawrence, *Music for Patriots, Politicians and Presidents* (New York: Macmil-
lan, 1975), 23.

1775   "May each unkind report," *Virginia Gazette* (Williamsburg) (17 February
1775), 2.

1776   "Hail, O America!" *New York Packet* (1 August 1776), 4.

1776   "Free states attend the Song," *Virginia Gazette* (Williamsburg) (24 August
1776), 8.

1777   "Fame, let thy Trumpet sound," *Boston Independent Chronicle* (4 December
1777), 4.

1778   "God Save America," *Maryland Journal* (Baltimore) (12 May 1778), 2.

1780   "God Save the Thirteen States," *Pennsylvania Packet* (1 January 1780), 4.

1781   "By Sacred Influence Hurl'd," *New-York Gazette* (2 July 1781), 3.

1781   "From the Americ' Shore," *New-Jersey Journal* (Chatham) (26 December
1781), 2.

1782   "God Save the Thirteen States!" *Pennsylvania Journal* (30 January 1782),
3.

1782   "Gallia's increasing Fame," *Pennsylvania Journal* (Philadelphia) (27 February 1782), 3.

1784   "Americans rejoice," *Independent Gazette; or The New-York Journal Revived*
(12 February 1784).

1786   "God Save Great Washington," *Philadelphia Continental Journal* (7 April 1786).

1786   Thomas Dawes, Jr., "Now let rich Musick sound," performed at Bunker Hill, 17 June 1786. *Boston Independent Chronicle* (22 June 1786).

1788   "Hail God-like Washington," in Lawrence, *Music for Patriots*, 96.

1789   Samuel Low, "Ode to be Sung on the Arrival of the President of the United States" ("Hail thou auspicious day"), *Gazette of the United States* (25 April 1789).

1789   "God save America!" in *The Philadelphia Songster* (Philadelphia: McCulloch, 1789).

1793   "God save Columbia's son!" *Columbian Centinel* (13 July 1793).

1793   William Billings, "A New Song" ("God save—'The Rights of Man'"), *Providence Gazette* (25 May 1793).

1795   "Rights of Woman" ("God save each Female's right"), *Philadelphia Minerva* (17 October 1795).

1796   "A Song" ("While others sing of Kings"), *Columbian Centinel* (20 February 1796), in Lawrence, *Music for Patriots*, 133.

1798   "Ode for the Fourth of July" ("Come all ye sons of song"), in *The American Musical Miscellany* (1798), 130–131.

1803   "Hail, Brother Masons, Hail!" in *The Songster's Museum* (Northampton, Mass., 1803), 109–110.

1816   "Let Mason's Fame Resound," in David Vinton, comp., *The Masonic Minstrel* (Dedham, Mass.: H. Mann, 1816), 11–12.

1816   "Hail, Masonry Divine," in Vinton, *The Masonic Minstrel*, 13–14.

1816   T. S. Webb, "Mark Master's Song" ("Mark masters, all appear!"), in Vinton, *The Masonic Minstrel*, 144–145.

1816   "Knight Templar's Song" ("God bless the noble band"), in Vinton, *The Masonic Minstrel*, 222–223.

1818   "Hymn for Consecration" ("Hail, universal Lord!"), in Luke Eastman, comp., *Masonic Melodies* (Boston: T. Rowe, 1818), 28.

1818   "Knight Templar's Song" ("God bless the worthy band"), in Eastman, *Masonic Melodies*, 84–85; and *The Templar's Chart* (New Haven, 1821), 120–122.

1829   John Pierpont, "Prayer of the Christian (With Thy Pure Dews and Rains)," performed at Park Street Church, Boston (4 July 1829), in *William Lloyd Garrison: The Story of His Life* (New York: Century, 1885), 126, and *The Anti-Slavery Poems of John Pierpont* (Boston: Oliver Johnson, 1843), 7–9.

1831   Samuel Francis Smith, "America" ("My Country, 'Tis of Thee"), first performed at Park Street Church, Boston (4 July 1831).

c. 1833   Reverend C. T. Brooks, "God Bless Our Native Land"; reprinted in

John Julian, ed., *Dictionary of Hymnology* (London: John Murray, 1915; originally published 1892) and *The Soldier's Hymn Book* (Charleston: South Carolina Tract Society, 1862), 222.

1834 William Lloyd Garrison, "Hope and Faith (Ye Who in Bondage Pine)," in Maria W. Chapman, comp., *Songs of the Free, and Hymns of Christian Freedom* (1836), 50–51.

1836 A. G. Duncan, "Day of Jubilee," in Chapman, *Songs of the Free*, 87–88.

1837 George Russell, "Hymn," performed at 4 July 1837 meeting of Plymouth County Anti-Slavery Society, *Liberator* (4 August 1837), 128.

1839 Theta, "America A Parody," *Liberator* (3 May 1839), 72.

1840 Maria W. Chapman, "Ode," *Liberator* (7 August 1840), 128.

1842 "Ode for the Fourth of July" ("Our Country's Banners Play"), in Reverend John Marsh, comp., *Temperance Hymn Book and Minstrel* (New York: American Temperance Union, 1842), 90–91.

1842 John Pierpont, "Fourth of July Ode" ("With patriotic glee"), in Charles T. Young, comp., *Temperance Song Book of the Mass. Temperance Union* (Boston: Kidder and Wright, 1842), 37.

1842 I. F. Shepard, "Thanksgiving Hymn" ("God of the spreading earth"), in Young, *Temperance Song Book of the Mass. Temperance Union*, 36–37.

1842 John Pierpont, "Ode, Sung by the Constituents of John Quincy Adams, on his return from Congress, September 17, 1842," in *The Anti-Slavery Poems of John Pierpont*, 60–61.

1843 Samuel F. Smith, "Hymn for the National Anniversary" ("Auspicious morning, hail!"), in Baron Stow and Smith, ed., *The Psalmist* (Boston: Gould and Lincoln, 1843), 596–597.

1844 "My Country," in George W. Clark, comp., *The Liberty Minstrel*, 7th ed. (New York: George W. Clark, 1844), 192–193.

1844 "The Liberty Army," in Clark, *The Liberty Minstrel*, 7th ed., 193.

1844 "Spirit of Freemen, Awake," in Clark, *The Liberty Minstrel*, 7th ed., 193.

1844 Rev. John Sullivan, "God bless our native land," in Julian, *Dictionary of Hymnology*.

1845 "Sing Me a Triumph Song," in H. S. Gilmore, comp., *A Collection of Miscellaneous Songs* (1845), reprinted in Vicki L. Eaklor, *American Antislavery Songs* (New York: Greenwood, 1988), 70.

1848 "My Country," in George W. Clark, comp., *The Free Soil Minstrel* (New York: Martyn and Ely, 1848), 193–194.

1852 L. Wilder, "Hymn," *African Repository and Colonial Journal* (June 1852): 185; reprinted in Eaklor, *American Antislavery Songs*, 12–13.

1852 D. S. Whitney, "Original Hymn," performed in Abington, Mass., 5 July 1852; *Liberator* (16 July 1852), 110.

1853   "Slave of the Cup" ("Slave of the cup, beware!"), in Phineas Stowe, ed., *Melodies for the Temperance Band* (Boston: Nathaniel Noyes, 1853), 60.

1853   John Pierpont, "For Young Persons" ("Let the still air rejoice") in Stowe, *Melodies for the Temperance Band*, 45; reprinted as "Temperance Hymn," in *The Soldier's Companion* (Boston: Walker, Wise, 1863), 3.

1853   "Overthrow of Alcohol" ("It comes, the joyful day"), in Stowe, *Melodies for the Temperance Band*, 58.

1853   Mrs. A. M. C. Edmond, "Prayer at Sea" ("Tossed on the stormy sea"), in Stowe, *Melodies for the Temperance Band*, 96.

1853   "The Pledge" ("As we are gathered here"), in A. D. Fillmore, comp., *The Temperance Musician* (Cincinnati: Applegate, 1853), 47.

1853   "God Save the State," *Kentucky Family Mirror* (Carrolton) (2 July 1853), in Robert Pettus Hay, "Freedom's Jubilee: One Hundred Years of the Fourth of July, 1776–1876" (Ph.D. diss., University of Kentucky, 1967), 142.

1854   Joshua McCarter Simpson, "Fourth of July in Alabama," in *The Emancipation Car* (Zanesville, Ohio: E. C. Church, 1854), 40–42.

1854   Joshua McCarter Simpson, "Song of the Aliened American," in *The Emancipation Car*, 17–18.

c. 1854   James Montgomery, "Praise to the God of Harvest" ("The God of harvest praise"); reprinted in *The Soldier's Companion*, 11.

1855   John Pierpont, "Hymn, to be sung at the erection of the monument on the grave of Asa R. Wing," *Liberator* (24 August 1855), 136.

1856   D. S. Whitney, "The Day of Jubilee," *Liberator* (1 August 1856), 214–215.

1856   "Freedom's Anthem" ("God guard the Freeman's cause!"), in *The Republican Campaign Songster* (New York: Miller, Orton and Mulligan, 1856), 91–92.

1857   S. G. C., "The Patriot's Hymn A Parody," *Liberator* (25 December 1857), 208.

1859   Justitia, "An Appeal to American Freemen" (21 June 1859), *Liberator* (1 July 1859), 104.

1861   "God Bless the Farmer's Toil," in *The Book of Popular Songs* (Philadelphia: G. G. Evans, 1861), 121.

1861   "God Save John Bull," in Richard Grant White, comp., *National Hymns* (New York: Rudd and Carleton, 1861).

1861   George Dow, "For Bunker Hill" ("Though many miles away"), performed by Union troops on 17 May 1861 in Alexandria, Virginia; reprinted in Frank Moore, ed., *The Rebellion Record* (New York: Putnam, 1862), 1:125.

1861   "A New Version of an Old Song" ("God save Cotton, our King!"), *New*

York Evening Post (29 May 1861); reprinted in Moore, *The Rebellion Record,* 1:120.

1861 James Walden, "God Save Our Native Land," *New York Times;* reprinted in Moore, *The Rebellion Record,* 1:17.

1861 George G. W. Morgan, "God Protect Us!" ("O Lord, we humbly pray"); reprinted in Moore, *The Rebellion Record* 1:85–86.

1861 Harriet Beecher Stowe, "Let Freedom's Banner wave" ("Here, where our fathers came"), *Independent* (13 June 1861), 1; reprinted as "Hymn for a Flag-Raising" in Moore, *The Rebellion Record,* 1:140.

c. 1861 Reuben Nason, "God Save the South!" (Mobile: Joseph Bloch, c. 1861).

c. 1861 H. De Marsan, "God Save the Union," Library Company of Philadelphia Song Sheet Collection.

1862 G. W. Rogers, "War," *Liberator* (10 January 1862), 8.

1862 R. S. A., "God Save the South" ("Wake, every minstrel strain"), *Richmond Dispatch;* reprinted in Moore, *The Rebellion Record,* 4:36–37.

1862 "Glory to God on high," in *The Soldier's Hymn Book* (Charleston, S.C.: South Carolina Tract Society, 1862), 62–63.

1862 "My Country 'tis of thee . . . Land of the Southron's pride," *The Soldier's Hymn Book,* 191–192.

1862 "Our Land, with mercies crowned," *The Soldier's Hymn Book,* 203–204.

1862 "Grateful Praises for the Gospel," *The Soldier's Hymn-Book; For Camp Worship* (Virginia: Southern Tract Society, 1862), 48–49.

c. 1862 "God Help Kentucky!" ("Lord from thy heavenly throne"), slip sheet, Library Company of Philadelphia Song Sheet Collection.

c. 1862 "God Save the President!" broadside, Library Company of Philadelphia Song Sheet Collection.

1863 "God Bless Our Southern Land," performed in a reception for Major General J. B. Magruder in Houston, Texas, 20 January 1863. Published in Francis D. Allan, comp., *Allan's Lone Star Ballads* (Galveston: J. D. Sawyer, 1874), 43.

1863 "God of the brave and free," *The Soldier's Hymn Book, 2nd ed..* (Charleston, S.C.: South Carolina Tract Society, 1863), 200–201.

1863 "Our dearly cherished land," *The Soldier's Hymn Book, 2nd ed.,* 232–233.

1863 "Mrs. W. D. G.," "Song of Freedom, Dedicated to Frederick Douglass" ("Come sing a cheerful lay"), *Liberator* (April 1863), 831.

1863 "Prayer for our Country" ("God bless our native land"), *The Soldier's Companion,* 3.

1863 "The Benediction," ("Up! 'Tis our country's cause"), *The Soldier's Companion,* 3.

1863   Robert Nicoll, "The Soldier's Prayer" ("Lord, from thy blessed throne"), *The Soldier's Companion*, 3.

1863   John Pierpont, "National Hymn" ("God of this glorious earth"), *The Soldier's Companion*, 5.

1864   "Come, let our voices raise," in *The Sabbath School Wreath* (Raleigh, N.C.: Spirit of the Age, 1864), 83.

1864   "God Bless Our Sunday School," *Cymbal: A Collection of Hymns for Sabbath Schools* (Augusta, Ga.: J. T. Patterson, 1864), 91.

1864   "Hymn of the Connecticut Twelfth," in Frank Moore, comp., *Songs of the Soldiers* (New York: Putnam, 1864), 153–154.

1864   Rev. J. F. Mines, "The Patriot's Hymn" ("While the loud drum and fife"), in Moore, *Songs of the Soldiers*, 317–318.

1865   "Eight-Hour Lyrics" ("Ye noble sons of toil"), *Fincher's Trades' Review* (23 September 1865), reprinted in Philip S. Foner, *American Labor Songs of the Nineteenth Century* (Urbana: University of Illinois Press, 1975), 217.

1866   "My Country," performed on 4 July at Harmony Grove, Framingham, Massachusetts. Broadside in Harris Collection, Brown University Library. Reprinted in John Greenway, *American Folksongs of Protest* (Philadelphia: University of Pennsylvania Press, 1953), 88–89.

1869   "Soldiers of Christ are We," "Welcome Meeting to the Delegates of the Y. M. C. A.," Fourteenth Annual Convention, Portland, Maine (14 July 1869), O. O. Howard Papers, Bowdoin College Special Collections, Brunswick, Maine.

c. 1869   Henry Wadsworth Longfellow, "Lord, let war's tempests cease," in S. J. Adair Fitz-Gerald, *Stories of Famous Songs, In Two Volumes* (Philadelphia: Lippincott, 1901) I:214–215.

1872   A. B. Curry, "Come Thou who made this earth," in *Songs for the Grange* (Washington, D.C.: Gibson Bros., 1872).

1877   Albert Welles, "My Country 'Tis of Thee," *National Labor Tribune* (20 October 1877).

1880   "Come With Us to the Spring" ("Why to the wine-cup's brim"), in J. N. Stearns, ed., *National Temperance Hymn and Song Book* (New York: National Temperance Society, 1880), 49.

1882   Ambrose Bierce, "A Rational Anthem" ("My country, 'tis of thee, / Sweet land of felony"), *San Francisco Wasp* (16 September 1882); 581.

1883   Elizabeth Boynton Harbert, "The New America" ("Our country now from thee"), composed for the Convention of the National Woman Suffrage Association, Washington, D.C., January, 1883. Reprinted in L. May Wheeler, comp., *Booklet of Song; A Collection of Suffrage and Temperance Melodies* (Minneapolis: Co-operative Printing, 1884), 14–16.

1884   L. May Wheeler, "My Native Country" ("I'll sing dear land, of thee"), in Wheeler, *Booklet of Song*, 16–17.

1885   "Foremothers' Hymn" ("My country 'tis to thee"), *New Era* (October 1885): 305; reprinted in Sally Wagner, *A Time of Protest* (Carmichael, Calif.: Sky Carrier Press, 1988), 125–126.

1886   "Our State" ("God bless our noble State"), in J. H. Leslie, comp., *The Good Templar Songster* (New York: Independent Order of Good Templars, 1886), 6.

1886   "Our Cause" ("God, bless our temp'rance band"), in Leslie, *The Good Templar Songster*, 6.

1886   Ella Alexander Boole, "For God and Home and Native Land" ("Our father's God! of thee"), in Leslie, *The Good Templar Songster*, 7.

1886   "Our Land Redeemed" ("My country! broad and fine"), in Leslie, *The Good Templar Songster*, 7.

1886   Rev. C. S. H. Dunn, "My Country, 'Tis to Thee," in Leslie, *The Good Templar Songster*, 7.

1886   "God of the Temp'rance cause," in Leslie, *The Good Templar Songster*, n.p.

1889   Samuel F. Smith, "Our joyful hearts to-day" (extra verse), in Smith, *Poems of Home and Country* (Boston: Silver, Burdett, 1895), 184.

1889   Walter K. Fobes, "Temperance, Thy Noble Name," in *Temperance Songs and Hymns* (Boston: Walter K. Fobes, 1889), 19.

1889   H. C. Dodge, "The Future 'America,'" ("My country 'tis of thee, / Land of lost liberty"), *Bakers' Journal* (23 March 1889); reprinted in Foner, *American Labor Songs of the Nineteenth Century*, 183.

1890   Ralph E. Hoyt, "America" ("Our Country, 'tis of thee, / Sweet land of knavery"), *Journal of the Knights of Labor* (3 July 1890); reprinted in Foner, *American Labor Songs of the Nineteenth Century*, 151–152.

1891   "Once More We Meet to Clasp," in Leopold Vincent, comp., *The Alliance and Labor Songster* (Indianapolis: Vincent Bros. Pub. Co., 1891), 4.

1891   H. W. Finson, "Awake! Be Free" ("Our country, great and grand"), in Vincent, *The Alliance and Labor Songster*, 5; reprinted and attributed to H. W. Fulson in Phillips Thompson, ed., *The Labor Reform Songster* (Philadelphia, 1892).

1891   Charles Chesewright, "Our Cause," in Vincent, *The Alliance and Labor Songster*, 5.

1891   Thomas Nicol, "A New National Anthem" ("My country, 'tis of thee, / Once land of liberty"), in Vincent, *The Alliance and Labor Songster*, 5.

1894   Samuel F. Smith, "Patriot's Day," in *Poems of Home and Country*, 138.

1895   O. J. Graham, "America—1895" ("Our country 'tis for thee / Land where once all were free"), *Labor Journal*, reprinted in *Coming Nation* (11

May 1895), reprinted in Foner, *American Labor Songs of the Nineteenth Century*, 251–252.

1897   "Bates College 'Tis to Thee," performed at the dedication of the "English Room" in Hawthorn Hall, Bates College (10 June 1897). Bates College Special Collections, Lewiston, Maine.

1898   Samuel F. Smith, "Our glorious Land to-day" (the "education" verses), in R. L. Paget, comp., *Poems of American Patriotism, 1776–1898* (Boston: Page, 1898), 1–3; reprinted in *School Life* (October 1933).

1900   Rose Alice Cleveland, "Hymn of the Toilers" ("O nation, strong and great"), in Charles H. Kerr, comp., *Socialist Songs; Pocket Library of Socialism*, no. 11 (Chicago: Charles H. Kerr, 15 January 1900), n.p.

Notes

Introduction

1. Joshua McCarter Simpson, *The Emancipation Car, Being an Original Composition of Anti-Slavery Ballads, Composed Exclusively for the Under Ground Rail Road* (Miami: Mnemosyne, 1969; originally published in Zanesville, Ohio, 1854; copyrighted in 1874), iii–vi; emphasis added.

2. For an overview of this claim, see Robert James Branham, "'Of Thee I Sing': Contesting 'America,'" *American Quarterly* 48 (December 1996): 623–652. For coverage of Cleveland's "Festival," see "The National Hymn," *Boston Post* (30 November 1894). For a select list of variations of "America," see appendix B.

3. Ernst Bloch, *Essays on the Philosophy of Music*, trans. Peter Palmer (Cambridge, England: Cambridge University Press, 1985; originally written in German in 1918), 140, 113, 93, 132–133. "Listening through" and "listening beyond" are not Bloch's terms but our attempt to explicate his often paradoxical and elliptical claims.

4. Nathan Irvin Huggins, *Revelations: American History, American Myths* (New York: Oxford University Press, 1995), 169. In contrast to this *exclusionary* model, in which nationalism is a process of "obliterating or subordinating" others, see Sacvan Bercovitch, *The Rites of Assent: Transformations in the Symbolic Construction of America* (New York: Routledge, 1993), where American nationalism is described as a voraciously *inclusive* process. Regarding Bercovitch's model of nationalism, see Stephen Hartnett and Ramsey Eric Ramsey, "'A Plain Public Road': Evaluating Arguments for Democracy in a Post-Metaphysical World," *Argumentation and Advocacy* 35:3 (winter 1999): 95–114.

5. George W. Clark, comp., *The Liberty Minstrel* (New York, 1844), 4.

6. Douglass Adair and John A. Schutz, eds., *Peter Oliver's Origin & Progress of the American Rebellion: A Tory View* (San Marino, Calif.: Huntington Library, 1961), 41.

7. "Rallying Song of the Tea Party," 1773, as reprinted in Henry Steele Commager and Richard B. Morris, eds., *The Spirit of 'Seventy-Six: The Story of the American Revolution as Told by Participants* (New York: Da Capo Press, 1995; originally published in 1958), 3.

8. Tom Paine, "The Liberty Tree" (1775), in *The Thomas Paine Reader*, Michael Foot and Isaac Kramnick, eds. (New York: Penguin, 1987), 63–64.

9. James Morton Smith, *Freedom's Fetters: The Alien and Sedition Laws and American Civil Liberties* (Ithaca: Cornell University Press, 1956), 8–9. See *An Act Respecting Alien Enemies* (6 July 1798) and *An Act for the Punishment of Certain Crimes Against the United States* (14 July 1798), both printed in *The Public Statutes at Large of The United States of America, etc.*, (Boston: Little & Brown, 1845), 1:577–578 and 596–597.

10. Vera Brodsky Lawrence, *Music for Patriots, Politicians, and Presidents: Harmonies and Discords of the First Hundred Years* (New York: Macmillan, 1975), 143.

11. Quoted in Smith, *Freedom's Fetters*, 161. See the story of the *Aurora's* battle against the Alien and Sedition Acts of 1798 in Richard Rosenfeld, *American Aurora: A Democratic-Republican Returns; The Suppressed History of Our Nation's Beginnings and the Heroic Newspaper That Tried to Report It* (New York: St. Martin's Press, 1997).

12. Lawrence, *Music for Patriots*, 141, 143; and see the facsimile of the original version of "Hail Columbia" reprinted on 144–145.

13. William C. Woodbridge, "Editor's Address," *American Annals of Education and Instruction* 1 (August 1830): 2.

14. Lowell Mason, *Address on Church Music: Delivered by Request, on the Evening of Saturday, October 7, 1826, In The Vestry of Hanover Church, and on the Evening of Monday Following, In The Third Baptist Church, Boston* (Boston: Hilliard, Gray, Little, and Wilkins, 1827), 40.

15. Gustave de Beaumont, *Marie; or, Slavery in the United States*, trans. Barbara Chapman (Baltimore: Johns Hopkins University Press, 1999; originally published in 1835), 38, 102.

16. Max Weber, *The Protestant Ethic and the Spirit of Capitalism* (London: Routledge, 1997; originally published as two essays in 1904, then as a book in German in 1920, and finally translated into English in 1930 by Talcott Parsons), 272, n. 64.

17. Weber, *Protestant Ethic*, 181–182.

18. Thomas Nicol, "A New National Anthem," in Leopold Vincent, comp., *The Alliance and Labor Songster* (Kansas, 1891); reprinted in Philip Foner, comp., *American Labor Songs of the Nineteenth Century* (Urbana: University of Illinois Press, 1975), 268.

19. See the lyrics of these songs printed in Foner, *American Labor Songs of the Nineteenth Century*, 268–273. For a contemporary version of such materials, see *Songs to Fan the Flames of Discontent: The Little Red Songbook of the IWW, International Edition* (Ypsilanti, Mich.: International Workers of the World, 1995), including "Food not Finance," Stephen Hartnett's musical tribute to progressive farmers, 22–23.

20. Harvey Moyer, "My Country, a New National Hymn," *Songs of Socialism*, 7th ed. (Chicago: Cooperative Printing, 1913), 1. And see "Democracy!"—another pro-labor version of America included on the inside cover of the booklet.

21. For an example of Adorno's towering condescension, see "Perennial Fash-

ion—Jazz," in his *Prisms*, trans. Samuel and Shierry Weber (Cambridge: MIT Press, 1984; originally published in 1967), 119–132. While Adorno was blind to the political power of popular and folk cultures, his critique of the culture industry as a whole was nonetheless brilliant and informs our discussion in the epilogue.

22. Anonymous, "A New Version of an Old Song," *New York Evening Post* (29 May 1861); reprinted in Frank Moore, ed., *The Rebellion Record: A Diary of American Events, with Documents, Narratives, Illustrative Incidents, Poetry, etc.* (New York: Putnam, 1862), 1:120.

23. David Kennedy, "The Truest Measure of Patriotism," *New York Times* (4 July 2000), A13.

24. Elise K. Kirk, *Music at the White House: A History of the American Spirit* (Urbana: University of Illinois Press, 1986), 206.

25. This claim is not meant to be nostalgic but rather a historical observation on the roles of songs and singing in a world prior to the culture industry. For analyses of some of the possibilities of music in the postmodern age, see the epilogue; Stephen Hartnett, "Cultural Postmodernism and Bobby McFerrin: A Case Study of the Production of Music as the Composition of Spectacle," *Cultural Critique* 16 (fall 1990): 61–85; "It's a Dirty, Rotten Business, but It Can't Kill the Music," *Cultural Studies* 11:1 (January 1997): 159–166; and Jacques Attali, *Noise: The Political Economy of Music*, trans. Brian Massumi (Minneapolis: University of Minnesota Press, 1985; French original published in 1977).

26. Smith's poem from the *Essex (Mass.) County Register* (18 September 1861); reprinted in Moore, *The Rebellion Record*, 3:48–49.

Chapter 1

1. Antonin Dvorak, "Music in America," *Harper's New Monthly Magazine* (February 1895), 432.

2. "American Music for Hymn 'America,'" *New York Times* (17 November 1918), 12; "Americanism in Song," *New York Times* (23 September 1889), 4.

3. *Legislation to Make "The Star-Spangled Banner" the National Anthem*, Hearing before the House Judiciary Committee (Washington, D.C.: Government Printing Office, 1930), 42–43.

4. See, for example, Stephen Kosokoff and Carl Campbell, "The Rhetoric of Protest: Song, Speech, and Attitude Change," *Southern Speech Journal* 35 (summer 1970): 295–302; James Irvine and Walter Kirkpatrick, "The Musical Form in Rhetorical Exchange: Theoretical Considerations," *Quarterly Journal of Speech* 58 (October 1972): 272–284; Cheryl Irwin Thomas, "'Look What They've Done to My Song, Ma': The Persuasiveness of Song," *Southern Speech Communication Journal* 39 (spring 1974): 260–268; Mark Booth, "The Art of Words in Songs," *Quarterly Journal of Speech* 62 (October 1976): 242–249; Ralph Knupp, "A Time for Every Purpose under Heaven: Rhetorical Dimensions of Protest Music," *Southern Speech Communication Journal* 46 (summer 1981): 377–389; Elizabeth Kizer, "Protest Song Lyrics as Rhetoric," *Popular Music and Society* 9 (1983): 3–11; Sheila Davis, "Pop Lyrics: A Mir-

ror and Molder of Society," *Etc.* 42 (summer 1985): 161–169; Ray Pratt, *Rhythm and Resistance: Explorations in the Political Uses of Popular Music* (New York: Praeger, 1990).

5. See Liah Greenfeld, *Nationalism: Five Roads to Modernity* (Cambridge: Harvard University Press, 1992), 3–6; Benedict Anderson, *Imagined Communities: Reflections on the Origin and Spread of Nationalism* (New York: Verso, 1983), 13–15; Graeme Turner, "Representing the Nation," in Tony Bennett, ed., *Popular Fiction: Technology, Ideology, Production, Reading* (London: Routledge, 1990), 117–127; Ernest Gellner, *Nations and Nationalism* (Ithaca: Cornell University Press, 1983), and E. J. Hobsbawm, *Nations and Nationalism since 1780: Programme, Myth, Reality* (Cambridge, UK: Cambridge University Press, 1990). For a case study of how Americans constructed such nationalism around the dream of empire, see Stephen Hartnett, "Senator Robert Walker's 1844 *Letter on Texas Annexation*; or, The Rhetorical 'Logic' of Imperialism," *American Studies* 38:1 (spring 1997): 27–54.

6. Margaret Canovan, *Nationhood and Political Theory* (Cheltenham, England: Elgar, 1996), 69.

7. See Michael C. McGee, "In Search of the "People": A Rhetorical Alternative," *Quarterly Journal of Speech* 61 (1975), 235–249; Maurice Charland, "Constitutive Rhetoric: The Case of the Peuple Québécois," *Quarterly Journal of Speech* 73 (1987), 133–150; and Stephen Hartnett and Ramsey Eric Ramsey, "'A Plain Public Road': Evaluating Arguments for Democracy in a Post-Metaphysical World," *Argumentation and Advocacy* 35:3 (winter 1999): 95–114. Quotation from Elias Nason, *A Monogram on Our National Song* (Albany: Joel Munsell, 1869), 9.

8. Walt Whitman, "One's Self I Sing" (1871), in Emory Holloway, ed., *The Collected Poems of Walt Whitman* (New York: Book League of America, 1942), 1.

9. E. L. Doctorow, "Standards," in Susan Sontag, ed., *The Best American Essays, 1992* (New York: Ticknor and Fields, 1992), 50.

10. Paul Nettl, *National Anthems* (New York: Storm, 1952), 1; F. Gunther Eyck, *The Voice of Nations: European National Anthems and their Authors* (Westport, Conn.: Greenwood, 1995), xii–xiii; Rey Longyear, *Nineteenth-Century Romanticism in Music* (Englewood Cliffs, N.J.: Prentice-Hall, 1969), 154–183.

11. The first publication is often wrongly cited as *Harmonia Anglicana* (1744), which does not include the song. See Donald W. Krummel, "God Save the King," *Musical Times* (March 1962): 159; Stanley Sadie, ed., "National Anthems," *The New Grove Dictionary of Music and Musicians* (London: Macmillan, 1980), 13:56.

12. Percy A. Scholes, *God Save the Queen! The History and Romance of the World's First National Anthem* (London: Oxford University Press, 1954), 4; quotation from *ibid.*, 6–7.

13. Lyrics printed in Scholes, *God Save the Queen!* 10–11. See the note to song 1 in appendix A regarding other possible sources of the third verse.

14. Scholes, *God Save the Queen!* 22, notes to plate 6; and see Linda Colley, *Britons: Forging the Nation 1707–1837* (New Haven: Yale University Press, 1992), 43–46.

15. Zdzislaw Mach, "National Anthems: The Case of Chopin as a National Composer," in Martin Stokes, ed., *Ethnicity, Identity and Music: The Musical Construction of Place* (New York: Berg, 1997), 61–62, emphasis added.

16. Scholes, *God Save the Queen!* 20, 22.

17. Ben Arnold, *Music and War: A Research and Information Guide* (New York: Garland, 1993), 52–61; Beethoven's *Wellington's Victory* was among his most popular pieces. And see "Annotated Listing of Classic and Early Romantic War Music," 62–97.

18. Scholes, *God Save the Queen!* 217.

19. Esmond Wright, *An Empire for Liberty: From Washington to Lincoln* (Cambridge, Mass.: Blackwell, 1995), 71; David Hackett Fischer, *Albion's Seed: Four British Folkways in America* (New York: Oxford University Press, 1989), 6; Richard L. Bushman, *King and People in Provincial Massachusetts* (Chapel Hill: University of North Carolina Press, 1985), 19–20; Fischer, *Albion's Seed*, 385; Bushman, *King and People*, 4.

20. Carleton Sprague Smith, "Broadsides and Their Music in Colonial America," in Barbara Lambert and Frederick Allis Jr., eds., *Music in Colonial Massachusetts, 1630–1820* (Boston: Colonial Society of Massachusetts, 1980), 254, n. 82; Jerrilyn Greene Marston, *King and Congress: The Transfer of Political Legitimacy, 1774–1776* (Princeton: Princeton University Press, 1987), 13; Proclamation, quoted in Bushman, *King and People*, 15.

21. Smith, "Broadsides," 157–58; John Anthony Scott, *The Ballad of America: The History of the United States in Song and Story* (Carbondale: Southern Illinois University Press, 1983), 2–6.

22. Russell Sanjek, *American Popular Music and Its Business: The First Four Hundred Years* (New York: Oxford University Press, 1988), 1:278–79; Gilbert Chase, *America's Music: From the Pilgrims to the Present*, 3rd ed. (Urbana: University of Illinois, 1987), 114. And see the preface by Richard Crawford to the facsimile version of *Urania* (New York: Da Capo, 1974), i–xxi.

23. "A New Song on the Success of 1759," set to the tune of "God Save the King" in celebration of the capture of Quebec, was published by Enoch Freeman of Falmouth, Maine; see James Leamon, *Revolution Downeast: The War for American Independence in Maine* (Amherst: University of Massachusetts Press, 1993), 31; Lester C. Olson, *Emblems of American Community in the Revolutionary Era* (Washington, D.C.: Smithsonian Institution Press, 1991), 58–60; Foxcroft quoted in Marston, *King and Congress*, 29; Christopher Moore, *The Loyalists: Revolution, Exile, Settlement* (Toronto: McClelland and Stewart, 1984), 62–63.

24. Louise Burnham Dunbar, "A Study of Monarchical Tendencies in the United States from 1776 to 1801," *University of Illinois Studies in the Social Sciences* 10 (March 1922): 10; William D. Liddle, "'A Patriot King, or None': Lord Bolingbroke and the American Renunciation of George III," *Journal of American History* 65 (March 1979): 960.

25. J. C. D. Clark, *The Language of Liberty 1660–1832: Political Discourse and Social Dynamics in the Anglo-American World* (Cambridge, England: Cambridge University Press, 1994), 296; Wright, *An Empire for Liberty*, 55.

26. *Virginia Gazette* (17 February 1775), 2, col. 1; Wright, *An Empire for Liberty*, 60.

27. *Rivington's Gazette* (20 April 1775), reprinted in Frank Moore, *The Diary of the American Revolution 1775–1781*, ed. John Anthony Scott (New York: Washington Square, 1967; originally published in 1876), 23.

28. Sylvia R. Frey, *Water from the Rock: Black Resistance in a Revolutionary Age* (Princeton: Princeton University Press, 1991), 110; Wallace Brown, *The Good Americans: The Loyalists in the American Revolution* (New York: Morrow, 1969), 37.

29. Odell's poem quoted in G. N. D. Evans, ed., *Allegiance in America: The Case of the Loyalists* (Reading, Mass.: Addison-Wesley, 1969), 20–21; also see Arthur F. Schrader, "Songs to Cultivate the Sensations of Freedom," in *Music in Colonial Massachusetts, 1630–1820.*

30. Eyck, *The Voice of Nations,* 39–56.

31. Scholes, *God Save the Queen!* 51–60; James J. Fuld, *The Book of World-Famous Music, 3rd ed.* (New York: Dover, 1985), 249; Scholes, *God Save the Queen!* 54.

32. Eyck, *The Voice of Nations,* 16–18; Turner, "Representing the Nation," 126–127.

33. "Extempore" version printed in Scholes, *God Save the Queen!* 157; on Whitefield, see Charles Seymour Robinson, *Annotations Upon Popular Hymns* (Cleveland: F. M. Barton, 1893), 140–141; Samuel W. Duffield, *English Hymns: Their Authors and History* (New York: Funk and Wagnall's, 1886), 113–114.

34. Lyrics printed in Scholes, *God Save the Queen!* 154–56; Anthony Trollope, *North America,* ed. Donald Smalley and Bradford A. Booth (New York: Knopf, 1951), 89; and see General Association of Connecticut, *Psalms and Hymns, for Christian Use and Worship* (New Haven: Durrie and Peck, 1845), 400.

35. Timothy D. Hall, *Contested Boundaries: Itinerancy and the Reshaping of the Colonial American Religious World* (Durham, N.C.: Duke University Press, 1994), 32–36; Duffield, *English Hymns,* 114.

36. Philip Davidson, *Propaganda and the American Revolution 1763–1783* (Chapel Hill: University of North Carolina Press, 1941), 188; Gillian B. Anderson, comp., *Freedom's Voice in Poetry and Song* (Wilmington, Del.: Scholarly Resources, 1977), x.

37. Perry quoted in Anderson, *Freedom's Voice,* x; Frank Moore, *Songs and Ballads of the American Revolution* (New York: D. Appleton, 1855), v–vi.

38. Adams quoted in Arthur M. Schlesinger, Sr., "A Note on Songs as Patriot Propaganda 1765–1776," *William and Mary Quarterly,* Third Series XI:1 (Jan., 1954): 79; Robert L. Davis, *A History of Music in American Life* (Malabar, Fla.: Krieger, 1982), 1:78.

39. Josiah Quincy, *Observations on the Act of Parliament Commonly Called the Boston Port-Bill* (Boston: Edes and Gill, 1774), 79; Marston, *King and Congress,* 39–54.

40. Oliver quoted in Douglas Adair and John A. Schutz, *Peter Oliver's Origin & Progress of the American Rebellion: A Tory View* (San Marino, Calif.: Huntington Library, 1961), 166; Thomas Paine, "Common Sense" (1776), in *The Thomas Paine Reader,* ed. Michael Foot and Isaac Kramnick (New York: Penguin, 1987), 87, 75. The best history of this slow transformation remains Gordon Wood, *The Creation of the American Republic, 1776–1787* (Chapel Hill: University of North Carolina Press 1998 — original in 1969).

41. "A New Song," reprinted in Anderson, *Freedom's Voice,* 375.

42. Stephen Lucas, "The Rhetorical Ancestry of the Declaration of Independence," *Rhetoric & Public Affairs* 1:2 (1998): 165.

43. Jan Willem Schulte Nordholt, *The Dutch Republic and American Independence*

(Chapel Hill: University of North Carolina Press, 1982), 70–74; "A SONG, written by a Dutch Lady at the Hague, for the Americans at Amsterdam, July 4, 1779," and "Another, written by a Dutch Gentleman at Amsterdam, July 4, 1779," *Providence Gazette and Country Journal* (1 January 1780), 4. Also see Oscar Sonneck, *Library of Congress Report on "The Star-Spangled Banner," "Hail Columbia," "America," "Yankee Doodle"* (Washington, D.C.: Government Printing Office, 1909), 77; Oscar Brand, *Songs of '76: A Folksinger's History of the Revolution* (New York: Evans, 1972), 166.

44. The song was published in the *Boston Independent Chronicle* (22 June 1786) and is reprinted in Vera Brodsky Lawrence, *Music for Patriots, Politicians, and Presidents: Harmonies and Discords of the First Hundred Years* (New York: Macmillan, 1975), 97. It was republished in the *Boston Commercial Gazette* of 9 June 1825 in anticipation of the laying of the cornerstone for the Bunker Hill monument.

45. Ernest Renan, "Qu'est-ce qu'une nation" (1882), in John Hutchinson and Anthony D. Smith, eds., *Nationalism* (New York: Oxford University Press, 1994), 17. Compare this translation to "What Is a Nation?" reprinted in Homi Bhabha, ed., *Nation and Narration* (London: Routledge, 1993), 8–22; quoted passage on 19.

46. Quotations from Louis C. Elson, *The National Music of America and Its Sources* (Boston: L.C. Page, 1899), 124–125; lyrics reprinted in Lawrence, *Music for Patriots*, 97. For discussion of some of these pre-Constitution conflicts, see David P. Szatmary, *Shay's Rebellion: The Making of an Agrarian Insurrection* (Amherst: University of Massachusetts Press, 1980).

47. Leon Plantinga, *Romantic Music: A History of Musical Style in Nineteenth-Century Europe* (New York: Norton, 1984), 341; Sadie, "National Anthems," 57.

48. Edward A. Maginty, "'America': The Origin of its Melody," *Musical Quarterly* 20 (July 1934): 259–61; Scholes, *God Save the Queen!* 186.

49. Stephen Salisbury, *An Essay on the Star Spangled Banner and National Songs* (Worcester, Mass.: Charles Hamilton, 1873), 14–15.

50. Elson, *The National Music of America,* 119–120; Beethoven quoted in Nettl, *National Anthems,* 47; *ibid.,* 47.

51. S. Frederick Starr, *Bamboula! The Life and Times of Louis Moreau Gottschalk* (New York: Oxford University Press, 1995), 85–86, 139, 157, 287.

52. Bishop James Madison, "Manifestation of the Beneficence of Divine Providence Towards America" (19 February 1795), in Ellis Sandoz, ed., *Political Sermons of the Founding Era* (Indianapolis: Liberty Press, 1991), 1319.

53. Gustave de Beaumont, *Marie; or, Slavery in the United States,* trans. Barbara Chapman (Baltimore: Johns Hopkins University Press, 1999; originally published in 1835), 106; and see Lawrence J. Friedman, *Inventors of the Promised Land* (New York: Knopf, 1975), 51–55.

54. *New-Jersey Journal* (26 December 1781), in Lawrence, *Music for Patriots,* 92; *Independent Gazette; or The New-York Journal Revived* (12 February 1784), reprinted in Lawrence, *Music for Patriots,* 96.

55. "God Save Great Washington," *Philadelphia Continental Journal* (7 April 1786), reprinted in Irwin Silber, *Songs America Voted By* (Harrisburg, Pa.: Stackpole Books, 1971), 21; 1788 version printed in Lawrence, *Music for Patriots,* 96.

56. "Ode to be Sung on the Arrival of the President of the United States," *Gazette of the United States* (25 April 1789), 3; broadside courtesy of the New York Historical Society. Also see Douglas Southall Freeman, *George Washington: A Biography* (New York: Scribner's, 1954), 6:180, and James Thomas Flexner, *George Washington and the New Nation* (Boston: Little Brown, 1970), 179.

57. Dunbar, "A Study of Monarchical Tendencies," 84, 117, 129, 46.

58. Reprinted in Lawrence, *Music for Patriots*, 128.

59. Lawrence, *Music for Patriots*, 146; "Ode" in Lawrence, *Music for Patriots*, 128.

60. Renan, "Qu'est-ce qu'une nation," 17; Elson, *The National Music of America*, 121–125; Donald L. Hixon, *Music in Early America: A Bibliography of Music in Evans* (Metuchen, N.J.: Scarecrow Press, 1970), 3, 69–70, 88–90.

61. Lyrics printed in Lawrence, *Music for Patriots*, 133.

62. *United States Gazette, for the Country* (25 October 1805), quoted in Lawrence, *Music for Patriots*, 14.

Chapter 2

1. Quoted in Daniel Feller, *The Jacksonian Promise: America, 1815–1840* (Baltimore: Johns Hopkins University Press, 1995), 6–7.

2. Alexis de Tocqueville, *Democracy in America* (New York: Vintage Books, 1990; originally published in 1835), 1:241, 386, 387.

3. Perry Miller, *The Life of the Mind in America: From the Revolution to the Civil War* (New York: Harcourt, Brace and World, 1965), 5–6.

4. Carol A. Pemberton, *Lowell Mason: His Life and Work* (Ann Arbor: UMI Research Press, 1985), 32–45.

5. Lowell Mason, *Address on Church Music: Delivered by Request, on the Evening of Saturday, October 7, 1825, in the Vestry of Hanover Church, etc.* (Boston: Hilliard, Gray, Little and Wilkins, 1827), 5, 15, 17, 6–7. Mason was so pleased with Beecher's request that he printed the letter in the revised edition. Regarding revivals and their use of music, see Nathan Hatch, *The Democratization of American Christianity* (New Haven: Yale University Press, 1999), 146–161.

6. Mason, *Address on Church Music*, 19; Russell Sanjek, *American Popular Music and Its Business: The First Four Hundred Years, vol. 2, 1790 to 1909* (New York: Oxford University Press, 1988), 204.

7. Charles C. Cole, Jr., *The Social Ideas of the Northern Evangelists, 1826–1860* (New York: Octagon Books, 1966), 13; Hatch, *Democratization of American Christianity*, 3–16. Debra Gold Hansen, *Strained Sisterhood: Gender and Class in the Boston Female Anti-Slavery Society* (Amherst: University of Massachusetts Press, 1993), 35.

8. William C. McLoughlin, *Revivals, Awakenings, and Reform* (Chicago: University of Chicago Press, 1978), 112; Feller, *The Jacksonian Promise*, 98.

9. Lyman Beecher, *The Practicability of Suppressing Vice, By Means of Societies Instituted for That Purpose, A Sermon Delivered before the Moral Society in East-Hampton (Long-Island), September 21, 1803* (New London, Conn.: Samuel Green, 1804), 8–9.

10. Charles Beecher, ed., *Autobiography, Correspondence, Etc., of Lyman Beecher* (New

York: Harper, 1865), 2:101; William G. McLoughlin, *Modern Revivalism: Charles Grandison Finney to Billy Graham* (New York: Ronald Press, 1959), 62–63; Charles G. Finney, *Lectures on Revivals* (New York, 1835), 12.

11. In 1832, Finney hired one of Lowell Mason's students, Thomas Hastings, as his musical assistant. Hastings directed Finney's choir, compiled popular songbooks, and composed the music for the hymn "Rock of Ages." McLoughlin, *Modern Revivalism*, 99. See also McLoughlin, *Revivals, Awakenings, and Reforms*, 128; and James F. Findlay, Jr., *Dwight L. Moody, American Evangelist, 1837–1899* (Chicago: University of Chicago Press, 1969), 214–217.

12. The Bowdoin Street Church replaced Beecher's Hanover Street Church, which burned on 1 February 1830. Beecher, *Autobiography, Correspondence, Etc., of Lyman Beecher*, 150; Pemberton, *Lowell Mason*, 64–65. Pemberton claims, perhaps questionably, that this 1830 concert was "one of the first, if not *the* first, in which children sang as a group in public in the United States" (48).

13. Pemberton, *Lowell Mason*, 235, n. 24, 59; for a listing of Mason's works, see "Appendix B: Lowell Mason's Music Publications," 223–225.

14. Frederick Binder, *The Age of the Common School, 1830–1865* (New York: Wiley, 1974), 27; William C. Woodbridge, "Music, as a Branch of Instruction in Common Schools," *American Journal of Education and Instruction* 1 (September 1830):4.

15. Arthur Lowndes Rich, *Lowell Mason: "The Father of Singing Among the Children"* (Chapel Hill: University of North Carolina Press, 1946), 96. The bibliography here of Mason's works is even more complete than Pemberton's; see "Lowell Mason's Writings," 138–172.

16. William C. Woodbridge, "Editor's Address," *American Journal of Education and Instruction* 1 (August 1830):2; William C. Woodbridge, "On Vocal Music As a Branch of Common Education, Communicated to the American Lyceum," *American Journal of Education and Instruction* 3 (April 1833):18.

17. This lecture was reprinted many times and in many variations, including as the essay cited previously, "On Vocal Music As a Branch of Common Education."

18. David Z. Kushner, "The 'Masonic' Influence on Nineteenth-Century American Musical Education," *Journal of Musicological Research* 4 (1983): 447; Woodbridge, "On Vocal Music As a Branch of Common Education," 17.

19. Oliver Wendell Holmes, "The Boys" (1859), in *The Complete Poetical Works of Oliver Wendell Holmes* (Boston: Riverside Press, 1895), 118–119.

20. Samuel F. Smith, "Recollections By the Author of 'America,'" *Harvard Graduates' Magazine* 2 (December 1893):161–170; quotation from Henry K. Rowe, *History of Andover Theological Seminary* (Newton, Mass.: Thomas Todd, 1933), 18. In its first twenty-five years, only 42 of the 607 Andover graduates had not first graduated from college; *ibid.*, 26. See also Robert E. Riegel, *Young America, 1830–1840* (Norman: University of Oklahoma Press, 1949), 251.

21. Letter from Samuel Francis Smith to Capt. George Henry Preble (12 September 1872), in George Henry Preble, *History of the Flag of the United States of America*, 2nd ed. (Boston: A. Williams, 1880), 742.

22. Samuel F. Smith, "Recollections of Lowell Mason," *New England Magazine* 11

(January 1895):650; "Corner Scrap-Book," *Congregationalist* (5 December 1895); Samuel Smith, *Poems of Home and Country* (Boston: Silver, Burdett, 1895), xvii; Long quoted in "Memories of the Author of 'America' By His Daughter, Mrs. J. F. Morton," undated typescript in Miller Library Special Collections, Colby College, Waterville, Maine, 3.

23. Smith quoted in Preble, *History of the Flag of the United States*, 742; Smith, *Poems of Home and Country*, 141–142. The last line in Smith's original manuscript was "Our God, Our King." Program of the "Celebration of American Independence, by the Boston Sabbath School Union, at Park Street Church, July 4, 1831." Copy in Chapin Library Special Collections, Williams College.

24. Marguerite E. Fitch, "What Happened to the Middle Verse of 'America'?" *Yankee* 40 (November 1976):248; Lowell Mason, comp., *The Choir: or Union Collection of Church Music* (Boston: Carter, Hendee, 1833).

25. Ralph Corydon Fitts, "The North End," unpublished manuscript, Newton Historical Society, Newton, Massachusetts.

26. Samuel F. Smith, "America: The Author's Own Account of How the National Hymn Was Written, Address of the Rev. S. F. Smith at the Testimonial Recognition Tendered Him by the Governors of All the States, in Boston, April 3, 1895." Broadside in Newton Historical Society, Newton, Massachusetts.

27. "'America' Author Consents," *Boston Post* (3 December 1894); Helen Johnson Kendrick, *Our Familiar Songs and Those Who Made Them* (New York: Henry Holt, 1881), 595; "The Story of the Hymn 'America,'" *Critic* (26 January 1895), 69.

28. Smith, *Poems of Home and Country*, xvii; Oscar Sonneck, *Library of Congress Report on "The Star-Spangled Banner," "Hail Columbia," "America," "Yankee Doodle"* (Washington, D.C.: Government Printing Office, 1909), 75.

29. James is quoted without reference in John Harris, *Historic Walks in Old Boston* (Chester, Conn.: Globe Pequot Press, 1982), 138; some of the material in the next paragraph is drawn from this source, 138–146.

30. For a discussion of such "memory sites," see Pierre Nora, "Between Memory and History: *Les Lieux de Memoire*," *Representations* 26 (spring 1989): 7–25.

31. Feller, *The Jacksonian Promise*, xiii.

32. Binder, *The Age of the Common School*, 68–69. The following year, Beecher would leave Boston for Lane Seminary in Ohio to battle for the soul of the West against "popery and paganism." See Beecher, *Autobiography, Correspondence, Etc., of Lyman Beecher*, 2:249.

33. Lyman Beecher, "The Necessity of Revivals of Religion to the Perpetuity of Our Civil and Religious Institutions," *The Spirit of the Pilgrims* IV:9 (Sept. 1831): 467–479, quotation from 467; William E. Channing, "The Perfect Life: The Essence of the Christian Religion," in *Channing's Works* (Boston: American Unitarian Association, 1895), 1003.

34. "Sabbath School Celebration the 4th of July," *Sabbath School Treasury* 4 (August 1831):168.

35. Edward Everett Hale, *A New England Boyhood and Other Bits of Autobiography* (Boston: Little, Brown, 1915), 78–79; "Sabbath School Celebration," 168.

36. Woodbridge, "On Vocal Music As a Branch of Common Education," 196; "Advancing," *Liberator* (9 July 1831), 1; "Sabbath School Celebration," 168.

37. Irving Sablosky, *American Music* (Chicago: University of Chicago Press, 1969), 71. In 1831, the nineteen Boston Sabbath schools, including two designated for "Africans," enrolled 1,303 boys and 1,507 girls. Thomas C. Richards, "When 'America' Was First Sung," *Congregationalist and Herald of Gospel Liberty* (16 June 1932), 767–768.

38. *Semi-Centennial of the Park Street Church* (Boston, 1859), 162–166; lyrics printed in "Sabbath School Celebration," 168.

39. Binder, *The Age of the Common School*, 32–33; Tocqueville, *Democracy in America*, 1:330.

40. Michael B. Katz, *The Irony of Early School Reform: Educational Innovation in Mid-Nineteenth Century Massachusetts* (Cambridge: Harvard University Press, 1968), 11–12; Ruth Miller Elson, *Guardians of Tradition: American Schoolbooks of the Nineteenth Century* (Lincoln: University of Nebraska Press, 1964), 5–6.

41. William C. Woodbridge, editorial, *American Journal of Education and Instruction* 8 (January 1838):44; "Music in America," *North American Review* 52 (April 1841):330.

42. James H. Stone, "Mid-Nineteenth-Century American Beliefs in the Social Values of Music," *Musical Quarterly* 43 (January 1957):41, n. 4; Sanjek, *American Popular Music and Its Business*, 2:205.

43. Joseph Harrington, letter to the editor, under heading of "Musical Instruction in Common Schools," *Boston Musical Gazette* 1:7 (25 July 1838), 53.

44. Pemberton, *Lowell Mason*, 116–117; "School Committee's Report," *Boston Musical Gazette* 1 (26 December 1838), 137.

45. "Singing in Common Schools," *Common School Journal* 3 (15 June 1841), 189–190; "Music in America," *North American Review* 52 (April 1841): 320, 325, 326; Stone, "Mid-Nineteenth-Century American Beliefs," 40.

46. "School Committee's Report," 138; Woodbridge, "On Vocal Music" 201; Michael Broyles, *"Music of the Highest Class": Elitism and Populism in Antebellum Boston* (New Haven: Yale University Press, 1992), 31.

47. Edgar O. Silver, "The Growth of Music Among the People," *National Educational Association Journal of Proceedings and Addresses, Session of the Year 1891* (New York: J. J. Little, 1891), 815; Ralph L. Baldwin, "Evolution of Public School Music in the United States from the Civil War to 1900," Music Teachers National Association, *Papers and Proceedings* (1922):169; Elson, *Guardians of Tradition*, 2, 282.

48. "'America's' Author Consents"; Rowe, *History of Andover Theological Seminary*, 42; Mason, dedication to *The Choir*, iii.

49. Stone, "Mid-Nineteenth-Century American Beliefs," 43, n. 9.

50. Smith, *Poems of Home and Country*, xii; Dumas Malone, ed., *Dictionary of American Biography* (New York: Scribner's, 1935), 17: 342–343; General Association of Connecticut, *Psalms and Hymns, for Christian Use and Worship* (New-Haven: Durrie and Peck, 1845), 609–610; Henry Ward Beecher, *Plymouth Collection of Hymns for the Use of Christian Congregations* (New York: A. S. Barnes, 1855), 608–609.

51. Regarding the war on drugs, see Dan Baum, *Smoke and Mirrors: The War on*

Drugs and the Politics of Failure (Boston: Little, Brown, 1996); Christine Jacqueline Johns, *Power, Ideology, and the War on Drugs* (New York: Praeger, 1992); Peter Dale Scott and Jonathan Marshall, *Cocaine Politics: Drugs, Armies, and the CIA in Central America* (Berkeley: University of California Press, 1991), and Stephen Hartnett, "Seven Theses regarding the CIA, the Drug War, and Democracy," *LIP* 10 (autumn 1998): 32–37.

52. "God Bless America" (1784), reprinted in Vera Brodsky Lawrence, *Music for Patriots, Politicians, and Presidents* (New York: Macmillan, 1975), 98.

53. Rush quoted in Mark Edward Lender and James Kirby Martin, *Drinking in America: A History*, rev. and expanded ed. (New York: Free Press, 1987), 38; Lyman Beecher, *Six Sermons on the Nature, Occasions, Signs, Evils, and Remedy of Intemperance* (Boston: T. R. Marvin, 1828), 61.

54. W. R. Rohrabaugh, *The Alcoholic Republic* (New York: Oxford University Press, 1979), 35, 92; Lender and Martin, *Drinking in America*, 10.

55. Cole, *The Social Ideas of the Northern Evangelists*, 120.

56. Lender and Martin, *Drinking in America*, 2–3, 9; J. C. Furnas, *The Life and Times of the Late Demon Rum* (New York: Putnam, 1965), 17, 22; Rohrabaugh, *The Alcoholic Republic*, 145–146; Lender and Martin, *Drinking in America*, 14, 46; Rohrabaugh, *The Alcoholic Republic*, 15.

57. Lender and Martin, *Drinking in America*, 71–72; Beecher, *Six Sermons on the Nature, Occasions, Signs, Evils, and Remedy of Intemperance*, 85, emphasis added; Riegel, *Young America*, 288.

58. See Walter K. Fobes, comp., *Temperance Songs and Hymns* (Boston: Walter K. Fobes, 1889), endpapers; Henry W. Blair, *The Temperance Movement: Or, The Conflict Between Man and Alcohol* (Boston: William E. Smythe, 1888), 521; Potter quoted in George Ewing, *The Well-Tempered Lyre* (Dallas: Southern Methodist University Press, 1977), 245.

59. Ewing, *The Well-Tempered Lyre*, 13; Preface to Charles T. Young, comp., *Temperance Song Book of the Mass. Temperance Union* (Boston: Kidder and Wright, 1842); Furnas, *The Life and Times of the Late Demon Rum*, 55.

60. Reverend John Marsh, comp., *Temperance Hymn Book and Minstrel; A Collection of Hymns, Songs and Odes, for Temperance Meetings and Festivals* (New York: American Temperance Union, 1842), 90–91.

61. Robert James Branham, "The Role of the Convert in *Eclipse of Reason* and *The Silent Scream*," *Quarterly Journal of Speech* 77 (1991): 409–410.

62. John Pierpont, "Fourth of July Ode," in Young, *Temperance Song Book*, 37.

63. "Slave of the Cup," in Phineas Stowe, comp., *Melodies for the Temperance Band: A Collection of Hymns and Songs* (Boston: Nathaniel Noyes, 1856), 60.

64. A. D. Fillmore, *The Temperance Musician* (Cincinnati: Applegate, 1853), 47.

65. Furnas, *The Life and Times of the Late Demon Rum*, 21; "Overthrow of Alcohol," in Stowe, *Melodies for the Temperance Band*, 58; "Praise of Water," National Temperance Society, *The Temperance Songster* (New York: Nafis and Cornish, 1845 [?]), 12.

66. "Temperance Celebrations," *Singer* (February 1841): 90–91.

67. John Pierpont, "For Young Persons," in Stowe, *Melodies for the Temperance*

Band, 45; later reprinted as "Children's Temperance Hymn," in J. H. Leslie, comp., *The Good Templar Songster for Temperance Meetings and the Home Circle* (New York: Independent Order of Good Templars, 1880), 7.

68. Furnas, *The Life and Times of the Late Demon Rum*, 90.

69. "Temperance Celebrations," 90; I. F. Shepard, "Thanksgiving Hymn," in Young, *Temperance Song Book*, 36–37.

70. William Lloyd Garrison, "The Dangers of the Nation" (4 July 1829), in *Selections From the Writings and Speeches of William Lloyd Garrison* (Boston: R. F. Wallcut, 1852), 45.

71. Robert Pettus Hay, "Freedom's Jubilee: One Hundred Years of the Fourth of July" (Ph. D. diss., University of Kentucky, 1967), 135–136; John Pierpont, "Fourth of July Ode," 37.

72. Gilbert Seldes, *The Stammering Century* (New York: John Day, 1928), 8; Beecher quoted in David Brion Davis, ed., *Antebellum American Culture: An Interpretive Anthology* (Lexington, MA: Heath, 1979), 397.

73. Blair, *The Temperance Movement*, 341–343; William Whipper, "The Slavery of Intemperance," in Philip Foner and Robert Branham, eds., *Lift Every Voice: African American Oratory, 1787–1900* (Tuscaloosa: University of Alabama Press, 1998), 145–154.

74. Benjamin Quarles, *Black Abolitionists* (New York: Oxford University Press, 1969), 93; Frederick Douglass, *My Bondage and My Freedom*, ed. William L. Andrews (Urbana: University of Illinois, 1987), 157.

75. "Slave of the Cup," 60.

76. See Joseph R. Gusfield, *Symbolic Crusade: Status Politics and the American Temperance Movement, 2nd ed.* (Urbana: University of Illinois, 1986).

77. Carroll Smith Rosenberg, "Beauty, the Beast, and Militant Woman: A Case Study in Sex Roles and Social Stress in Jacksonian American," and Jed Dannenbaum, "The Origins of Temperance Activism and Militancy among American Women," in Nancy F. Cott, ed., *History of Women in the United States* (Munich: Saur, 1994), 17:24–25, 71–75.

78. Ellen Carol DuBois, *Feminism and Suffrage: The Emergence of an Independent Women's Movement in America, 1848–1869* (Ithaca: Cornell University Press, 1978), 38–39; Janna MacAuslan, "Protest Songs of the Suffrage Era," *Hot Wire* 7 (September 1981): 12–13.

79. Bertha M. Stearns, "Early Philadelphia Magazines for Ladies," *Pennsylvania Magazine of History and Biography* 59 (October 1940): 479–483.

80. "A Lady," "Rights of Woman," *Philadelphia Minerva* (17 October 1795).

81. Sally Rosech Wagner, *A Time of Protest: Suffragists Challenge the Republic, 1870–1887* (Carmichael, Calif.: Sky Carrier Press, 1988), 31; Elizabeth Cady Stanton, Susan B. Anthony, and Matilda Joslyn Gage, *History of Woman Suffrage* (Rochester: Susan B. Anthony, 1881) III:iv.

82. Elizabeth Sanders, "Songs of the First Wave," *Paid My Dues* 3 (1978): 17–18, 41.

Chapter 3

1. Leonard R. Richards, "The Jacksonians and Slavery," in Lewis Perry and Michael Fellman, eds., *Antislavery Reconsidered: New Perspectives on the Abolitionists* (Baton Rouge: Louisiana State University Press, 1979), 104–109; Harry L. Watson, *Liberty and Power: The Politics of Jacksonian America* (New York: Hill and Wang, 1990), 104–113; Peter M. Bergman, *The Chronological History of the Negro in America* (New York: Harper and Row, 1969), 142–143.

2. Marilyn Richardson, ed., *Maria W. Stewart, America's First Black Woman Political Writer: Essays and Speeches* (Bloomington: Indiana University Press, 1987), 13–14; Wendell Phillips Garrison and Francis Garrison, eds., *William Lloyd Garrison 1805–1879: The Story of His Life Told By His Children* (New York: Century, 1885), 1:253; "Advancing," *Liberator* 1 (9 July 1831), 111.

3. For an analysis of the early abolitionist movement, which used the Declaration of Independence in much the same way later abolitionists used "America," see Stephen Hartnett and Michael Pfau, "The Confounded Rhetorics of Race in Revolutionary America," in Stephen Lucas, ed., *Rhetoric, Independence, and Nationhood*, vol. 1 of *The Rhetorical History of the United States* (East Lansing: Michigan State University Press, forthcoming).

4. Benjamin Quarles, *Black Abolitionists* (New York: Oxford University Press, 1969), 3–22; James Oliver Horton and Lois E. Horton, *Black Bostonians: Family Life and Community Struggle in the Antebellum North* (New York: Holmes and Meier, 1979), 81; Ronald G. Walters, "The Boundaries of Abolitionism," in Perry and Fellman, *Antislavery Reconsidered*, 4.

5. Gilbert Hobbs Barnes, *The Antislavery Impulse, 1830–1844* (New York: Harcourt, Brace and World, 1933/1964), 29–33.

6. William Lloyd Garrison, "To The Public," *Liberator* (1 January 1831), 1.

7. Richards, "The Jacksonians and Slavery," 108. Regarding the abolitionists, the "print revolution," and the resulting conspiracy charges, see Leonard Richards, *"Gentlemen of Property and Standing": Anti-Abolition Mobs in Jacksonian America* (Oxford: Oxford University Press, 1970), 71–73, 166–169; and Stephen Hartnett, *Democratic Dissent and the Cultural Fictions of Antebellum America* (Champaign: University of Illinois Press, 2002).

8. George W. Clark, comp., *The Liberty Minstrel* (New York: George W. Clark, 1844), 99, 3.

9. *Liberator* (23 July 1847), 119, quoted in Vicki L. Eaklor, *American Antislavery Songs: A Collection and Analysis* (New York: Greenwood Press, 1988), xxii; "New England Anti-Slavery Convention," *Liberator* (30 June 1843), 102.

10. Jairus Lincoln, *Anti-Slavery Melodies for the Friends of Freedom* (Hingham, MA: Elijah B. Gill, 1843), 3; Maria Weston Chapman, "Ode," *Liberator* (7 August 1840), 128.

11. John A. Collins, comp., *The Anti-Slavery Picnick: A Collection of Speeches, Poems, Dialogues and Songs; Intended for Use in Schools and Anti-Slavery Meetings* (Boston: H. W. Williams, 1842), 3.

12. *Liberator* (31 May 1834), 87; lyrics in Maria Weston Chapman, *Songs of the Free, and Hymns of Christian Freedom* (Boston: Isaac Knapp, 1836), 50–51.

13. Vicki L. Eaklor, "The Songs of *The Emancipation Car:* Variations on an Abolitionist Theme," *Bulletin of the Missouri Historical Society* 36 (January 1980): 92.

14. Paul reprinted in Dorothy Porter, ed., *Early Negro Writing, 1760–1837* (Boston: Beacon Press, 1971), 287; resolution quoted in Earl Ofari, *"Let Your Motto Be Resistance": The Life and Thought of Henry Highland Garnet* (Boston: Beacon Press, 1972), 44; *The Poetical Works of James Madison Bell* (Lansing, Mich.: Wynkoop Hallenbeck Crawford, 1901), 36, emphasis added. As discussed hereafter, Bell also composed a "Song For the First of August" to the tune of "God Save the Queen," 198–199. For further information on the life and writings of Bell, see Blyden Jackson, *A History of Afro-American Literature* (Baton Rouge: Louisiana State University Press, 1989), 254–256; and Joan R. Sherman, *Invisible Poets: Afro-Americans of the Nineteenth Century* (Urbana: University of Illinois Press, 1974), 80–87.

15. Purvis reprinted in C. Peter Ripley, ed., *Witness for Freedom: African American Voices on Race, Slavery, and Emancipation* (Chapel Hill: University of North Carolina Press, 1993), 175–176.

16. *The Address and Reply on the Presentation of a Testimonial to S. P. Chase, by the Colored People of Cincinnati* (Cincinnati: Henry W. Derby, 1845), 11; Herbert Marcuse, *Counterrevolution and Revolt* (Boston: Beacon Press, 1972), 80; Eaklor, *American Antislavery Songs*, xxxvi.

17. Theta, "America—A Parody," *Liberator* (3 May 1839), 72; Walters, "The Boundaries of Abolitionism," 8.

18. John Pierpont, "Ode," in *The Anti-Slavery Poems of John Pierpont* (Boston: Oliver Johnson, 1843), 60–61; Paul C. Nagel, *John Quincy Adams: A Public Life, A Private Life* (New York: Knopf, 1997), 389; regarding the tribute to Asa Wing, see John Pierpont, "Hymn," *Liberator* (24 August 1855), 136. For additional examples, see "My Country," in George W. Clark, comp., *The Liberty Minstrel* (New York: Martyn and Ely, 1848), 193–194; and S. G. C., "The Patriot's Hymn: A Parody," *Liberator* (25 December 1857), 208.

19. "The Liberty Army," in Clark, *The Liberty Minstrel* (1848 version), 193; William Wells Brown, *The Anti-Slavery Harp; A Collection of Songs for Anti-Slavery Meetings* (Boston: Bela Marsh, 1854), 13. This is an expanded version of "Spirit of Freemen, Awake," published in Clark, *The Liberty Minstrel* (1848 version), 193.

20. Eaklor, "The Songs of *The Emancipation Car*," 92–93; on the etymological history of *alien, alienating,* and *alienation* as terms of property and selfhood, see Gary Wills, *Inventing America: Jefferson's Declaration of Independence* (New York: Vintage Books, 1978), 213–217; Joshua McCarter Simpson, "Song of the 'Aliened American'," in his *The Emancipation Car, Being an Original Composition of Anti-Slavery Ballads* (Zanesville, OH: E. C. Church, 1854; Sullivan and Brown, 1874), 17–18.

21. Stuart Hall, "Encoding/decoding," in Hall, ed., *Culture, Media, Language: Working Papers in Cultural Studies, 1972–1979* (London: Hutchinson, 1980), 137–138.

22. Howard H. Martin, "The Fourth of July Oration," *Quarterly Journal of Speech* 44 (1958), 393; *Journals of Congress* (24 June 1779), 5:204, quoted in Catherine L. Al-

banese, *Sons of the Fathers: The Civil Religion of the American Revolution* (Philadelphia: Temple University Press, 1976), 188.

23. John Adams to Abigail Adams (3 July 1776), quoted in Len Travers, *Celebrating the Fourth: Independence Day and the Rites of Nationalism in the Early Republic* (Amherst: University of Massachusetts Press, 1997), 15; "Independence Day: Anti-Slavery Celebration at Framingham," *Liberator* (13 July 1860), 1; Martin, "The Fourth of July Oration," 394, 399; Cedric Larson, "Patriotism in Carmine: 162 Years of July 4th Oratory," *Quarterly Journal of Speech* 26 (1940): 14. See also Robert Bellah, "Civil Religion in America," *Daedalus* 96 (1967): 3–21; W. Lloyd Warner, *American Life: Dream and Reality* (Chicago: University of Chicago Press, 1953), 1–26; and Conrad Cherry, ed., *God's New Israel* (Englewood Cliffs, N.J.: Prentice-Hall, 1971).

24. "Independence Day," *Liberator* (2 July 1852), 106.

25. Michael Kammen, *Mystic Chords of Memory: The Transformation of Tradition in American Culture* (New York: Knopf, 1991), 49; "Dreadful Riots," *National Anti-Slavery Standard* (11 July 1857), unnumbered second page; Octavius B. Frothingham, "American Independence, A Sermon," *National Anti-Slavery Standard* (11 July 1857), unnumbered second page. For examples of political spectacle, see Edmund Morgan, *Inventing the People: The Rise of Popular Sovereignty in England and America* (New York: Norton, 1988), 174–208.

26. Larson, "Patriotism in Carmine," 12; Stanley Matthews (13 February 1879), quoted in William Safire, *The New Language of Politics* (New York: Collier Books, 1972), 221; Walt Whitman, "New York Amuses Itself—The Fourth of July," *Life Illustrated* (12 July 1856), reprinted in Walt Whitman, *New York Dissected* (New York: Wilson, 1936), 84; Mauger quoted in Larson, "Patriotism in Carmine," 17; Lance quoted in Martin, "The Fourth of July Oration," 395. Mann quoted in Larson, "Patriotism in Carmine," 16.

27. "Fourth of July," *Liberator* (23 July 1831), 119.

28. Dalcho quoted in the *Anti-Slavery Record* (October 1835), 115.

29. Leonard I. Sweet, "The Fourth of July and Black Americans in the Nineteenth Century," *Journal of Negro History* 61 (July 1976): 262–263; Charleston *City Gazette* (1 July 1799), quoted in Travers, *Celebrating the Fourth*, 150.

30. William Wells Brown, "Speech of William Wells Brown," *Liberator* (8 July 1859), 107.

31. Frederick Douglass, "What, to the Slave, is the Fourth of July?" in Philip S. Foner and Robert James Branham, eds., *Lift Every Voice: African American Oratory, 1787–1900* (Tuscaloosa: University of Alabama Press, 1998), 258.

32. Peter Williams, Jr., "Slavery and Colonization," in Foner and Branham, *Lift Every Voice*, 115; Quarles, *Black Abolitionists*, 122; *Colored American* (21 July 1838), quoted in Quarles, *Black Abolitionists*, 122.

33. "Speech of H. Ford Douglass," *Liberator* (13 July 1860), 1; Bell, "Song for the First of August," in *Poetical Works of James Madison Bell*, 198–199. Prior to the issuance of the Emancipation Proclamation, Frederick Douglass was among those who celebrated 1 August, rather than 4 July. Waldo Martin, *The Mind of Frederick Douglass* (Chapel Hill: University of North Carolina Press, 1984), 53. On 1 August celebra-

tions, see William H. Wiggins, Jr., *O Freedom! Afro-American Emancipation Celebrations* (Knoxville: University of Tennessee Press, 1987), xix–xx.

34. Queen Victoria was a popular figure among abolitionists and was frequently invoked in songs and poems. In *The Emancipation Car,* Joshua McCarter Simpson offers an imaginary dialogue of "Queen Victoria Conversing With Her Slave Children," set to the tune of "Come, Come Away." The Queen urges African Americans to come north to Canada, where they will be greeted "with open arms and outstretched hands; / from tyrant Columbia's land" (Simpson, *The Emancipation Car,* 59–63).

35. Austin Steward, "Twenty-Two Years a Slave and Forty Years a Freeman" (1856), in Foner and Branham, *Lift Every Voice,* 107.

36. Quarles, *Black Abolitionists,* 119–122; Peter Osborne, "It is Time for Us to be Up and Doing," *Liberator* (1 December 1832), reprinted in Foner and Branham, *Lift Every Voice,* 124; Sweet, "The Fourth of July and Black Americans," 259.

37. Arna Bontemps, *Free at Last: The Life of Frederick Douglass* (New York: Dodd, Mead, 1971), 194–196; Frederick Douglass, *Oration Delivered in Corinthian Hall* (Rochester, N.Y., 1852); reprinted in Foner and Branham, *Lift Every Voice,* 255.

38. Williams, Jr., "Slavery and Colonization," 115; William J. Watkins, "Our Rights as Men," in Philip S. Foner, *The Voice of Black America* (New York: Capricorn Books, 1975), 1:157; Sara G. Stanley, "Address to the Ohio Convention of Negro Men," in Herbert Aptheker, *A Documentary History of the Negro People in the United States* (New York: Citadel Press, 1951), 1:382.

39. Douglass, "What, to the Slave, is the Fourth of July?" 258; Molefi Kete Asante, *The Afrocentric Idea* (Philadelphia: Temple University Press, 1987), 126.

40. Simpson, "Fourth of July in Alabama," in *The Emancipation Car,* 41–42.

41. Toast quoted in Philip S. Foner, ed., *We the Other People: Alternative Declarations of Independence by Labor Groups, Farmers, Woman's Rights Advocates, Socialists, and Blacks, 1829–1975* (Urbana: University of Illinois Press, 1976), 1; Travers, *Celebrating the Fourth,* 11; Frances Wright, *Course of Popular Lectures,* 6th ed. (New York: G. W. and A. J. Matsell, 1836), 195, 181; and see Celia Morris Eckhardt, *Fanny Wright: Rebel in America* (Cambridge: Harvard University Press, 1984), 171.

42. From a story in the *Newark Eagle* quoted in William C. Nell, *The Colored Patriots of the American Revolution* (Boston: Robert F. Wallcut, 1855), 164; George Buchanon, *An Oration Upon the Moral and Political Evil of Slavery* (Baltimore: Philip Edwards, 1793).

43. Quarles, *Black Abolitionists,* 3–8; Robert Hay, "Freedom's Jubilee: One Hundred Years of the Fourth of July" (Ph.D. diss., University of Kentucky, 1967), 129–130, 132; Lawrence J. Friedman, *Inventors of the Promised Land* (New York: Knopf, 1975), 188–189; William Lloyd Garrison, "The Dangers of the Nation," in *Selections From the Writings and Speeches of William Lloyd Garrison* (Boston: R. F. Wallcut, 1852), 46; John L. Thomas, *The Liberator: William Lloyd Garrison* (Boston: Little, Brown, 1963), 92–101.

44. Anna Elizabeth, "A Short Address to Females of Color," *Liberator* (18 June 1831), 98; "Independence and Slavery," *Liberator* (16 June 1832), 94–95.

45. "Fourth of July," *Liberator* (9 July 1831), 111.

46. William Lloyd Garrison to Ebenezer Dole, 29 June 1832, in Walter M. Merrill, ed., *I Will Be Heard! The Letters of William Lloyd Garrison* (Cambridge: Harvard University Press, 1971), 1:66.

47. For examples, see the *Liberator* (28 June 1834), *Liberator* (27 June 1835), 103, and *Liberator* (4 July 1835), 107; "Fourth of July," *Liberator* (11 July 1834), 110, and "Fourth of July at Plymouth," *Liberator* (12 July 1835), 110; "Libertas," "Fourth of July," *Liberator* (13 June 1835), 94.

48. Chapman, *Songs of the Free;* on Texas annexation, see Stephen Hartnett, *Democratic Dissent* chapter 3; George Russell, "Hymn," *Liberator* (4 August 1837), 128.

49. Austin Willey, *The History of the Antislavery Cause in State and Nation* (Portland, ME: Brown, Thurnston, 1886), 318, 442–445.

50. "Anti-Slavery Demonstration," *Liberator* (23 July 1852), 119; "Anti-Slavery Celebration at Abbington," *Liberator* (9 July 1852), 110; D. S. Whitney, "Original Hymn," *Liberator* (16 July 1852), 116 [mistakenly numbered p. 110 in the *Liberator*].

51. Stephen W. Herring, "The Halcyon Days of Harmony Grove," Framingham Historical Society (n.d.); *Gleason's Pictorial Drawing Room Companion* 2 (12 June 1852): 384; Nason quoted in Edgar Potter, *Old Harmony Grove: Its Great Meetings and Some Reminiscences of its Days of Glory, Now Gone by* (South Framingham, MA: Gazette, 1896), 1; "Anti-Slavery Celebration of Independence Day," *National Anti-Slavery Standard* (11 July 1857), unnumbered second page; speakers advertised in the *National Anti-Slavery Standard* (27 June 1857).

52. Wendel and Francis Garrison, *William Lloyd Garrison: The Story of His Life, 1805–1879,* III: 412; Potter, *Old Harmony Grove,* 2.

53. "C. K. W.," "Independence Day," *Liberator* (13 July 1860), 111; see Ronald F. Reid, *The American Revolution and the Rhetoric of History* (Annandale, Va.: Speech Communication Association, 1978), 68–69; James H. Eels, *The American Revolution, Compared with the Present Struggle for the Abolition of Slavery in the United States,* quoted in Ibid 70.

54. Theodore Parker, for example, emphasized this coincidence in his 5 July 1852 oration at the Abington antislavery observance: "In 1776, there were less than 3,000,000 persons in the United States. Now, more than 3,000,000 voters. But, alas! there are also more than 3,000,000 slaves." *Liberator* (30 July 1852), 122.

55. "Declaration of the National Anti-Slavery Convention (1833)," in David Brion Davis, ed., *Antebellum American Culture: An Interpretive Anthology* (Lexington, Mass.: Heath, 1979), 426; Douglass, "What, to the Slave, Is the Fourth of July?" 250–254.

56. "The Insurrection of 1776!" *Liberator* (8 June 1860), 90; *Florida Herald* (1 July 1829), quoted in Hay, "Freedom's Jubilee," 82; Ibid., 192–193; "Declaration of the National Anti-Slavery Convention (1833)," 426–427.

57. On proslavery arguments, see Hartnett, *Democratic Dissent,* chapter 2; Eels quoted in Reid, *The American Revolution and the Rhetoric of History,* 70; "The Liberty Army," reprinted in Eaklor, *American Antislavery Songs,* 77–78; Reverend La Roy Sunderland, *Anti-Slavery Manual, Containing a Collection of Facts and Arguments on American Slavery,* 3rd ed. (New York: S. W. Benedict, 1839), 86–91.

58. William Lloyd Garrison, "More Treason," *Liberator* (23 July 1831), 120;

William Lloyd Garrison, "Walker's Appeal," in William E. Cain, ed., *William Lloyd Garrison and the Fight against Slavery* (Boston: St. Martin's Press, 1995), 77; Alonzo Lewis, "Independence and Slavery," *Liberator* (16 June 1832), 24; Herbert Aptheker, *American Negro Slave Revolts* (New York: International Publishers, 1943), 297.

59. Travers, *Celebrating the Fourth*, 148. In 1859 Harriet Tubman suggested to John Brown that the Fourth of July would be an ideal occasion to "raise the mill" in an armed raid on the federal arsenal at Harper's Ferry. Although circumstances delayed his attack until October, July Fourth continued to play an important part in the rhetorical justification of his deeds. When captured, Brown carried with him a leather bag containing an alternative Declaration of Independence, borrowing language from the original document. On 4 July 1860, following Brown's execution, an antislavery observance was held at the site of his grave in North Elba, New York. Brown's eldest son, John Brown, Jr., read the Declaration of Independence, and his youngest son, Simon, read the Sermon on the Mount. See Earl Conrad, *Harriet Tubman* (Washington, D.C.: Associated Publishers, 1943), 122; and "Celebration at North Elba," *Liberator* (27 July 1860), 120.

60. "Declaration of the National Anti-Slavery Convention (1833)," 426; Reid, *The American Revolution and the Rhetoric of History*, 70; Justitia, "An Appeal to American Freemen," *Liberator* (1 July 1859), 104.

61. Travers, *Celebrating the Fourth*, 7; "Our Fourth," *Liberator* (13 July 1860), 112; William Lloyd Garrison, "Letter From the Editor," *Liberator* (9 July 1836), 111.

62. Brown quoted in *Liberator* (8 July 1859); James Russell Lowell, "That's My Country," in Clark, *The Liberty Minstrel* (1848 version), 127.

Chapter 4

1. Richard Grant White, *National Hymns: How They Are Written and How They Are Not Written; A Lyric and National Study of the Times* (New York: Rudd and Carleton, 1861), 12–14.

2. Allan Neins and Milton Halsey Thomas, eds., *The Diary of George Templeton Strong* (New York: Macmillan, 1952), 3:161.

3. White, *National Hymns*, 31. The charge of being a "Black Republican" was commonly hurled at Republicans, including Lincoln, who were thought to be too cozy with abolitionists.

4. Vera Brodsky Lawrence, *Music for Patriots, Politicians, and Presidents: Harmonies and Discords of the First Hundred Years* (New York: Macmillan, 1975), 341.

5. Philip D. Jordan and Lillian Kessler, eds., *Songs of Yesterday: A Song Anthology of American Life* (Garden City, N.Y.: Doubleday, Doarn, 1941), 16–17.

6. Kenneth E. Olson, *Music and Musket: Bands and Bandsmen of the American Civil War* (Westport, Conn.: Greenwood Press, 1981), 36; C. A. Browne, *The Story of Our National Ballads* (New York: Crowell, 1919), 103.

7. Interview with George Coblyn, grandson of Eli Biddle, in the documentary film *The Massachusetts 54th Colored Infantry* (Jacqueline Shearer, 1990).

8. *Herald* quoted in Lawrence, *Music for Patriots*, 363; Lee and Soldier quoted in

National Historical Society, *Shadows of the Storm, vol. 2, The Image of War, 1861–1865,* (Garden City, N.Y.: Doubleday, 1982), 184–185.

9. Charles K. Wolfe, "Music," in Richard N. Current, ed. *Encyclopedia of the Confederacy* (New York: Simon and Schuster, 1993), 1104; Olson, *Music and Musket,* 4; Elias Nason, *A Monogram on Our National Song* (Albany: Joel Munsell, 1869), 55; Bell Irvin Wiley, *The Life of Billy Yank: The Common Soldier of the Union* (Baton Rouge: Louisiana State University Press, 1993; originally published in 1952), 157.

10. Frank Moore, ed., *The Rebellion Record: A Diary of American Events, with Documents, Narratives, Illustrative Incidents, Poetry, Etc.* (New York: Putnam, 1862), 1:125.

11. "God Bless Our Southern Land," in Francis D. Allan, comp., *Allan's Lone Star Ballads, A Collection of Southern Patriotic Songs Made During Confederate Times* (Galveston, Tex.: J. D. Sawyer, 1874), 43.

12. Olson, *Music and Musket,* 200; George F. Root, *The Story of a Musical Life* (Cincinnati: John Church, 1891), 243; Nason, *A Monogram on Our National Song,* 59; William Carter White, *A History of Military Music in America* (New York: Exposition Press, 1944), 67–68; Olson, *Music and Musket,* 76, 79, 182–183; John G. Whittier to Samuel F. Smith (18 October 1888), quoted in "Boston Letter," *Chicago Standard* (1 November 1888), 1.

13. Bruce Catton, *The American Heritage Picture History of the Civil War* (New York: Doubleday, 1960), 379; Soldier quoted in Lawrence, *Music for Patriots,* 363; Wiley, *The Life of Billy Yank,* 159; Bell Irvin Wiley, *The Life of Johny Reb: The Common Soldier of the Confederacy* (Baton Rouge: Louisiana State University Press, 1978; originally published in 1948), 151–152.

14. "National Hymn," "Praise to the God of Heaven," "The Soldier's Prayer," "Temperance Hymn," and "A Prayer for Our Country" all in *The Soldier's Companion* (Boston: Walker and Wise, 1863), 1–11.

15. "Smith Memorial Service," *Boston Standard* (2 December 1895).

16. "Our Land" in *The Soldier's Hymn Book* (Charleston: South Carolina Tract Society, 1862), 20–21, 62–63, 191–192, 203–204, 222.

17. *The Soldier's Hymn Book,* 2nd ed. (Charleston: South Carolina Tract Society, 1863), 200–201, 232–233.

18. *Dwight's Journal* quoted in Olson, *Music and Musket,* 242; *Examiner* quoted in George Henry Preble, *History of the Flag of the United States of America,* 2nd ed. (Boston: A. Williams, 1880), 510–517; Bloch quoted in Frank W. Hoogerwerf, *Confederate Sheet-Music Imprints* (New York: Institute for Studies in American Music, 1984), xv.

19. Wiley, *Life of Billy Yank* and *Life of Johny Reb;* Wolfe, "Music," 1103; Catton, *The American Heritage Picture History of the Civil War,* 379; Lawrence, *Music for Patriots,* 352; Cooley quoted in Moore, *The Rebellion Record,* 1:73; Ibid., 1:149; C. A. Browne, *The Story of Our National Ballads, Revised Edition* (New York: Crowell, 1931), 155.

20. Moore, *The Rebellion Record,* 3:35; Brander Matthews, "The Songs of the War," *Century Magazine* 34 (August 1887): 622; Kenneth A. Bernard, *Lincoln and the Music of the Civil War* (Caldwell, Idaho: Caxton, 1966), 232; Browne, *The Story of Our National Ballads,* 91–92.

21. L. D. Young, *Reminiscences of a Soldier of the Orphan Brigade,* as quoted in Olson, *Music and Musket,* 169.

22. Richard Crawford, comp., *The Civil War Songbook* (New York: Dover, 1977), v; Hoogerwerf, *Confederate Sheet-Music Imprints*, xv; Crawford, *The Civil War Songbook*, vi; Michael Broyles, *"Music of the Highest Class": Elitism and Populism in Antebellum Boston* (New Haven: Yale University Press, 1992), 89; James J. Fuld, "Patriotic Music," in H. Wiley Hitchcock and Stanley Sadie, eds., *The New Grove Dictionary of American Music* (New York: Grove, 1986), 3:487; Root, *The Story of a Musical Life*, 216.

23. Rusell Sanjek, *American Popular Music and Its Business: the First Four Hundred Years* (New York: Oxford University Press, 1988), 2:225; Geoffrey C. Ward, *The Civil War: An Illustrated History* (New York: Knopf, 1990), 104; Lawrence, *Music for Patriots*, 364. Wolfe, "Music," 1101. I (Stephen Hartnett) write from Lincoln Hall, an architectural wonder completed in 1913 on the campus of the University of Illinois. Along with bearing Lincoln's name, the building features the Gettysburg Address etched in bronze in the lovely front hallway, a giant bronze bust of Lincoln (made by Hermon Atkins MacNeil), and ten terra cotta panels (designed by Karl Schneider) depicting various phases of Lincoln's life. Panel 6, clearly paying tribute to Gibbons's poem/song, is entitled "We are coming, Father Abraham, One Hundred Thousand Strong," and depicts Lincoln directing troops, complete with what appears to be the Capitol building in the background.

24. Root, *The Story of a Musical Life*, 130–131; Philip Shaw Paludan, *"A People's Contest": The Union and Civil War* (New York: Harper and Row, 1988), 23; Greeley, quoted in Ibid., 23; Crawford, *The Civil War Songbook*, iv.

25. Mark Twain (Samuel Clemens), "Fourth of July," in Edgar M. Branch, ed., *Clemens of the Call* (Berkeley: University of California Press, 1969), 87–90.

26. G. W. Rogers, "War," *Liberator* (10 January 1862), 8; "The Patriot's Hymn," printed in Frank Moore, ed., *Songs of the Soldiers* (New York: Putnam, 1864), 317–318. Mines's "Hymn" was later included in Moore's massive anthology *The Rebellion Record*, 2:48–49, in the "Poetry, Rumors, and Incidents" section, which is preceded by another six hundred pages of material. Crawford, *The Civil War Songbook*, ix; emphasis added.

27. "God Bless Our Sunday School," in *Cymbal: A Collection of Hymns for Sabbath Schools* (Augusta, Ga.: J. T. Patterson, 1864), 91.

28. See Bernard, *Lincoln and the Music of the Civil War*, 177–179.

29. The Christian Commission was a civilian relief agency headed by Philadelphia merchant George H. Stuart, which provided food, clothing, and medical supplies to the union army. The Commission raised funds at church services and "patriotic meetings" featuring musical performances. See Bernard, *Lincoln and Music in the Civil War*, 209–221, 224–225.

30. The classic texts articulating the southern hatred of how modernity was turning the North into a Manchester- or Birmingham-like hell on earth of factories and poor workers are George Fitzhugh's 1854 *Sociology for the South, or The Failure of Free Society*, and his 1857 *Cannibals All! Or, Slaves Without Masters* (reprint, Cambridge: Harvard University Press, 1960). Lyrics printed in Moore, *The Rebellion Record*, 4:69.

31. Benjamin Quarles, *The Negro in the Civil War* (Boston: Little, Brown, 1969; originally published in 1953), 43; "Doc. 48—Speech of A. H. Stephens," in Moore,

The Rebellion Record, 1:45; John S. Rock, "What If the Slaves are Emancipated?" *Liberator* (4 February 1862), reprinted in Philip S. Foner and Robert J. Branham, eds., *Lift Every Voice: African American Oratory, 1787–1900* (Tuscaloosa: University of Alabama Press, 1998), 359.

32. Wightman quoted in Bernard, *Lincoln and the Music of the Civil War*, 87, 300; Lincoln quoted in Quarles, *The Negro in the Civil War*, 105–106; Jordan and Kessler, *Songs of Yesterday*, 334.

33. Lyrics printed in Moore, *The Rebellion Record*, 1:17. Unlike most of the alternative versions of "America" that appeared during the Civil War, Walden's "God Save Our Native Land" continued in use after the war. For example, it was featured in New York's Decoration Day ceremony in 1869 to mark the sacrifice of Union soldiers; see *New York Times* (30 May 1869), 1. And see Eric Foner, *Free Soil, Free Labor, Free Men: The Ideology of the Republican Party before the Civil War* (Oxford: Oxford University Press, 1970).

34. Mark Perry, *Conceived in Liberty: Joshua Chamberlain, William Oates, and the American Civil War* (New York: Viking, 1997), 189, 449.

35. Joan Hedrick, *Harriet Beecher Stowe: A Life* (New York: Oxford University Press, 1994), 300; Henry K. Rowe, *History of Andover Theological Seminary* (Newton, Mass.: Thomas Todd, 1933), 77–78.

36. Ibid., 77.

37. "Hymn for a Flag-Raising" printed in Moore, *The Rebellion Record*, 1:140.

38. "Thirty-Four" printed in Ibid., 3:48–49.

39. Harriet Beecher Stowe, "Letter From Andover," *Independent* (20 June 1861), 1; Benjamin Quarles, "Ministers without Portfolios," *Journal of Negro History* 39 (January 1954): 27–42. For an example of African American oratory in Britain during the war, see Sarah Parker Remond, "The Negroes in the United States of America," *Journal of Negro History* 27 (April 1942): 216–218, reprinted in Foner and Branham, *Lift Every Voice*, 377–380.

40. "God Save the South" reprinted in Moore, *The Rebellion Record*, 4:36–37; Perry, *Conceived in Liberty*, 370–371.

41. "New Version" reprinted in Moore, *The Rebellion Record*, 1:120.

42. Suvir Kaul, *Poems of Nation, Anthems of Empire: English Verse in the Long Eighteenth Century* (Charlottesville: University of Virginia Press, 2000), 2, 1; and see Quarles, *The Negro in the Civil War*, 280.

43. "God Protect Us!" reprinted in Moore, *The Rebellion Record*, 1:85–86.

44. Stephen V. Ash, *When the Yankees Came: Conflict and Chaos in the Occupied South, 1861–1865* (Chapel Hill: University of North Carolina Press, 1995), 150–151; "Hymn of the Connecticut Twelfth" printed in Moore, *Songs of the Soldiers*, 153–154.

45. Ash, *When the Yankees Came*, 150–151; Lincoln's letter in Roy P. Basler, ed., *The Collected Works of Abraham Lincoln* (New Brunswick: Rutgers University Press, 1953), 5:388–389; Quarles, *The Negro in the Civil War*, 180.

46. Eric Foner, *Reconstruction: America's Unfinished Business, 1863–1877* (New York: Perennial, 1988), 220.

47. Garry Wills, *Lincoln at Gettysburg: The Words That Remade America* (New York:

Philadelphia, Pa., September, 1885 (New York: National Temperance Society, 1886), 477, 479, 488.

6. The Reverend C. S. H. Dunn, "My Country 'Tis to Thee," in J. H. Leslie, comp., *The Good Templar Songster for Temperance Meetings and the Home Circle* (New York: Independent Order of Good Templars, 1880), 6–7.

7. S. W. Straub, comp., *Temperance Battle Songs* (Chicago: S. W. Straub, 1884); advertised in A. J. Jutkins, *Hand-Book of Prohibition* (Chicago: National Prohibition Home Protection Party, 1884), endpaper.

8. National Temperance Society, *Temperance Chimes* (New York: J. N. Stearns, 1867); *The Temperance Songster* (New York: Nafis and Cornish, 1845 [?]); Miss L. Penney, ed., *The National Temperance Orator. A New and Choice Collection of Prose and Poetical Articles and Selections, etc.* (New York: National Temperance Society, 1874), endpapers.

9. Blair, *The Temperance Movement*, 489, 296, 304.

10. Shaw quoted in George Ewing, *The Well-Tempered Lyre* (Dallas: Southern Methodist University Press, 1977), 245; verse 4 of E. A. Hoffman, "Mother Is Dead," in J. H. Tenney and Reverend Hoffman, comps., *Temperance Jewels: for Temperance and Reform Meetings* (Boston: Oliver Ditson, 1879), 50. For the visual equivalent of this argument, see the illustration entitled "Come Home, Mother," in J. N. Stearns, ed., *The National Temperance Almanac, 1871* (New York: National Temperance Society, 1871), 33.

11. "Come with Us to the Spring," in Stearns, *National Temperance Hymn and Song Book*, 49.

12. J. N. Stearns, ed., *The National Temperance Almanac and Teetotaler's Year Book for The Year of Our Lord 1880* (New York: National Temperance Society, 1880); prose discussion on 51–52; illustration on 50.

13. Harriet D. Castle, "America's New Tyrant," in E. S. Lorenz, comp., *New Anti-Saloon Songs* (New York: Lorenz, 1905), 103.

14. Windom quoted in Blair, *The Temperance Movement*, 361.

15. "Our Lord Redeemed," in Leslie, *The Good Templar Songster*, 7.

16. Fobes, "Temperance, Thy Noble Name," *Temperance Songs and Hymns*, 19.

17. "Overthrow of Alcohol," in Phineas Stowe, comp., *Melodies for the Temperance Band: A Collection of Hymns and Songs* (Boston: Nathaniel Noyes, 1856), 58.

18. Hitchcock quoted in Leslie, *The Good Templar Songster*, 36; Blair, *The Temperance Movement*, 284–285; quotation from Mark Wahlgren Summers, *The Gilded Age* (Upper Saddle River, N. J.: Prentice Hall, 1997), 175.

19. For historical comparisons, see Clarence Lusane, *Pipe Dream Blues: Racism and the War on Drugs* (Boston: South End Press, 1991); Eva Bertram et. al., eds., *Drug War Politics: The Price of Denial* (Berkeley: University of California Press, 1996); and Stephen Hartnett, "A Rhetorical Critique of the Drug War, Slavery, and the Nauseous Pendulum of Reason and Violence," *Journal of Contemporary Criminal Justice* 16:3 (August 2000): 247–271.

20. Ewing, *The Well-Tempered Lyre*, 84.

21. Ellen Carol DuBois, *Feminism and Suffrage: The Emergence of an Independent Women's Movement in America, 1848–1869* (Ithaca: Cornell University Press, 1978), 55;

Foremother's Hymn quoted in Sally Rosech Wagner, *A Time of Protest: Suffragists Challenge the Republic, 1870–1887* (Carmichael, Calif.: Sky Carrier Press, 1988), 125.

22. See Charlotte Perkins Gilman, comp., *Suffrage Songs and Verses* (New York: Charlton, 1911); Pauline Russell Brown, comp., *Woman's Suffrage Songs* (Indianapolis: P. R. Browne, 1913); Eugénie M. Rayé-Smith, comp., *Equal Suffrage Song Sheaf* (New York: E. M. Rayé-Smith, 1912); and *The National Altrusa Song Book* (n.p.: National Association of Altrusa Clubs, 1930). L. May Wheeler, comp., "My Native Country," in Wheeler, *Booklet of Song: A Collection of Suffrage and Temperance Melodies* (Minneapolis: Co-operative Printing, 1884), 14.

23. *Songs of the Suffragettes*, Folkways FH 5281 (1958); quotations from Wheeler, *Booklet of Song*, 15–17.

24. Harriet May Mills and Isabel Howland, *Manual for Political Equality Clubs* (Philadelphia: Alfred J. Ferris, 1896), 1–2, 15–21.

25. Samuel Smith, "Women's Rights," in his *Poems of Home and Country. Also, Sacred and Miscellaneous Verse* (Boston: Silver, Burdett, 1895), 116–118; Mary Ann Shadd Cary, "The Right of Women to Vote," in Philip S. Foner and Robert James Branham, eds., *Lift Every Voice: African American Oratory, 1787–1900* (Tuscaloosa: University of Alabama Press, 1998), 516–517.

26. See Philip N. Cohen, "Nationalism and Suffrage: Gender Struggle in Nation-Building America," *Signs* (spring 1996): 707–717.

27. While the list of possible sources here is extensive, one would be hard pressed to find a better place to begin studying such questions than Hannah Arendt, *The Human Condition* (Chicago: University of Chicago Press, 1998; originally published in 1958). Additional historical sources are cited hereafter.

28. Wright quoted in Philip S. Foner, ed. and comp., *American Labor Songs of the Nineteenth Century* (Urbana: University of Illinois Press, 1975), xv; Ibid., 17; Clark D. Halker, *For Democracy, Workers, and God: Labor Song-Poems and Labor Protest, 1865–95* (Urbana: University of Illinois Press, 1991), 31; Duncan Emrich, "Songs of the Western Miners," *California Folklore Quarterly* 1 (1942): 213–214; Richard A. Reuss, *Songs of American Labor, Industrialization and the Urban Work Experience: A Discography* (Ann Arbor: University of Michigan, 1983), 101; Karl Reuber, comp., *Hymns of Labor* (Pittsburgh: Barrows & Osbourne, 1871).

29. Anonymous version reprinted in Foner, *American Labor Songs of the Nineteenth Century*, 217.

30. Philip S. Foner, *History of the Labor Movement in the United States*, vol. 1 (New York: International Publishers, 1947), 365.

31. Sean Dennis Cashman, *America in the Gilded Age: From the Death of Lincoln to the Rise of Theodore Roosevelt* (New York: New York University Press, 1984), 282; wheat prices from this same page.

32. Quotations from *The Book of Popular Songs* (Philadelphia: G. G. Evans, 1861), 121.

33. Carleton Beals, *The Great Revolt and Its Leaders* (New York: Abelard-Schuman, 1968), 68; Solon Justus Buck, *The Granger Movement* (Cambridge: Harvard University Press, 1913), 35, 41, 66; Curry's version from *Songs of the Grange* (Washington, D.C.: Gibson Brothers, 1872), n.p.

34. Halker, *For Democracy, Workers, and God*, 1; Powderly quoted in Ibid., 37.

35. Ibid., 37, 59, 74, 96; Foner, *History of the Labor Movement in the United States*, 1:437.

36. Ibid., 1:507–510; Foner, *American Labor Songs of the Nineteenth Century*, 145.

37. Ralph E. Hoyt, "America," *Journal of the Knights of Labor* (3 July 1890); quoted in Foner, *American Labor Songs of the Nineteenth Century*, 151–152.

38. Thomas Nicol, "A New National Anthem," in Leopold Vincent, comp., *The Alliance and Labor Songster* (Indianapolis: Vincent Bros., 1891), 5, emphasis added.

39. Dodge reprinted in Foner, *American Labor Songs of the Nineteenth Century*, 183. This song was reprinted (with slight alterations and without credit) in Vincent, *The Alliance and Labor Songster*, and recorded by Cincinnati's University Singers, Earl Rivers, dir., *The Hand That Holds the Bread* (New World Records, 1978).

40. Sean Dennis Cashman, *America in the Gilded Age*, 3rd ed. (New York: New York University Press, 1993), 271; and see Samuel T. McSeveney, *The Politics of Depression: Political Behavior in the Northeast, 1893–1896* (New York: Oxford University Press, 1972).

41. Philip S. Foner, *History of the Labor Movement in the United States*, vol. 2 (New York: International Publishers, 1955), 235–243; see the portrayal of this depression- and racism-triggered violence in Toni Morrison, *Jazz* (New York: Plume, 1992).

42. Graham's version was published in the *Labor Journal* and in *Coming Nation* (11 May 1895); it is quoted here from Foner, *American Labor Songs of the Nineteenth Century*, 251–252.

43. Rose Alice Cleveland, "Hymn of the Toilers," in Charles H. Kerr, comp., *Socialist Songs* (Chicago: Charles H. Kerr, 1900), 13–14.

44. Floaten quoted in Sidney Lens, *The Labor Wars: From the Molly Maguires to the Sitdowns* (New York: Doubleday, 1973), 123–134.

45. Paul Fatout, *Ambrose Bierce: The Devil's Lexicographer* (Norman: University of Oklahoma Press, 1951), 136–137; Roy Morris, Jr., *Ambrose Bierce: Alone in Bad Company* (New York: Crown, 1995), 173–177; Bierce quoted in Fatout, *Ambrose Bierce*, 146.

46. Ambrose Bierce, "A Rational Anthem," San Francisco *Wasp* (16 September 1882), 581. Signed "B.," the song appears above Bierce's column, then entitled "Prattle."

47. "Land of the Pilgrims' Pride," in *The Collected Works of Ambrose Bierce* (New York: Neale, 1910), 4:78–80.

48. Frederick Keller, "Patriotism, Past and Present," San Francisco *Wasp* (26 May 1882), back page. For a sampling of such images, see Kenneth Johnson, *The Story of the Wasp: Political and Satirical Cartoons from The Turbulent Early San Francisco Weekly* (San Francisco: Book Club of California, 1967).

49. C. A. Browne, *The Story of Our National Ballads* (New York: Crowell, 1931), 103–104.

50. Henry B. Carrington, *Beacon Lights of Patriotism, or, Historic Incentives to Virtue and Good Citizenship* (Boston: Silver, Burdett, 1894), 401–403. "America" was not suggested for programs on Memorial and Decoration Days, perhaps because of beliefs that "America" was more pacifist than the occasions required.

51. Anna D. Cooper, *My Country, 'Tis of Thee: An Illustrated Pantomime* (New York: Dick and Fitzgerald, 1907), 3, 7.

52. The verses first appeared in R. L. Paget, ed., *Poems of American Patriotism, 1776–1898* (Boston: L. C. Page, 1898), 1–3; quotations below from this source.

53. See "The Centennial of a Famous Song," *National Education Association Journal* 21 (November 1932): 262; see "Education Week," and "Two Little Known Stanzas of 'America,'" *School Life* XIX:2 (October 1933): 28; H. L. Fisher, "Are 50,000,000 Americans Wrong about America?" *Boston Herald* (8 December 1935), 5.

54. "The Seal Once Laid On Pliant Wax," in Smith, *Poems of Home and Country*, 79.

55. Frank Damrosch, "Music in the Public Schools," in W. L. Hubbard, ed., *History of American Music* (Toledo: Irving Squire, 1908), 32.

56. William Carter White, *A History of Military Music in America* (New York: Exposition Press, 1944), 235.

57. Wilson asked Congress for an official declaration of war on 2 April 1916; Congress complied on 6 April. Frank V. Thompson, *Schooling of the Immigrant* (New York: Harper, 1920), 1, 121, 286–287; National Conference of Music Supervisors quoted in Augustus Delafield Zanzig, *Music in American Life: Present and Future* (London: Oxford University Press, 1932), 255–256.

58. Quotation from Bessie Louise Pierce, *Citizens' Organizations and the Civic Training of Youth* (New York: Scribner's, 1933), 31.

59. Oscar Sonneck, *Library of Congress Report on "The Star-Spangled Banner," "Hail Columbia," "America," "Yankee Doodle"* (Washington, D.C.: Government Printing Office, 1909), 76; Edward Ninde, *The Story of the American Hymn* (New York: Abandon, 1921), 279.

Epilogue

1. Popular music historian Joel Whitburn estimated chart positions of early recordings according to sheet music sales and monthly lists of top songs published in *Phonogram* (1890–1895), *Phonoscope* (1896–99), *Talking Machine World*, and *Billboard*. See his *Pop Memories, 1890–1954: The History of American Popular Music* (Menomonee Falls, Wis.: Record Research, 1986), 7–13, 22, 95, 183, 271, 400.

2. Michael Hicks, *Mormonism and Music: A History* (Urbana: University of Illinois Press, 1989), 156.

3. William G. McLoughlin, Jr., *Billy Sunday Was His Real Name* (Chicago: University of Chicago Press, 1955), 86.

4. For the legislation relating to these icons of nationalism, see *The United States Code, 1994 Edition, Containing the General and Permanent Laws of the United States, etc.* (Washington, D.C.: Government Printing Office, 1995), 782–787. And see Carolyn Marvin, *Blood Sacrifice and the Nation: Totem Rituals and the American Flag* (Cambridge, England: Cambridge University Press, 1999).

5. Fredric Jameson, *Postmodernism: or, The Cultural Logic of Late Capitalism* (Durham, N.C.: Duke University Press, 1991), 17, emphasis added.

6. See Jody Rosen, "Two American Anthems in Two American Voices," *New York Times* (2 July 2000), sect. 2, 1, 28.

7. The show opened on 26 December 1931 and ran for 446 performances. Ken Bloom, *American Song: The Complete Musical Theater Companion,* 2nd ed. (New York: Schirmer, 1996), 1:823.

8. George S. Kaufman and Morrie Ryskind, *Of Thee I Sing: A Musical Play* (London: Victor Gollancz, 1933), 55, 105, 111, 126.

9. "Vote for Mr. Rhythm," by Ralph Rainger, Leo Robin, and Richard Siegal, on *Ella Fitzgerald with the Chick Webb Orchestra* (Laserlight: 17–003; 1993 reissue).

10. Robert Fripp, liner notes to *God Save the Queen* (E. G. Music/Polygram, 1980); the "Frippertronic" version is track 2.

11. *New York Times* (9 May 2000), A15.

Index

Page numbers in *italics* indicate illustrations.